Christian Missions in East Bengal

Christian Missions in East Bengal

The Life and Times of
Archbishop Theotonius Amal Ganguly, CSC
(1920–1977)

S. M. TANVEER AHMED

Foreword by David B. Burrell, CSC

RESOURCE *Publications* • Eugene, Oregon

CHRISTIAN MISSIONS IN EAST BENGAL
The Life and Times of Archbishop Theotonius Amal Ganguly, CSC (1920–1977)

Copyright © 2018 S. M. Tanveer Ahmed. All rights reserved. Except for brief quotations in critical publications or reviews, no part of this book may be reproduced in any manner without prior written permission from the publisher. Write: Permissions, Wipf and Stock Publishers, 199 W. 8th Ave., Suite 3, Eugene, OR 97401.

Resource Publications
An Imprint of Wipf and Stock Publishers
199 W. 8th Ave., Suite 3
Eugene, OR 97401

www.wipfandstock.com

PAPERBACK ISBN: 978-1-5326-1642-6
HARDCOVER ISBN: 978-1-4982-4019-2
EBOOK ISBN: 978-1-4982-4018-5

Manufactured in the U.S.A.   JANUARY 25, 2018

The book is dedicated to the memory of my ancestors and my grandfather Md. Abdul Hamid Miah who, belonged to the peasant class of East Bengal (Bangladesh) and participated in the First World War in the Mesopotamian region as a British-Indian soldier, and his beloved wife, my grandmother Ful Banu, who left us so many years ago;

And

My teacher, Dr. A. H. Ahmed Kamal, Professor, Department of History, University of Dhaka who, taught me first how to work with history through methodology and created the deepest interest in history;

And

To my guide, supervisor and philosopher, David B. Burrell, CSC, Hesburgh Professor Emeritus, Philosophy and Theology, University of Notre Dame, Notre Dame, IN 46556, USA. Basically the book is the fruit of that historical, philosophical as well as literary training, which I have been receiving from my Professor David B. Burrell, CSC for the last two and half years. He has created a new motto for my writings: "Less is more". I show my highest gratitude to him for his liberal judgment of my work, which is creating in me a new way of thinking philosophically, showing a path for my better future behind the screen.

Contents

Foreword by David B. Burrell, CSC | ix
Preface and Acknowledgments | xi
Abbreviations | xviii

1   Introduction | 1
2   Social Structure of East Bengal in Colonial and Post-Colonial Period | 9
3   Background of Missionary Activities in East Bengal | 16
4   Family Background of Theotonius Amal Ganguly | 38
5   Educational Career | 44
6   The Philosophical Thoughts of Father T. A. Ganguly, CSC | 53
7   The Activities of T. A. Ganguly | 64
8   The Role of Archbishop T. A. Ganguly in the Liberation War of Bangladesh and the Aftermath | 94
9   The Early Phase of Reformation in Christianity in East Bengal and Archbishop T. A. Gaguly, CSC: 1959–1977 | 117
10 Death and Aftermath | 132
11 Conclusion | 136

Appendix I: Holy Cross Priests in East Bengal, 1853–2003 | 141
Appendix II: Holy Cross Priest Religious Superiors, 1920–1982 | 151

Contents

Appendix III: Former Archbishops of Dhaka, 1947–2005 (Archdiocese est. 15 July, 1950) | 153

Appendix IV: Holy Cross Bishops of East Bengal, 1891–2011 | 154

Appendix V: PIME Missionaries in West Bengal and East Bengal Bangladesh, 1855–2012 | 155

Appendix VI: Former Bishops of Dinajpur Diocese, 1927–2011 | 162

Appendix VII: Xaverian Missionaries in East Bengal, 1952–2010 | 163

Appendix VIII: Former Bishops of Khulna Diocese, 1952–2005 | 169

Appendix IX: Population by Religious Communities in Percentage, 1901–2001 | 170

Appendix X: Archbishop's Easter Message (March 29, 1964) | 171

Appendix XI: Archbishop's Pastoral Letter (July 26, 1964) | 173

Appendix XII: Archbishop Ganguly's Address at Reception on Jan. 21, 1968 | 175

Appendix XIII: Muhammad Ali Jinnah's First Presidential Address to the Constituent Assembly of Pakistan (August 11, 1947) | 178

Appendix XIV: Demographic Difference between East and West Pakistan, 1951 and 1961 | 182

Appendix XV: Frequency of Languages Commonly Spoken as Mother Tongue in Pakistan (Percentage of population) | 183

Appendix XVI: Twenty-One Point Programme, 1954 | 184

Appendix XVII: Six-Point Programme, 1966 | 187

Appendix XVIII: Some Economic Indicators between East Pakistan and West Pakistan | 189

Appendix XIX: Representation of the Civil Service of Pakistan in East Pakistan and West Pakistan, 1948-1967 | 191

Glossary | 193

Bibliography | 197

Index | 207

Foreword

MANY WORLDS WILL MEET in this account of the life of the first Bengali archbishop of Dhaka. But that is the way of Bengal, and particularly of east Bengal, where Theotonius Ganguly was born into the community of Christians evangelized by the Portuguese a few centuries earlier. Tanveer Ahmed is a generation or two younger than his subject, and himself a Muslim historian, fascinated with the scenario of westerners who came to Bengal as missionaries in the mid-nineteenth century. So we have a double stretch: Theotonius, going abroad for the education needed to teach in his own country, and Tanveer, who seeks to understand this talented Christian so dedicated to his own Bengali people. We will read the details, and notably how his early talent for philosophy moved him to penetrate Indian philosophy as an intellectual entree into his own culture. For some of us, philosophy has a way of honing the cultural issues explicitly so we can grasp them. Theotonius completed his doctor studies at the University of Notre Dame in Indiana, where his Indian physiognomy and his serene demeanor seemed to fit him to his subject. It was also natural that on his return he teach in the fledgling Notre Dame College, which his religious community of Holy Cross has just begun in what was then East Pakistan.

As the only Bengali among Americans, he was given (or took) multiple responsibilities, though his teaching program of logic hardly included the love of Indian philosophy shown in his dissertation. Yet 'the college' became his entree into the larger Bengali and Muslim society, as parents wanted their young men to profit from the education offered. But the times were parlous, as Pakistan never quite accepted east Bengal into their Punjabi mindset, as the twin issues of language and of economy were to

Foreword

reveal. For the Punjabis, Urdu would be the language, while Bengalis had no choice but to adopt their mother tongue, and literary language of the Asian subcontinent. So when the Pakistani generals proposed Urdu, a 'barracks language' as the lingua franca of Pakistan, Bengal broke out in revolt. Economic exploitation had been the name of the game between the east and west wings of the fractured country, but the prospect of their mother tongue being eliminated seared the hearts of all in the east.

Yet it was not this split which exercised the then Archbishop of Dhaka, but the fate of the indigenous (Mandy) people at the hands of the Bengalis themselves. And since some of them had become Catholic, Archbishop Graner, feeling the need to protest seizure of Garo lands, issued a dispatch which the UN transmitted, to the embarrassment of the generals. So they lost no time in informing him that his visa (to work in east Bengal) would not be renewed once he left the country. Since US power had supported West Pakistan in the subsequent genocide, there was no political room to assist an American archbishop in a Bengali fray. So Graner had to resign, and Rome appointed the mild-mannered philosopher as the new Archbishop. So our story begins.

Professor David B. Burrell, CSC
Theodore Hesburgh C.S.C. Professor Emeritus
Philosophy and Theology
University of Notre Dame, IN, USA.

Preface and Acknowledgments

NEEDLESS TO POINT OUT, the importance of the history of the Catholic missionary activities in East Bengal has been neglected by the historians. I have examined the life and times of Archbishop Theotonius Amal Ganguly, CSC with special reference to the social structure as well as the background of missionary activities in East Bengal.

This book attempts to raise a question by examining the life and times of Archbishop Theotonius Amal Ganguly, CSC: how he became the central character of the Catholic Church in East Bengal and why his life and times are very important in the history of this region. This book should help fill in the gap that exists in the history of religion in East Bengal.

I started the work several years ago. In 2011, when I joined my present University (Jagannath) as a lecturer, I began work on a project with my colleagues for writing a short biography of the 'Foreign Friends of Bangladesh,' for their selfless contribution during the struggle for independence of our country in 1971. The names were given us to from the Foreign Ministry of Bangladesh; later the Bangladesh government honored them.

During this time, I got to know Father Richard William Timm, CSC, who had been residing in the country for last fifty years and stood by the Bengali people in their struggle for liberation. So, I decided to meet with Fr. Timm and I met with him. He told me that he along with other missionaries in East Bengal also took steps in favor of Bengali people during the liberation war of Bangladesh. He also provided me the names of Archbishop Theotonius Amal Ganguly, CSC, Father Homrich, CSC, Father Marino Rigon, S.X., Father Corba, PIME, and many other priests who played laudatory roles in our freedom struggle and stood by the people of their

PREFACE AND ACKNOWLEDGMENTS

own diocese and parish. I wrote an article titled 'The Role of Father Timm in the Liberation War of Bangladesh', which I read at the Institute of Bangladesh Studies in Rajshahi. Later, the article was published from *Journal for the Arts faculty of Jagannath University*, Vol.02, Number-01, pp. 119–128, title as 'Father Timm and His Role in the Liberation War of Bangladesh'. In connection with my research, I had visited Tangail, where Father Homrich, CSC resides. After I met and interviewed Fr. Homrich at his present mission, at St. Paul's Church, Pirgacha, Madhupur, Tangail, he handed me most of the documents to improve and develop the article. On 28 May 2011, I met and interviewed him there and spent some time to get the details of his works especially during the Liberation War. Later, at a different time, I visited him and wrote an article on 'The Role of Father Homrich, CSC in the Liberation War of Bangladesh' and read it at the conference of Bangladesh Historical Association in 2012, which was held at Khulna University of Engineering and Technology (KUET). This was later published in the Journal of *Bangladesh Historical Studies*, Vol. XXIII, 2012–2014 titled 'Father Eugene E. Homrich and his role in the Liberation War of Bangladesh.' pp. 231–250.

Between 2011–2014, while researching the role of missionaries in the Liberation War of Bangladesh I came across the name of Archbishop Theotonius Amal Ganguly, CSC, a popular name in the history of Catholic missionaries of Bangladesh. By that time, I became interested in him and began to investigate his life and times. During the period of research, I had visited different libraries and met scholars of my country to get information about him, but very little was available. Though three biographies were written on him, but they are inadequate to meet the satisfaction of scholars. So, I started to research on Archbishop Theotonius Amal Ganguly, CSC. Finally, I got access to a substantial number of primary sources on T. A. Ganguly, CSC, which is now going to be published.

In the course of the book I have experienced many debts: to my teacher Professor Dr. A. H. Ahmed Kamal, Professor, Department of History, Dhaka University, for his constructive criticism and useful suggestions on the earlier version of this book. He also generated a lot of ideas so that my research work could progress. This book is the fruit of that training, which I have been receiving from my professor for the last six years as his student.

I owe to Professor David B. Burrell, CSC, Hesburgh Professor Emeritus, University of Notre Dame, Indiana (USA), and currently emeritus professor at Notre Dame University Bangladesh, for his critical comments

Preface and Acknowledgments

on my manuscript. He has given many hours of careful consideration for unrestrained development of thoughts, which he encouraged and for his useful criticism and advice for my book. Actually, he became the supervisor of my research through his unconditional help. I show my highest gratitude to him for writing the 'Foreword'. My special thanks are due to Professor David B. Burrell CSC for his great initiative so that my research could see the light of day in a form of a book.

My very special thanks are due to Stephen B. Bevans SVD, Louis J. Luzbetak, SVD Professor Emeritus of Mission and Culture, Catholic Theological Union, 5401 S. Cornell Avenue, Chicago, IL 60615, USA, for his encouragement of my study. He also showed a keen interest for my further study. He always stimulated behind the screen as my work could see the light. I show my highest gratitude to him for his constant support for my study.

I do not know how to show my gratitude to Father Richard William Timm, CSC for his great contribution for my research work. He provided me with a huge number of primary sources from his collection, and made sure that I can use the archive of Holy Cross Mission at Banasree, Rampura, Dhaka. I have used his residing place at Notre Dame College, Dhaka and his office at Caritas, Bangladesh as my research room. I was warmly received by him and his office staffs. Especially Miss Rosaline Costa, who always encouraged me and provided valuable suggestions and advice for my research work.

My special thanks are due to Rev. Joseph S. Peixotto, CSC; who gave me the opportunity to use the archive of Holy Cross Mission. For his unconditional and continuous help for my research it became easier to access information. My thanks are also due to the authority of Banani Seminary and Fr. Jyoti Francis Costa, former Dean of the faculty, for their kind permission to work in the library, and obviously Fr. Louis Susil Pereira, who personally helped me in the library, where I also found a large store of information for my work.

It makes me sad to think that the former Archbishop of Dhaka diocese Most Rev. Paulinus Costa, DD, who arranged for my access to the unpublished official documents of Catholic Church from different places and provided a huge number of published and unpublished primary and secondary sources for my research work, and was deeply interested in my research work, is no longer to read my book. In a sense, he became my mentor for the work. He had given me a number of valuable suggestions and criticisms

Preface and Acknowledgments

as the research progressed. We spend a lot of time at his last residing place Holy Rosary Church, Tejgaon, Dhaka, specially last three and half years.

My teacher Professor Munatssir Mamoon introduced me to Professor Dr. A. F. Salahuddin Ahmed, an eminent scholar and historian of the South Asian subcontinent, and National Professor of Bangladesh. I met him with the draft of my manuscript at his residence. He also showed a keen interest for my research work. He became interested in my research and agreed to write a 'foreword' for my book. He gave me the responsibility to write a chapter titled 'Christianity in Bangladesh' for his upcoming project, where he was the editor of the book. He is no more to see my book and I could not work in his project. He died on 19 October 2014. He could not write the 'foreword' for my book before his death.

It pains me to think that when the book will see the light of day I will miss the enthusiasm and the soul-stirring smile of Professor Dr. A. F. Salahuddin Ahmed and former Archbishop of Dhaka diocese Most Rev. Paulinus Costa, DD.

I am immensely grateful to the Ganguly family, and particularly to Mr. Pius Ganguly, nephew of Archbishop Ganguly and his wife Mrs. Rakhi Ganguly and other members of Ganguly family, staying at Dhaka and in the USA for their encouragement and unconditional help of my research work. Mr. Ganguly's residence and office, PM enterprise at Gulshan, Dhaka became an integral part of this work, and served as the base for my research work. To ensure availability of both Masters and PhD dissertations of Archbishop Ganguly at the Notre Dame University, USA, Mr. Ganguly invested all efforts to see them at my hands in time. The intellectual stimulation of this book came from Dr. James Tejosh S Das, a Professor of Dhaka University. Many arguments were generated and debated during numerous sittings at PM Enterprises, where the argumentative minds of Dr. Das and Mr. Ganguly established many historical facts, a valuable part of this book. Dr. Das also volunteered to read the entire manuscript and gave some valuable advice and comments, fully added into this book. Besides Mr. Ganguly, some primary but valuable information was provided by Major (rtd) Nizanur Rahman, an ex-student of Bandura Holy Cross High School, which proved worth adding.

In Rajshahi University, Department of History, I am especially grateful to Dr. Mahbubar Rahman, Dr. Abul Kashem, Professor M. Farukuzzaman, Saikhul Islam Mamun Ziad for their help and who also made easier to use the library of Rajshai University. I am particularly indebted to

Preface and Acknowledgments

Dr. Mahbubur Rahman for his most needed support and guidance at his personal archive.

I am also grateful to Dr. Sonia Nishat Amin, Professor, Department of History, University of Dhaka, for her keen interest in my research and for providing me a huge number of books on medieval church from her personal library. And also Dr. Nurul Islam Manjur, Professor, Department of History, Jahangirnagar University, Dhaka for his criticism on the earlier version of my few chapters.

I was extremely benefitted from conversations and their personal materials with Professor Muntassir Mamoon, Professor, Department of History, Dhaka University, Fr. Eugene E. Homrich, CSC, Fr. Jyoti F. Costa, Fr. Francis Gomes Sima, Brother Jarlath D'Souza, CSC, Brother Herald Bijoy Rodrigues, CSC, Fr. Marino Rigon, S.X., Father Adolfo L'imperio, PIME, Fr. Enzo Corba, PIME, Fr. Gianantonio Baio, PIME, Fr. Apollo, Father Silvano Garello, SX, Sr. Joseph Costa, SSMI, Dr. Md. Aminul Islam Jewel, Mr. Sunil Pereira, Kabbo Kamrul. I am particularly grateful to Fr. Francis Sima for his great co-operation with chapter 9. The chapter grew under his supervision. Many arguments and narratives come from his ideas. So, the particular chapter on religious reformation in Christianity is the fruit of the hard work of Fr. Francis Sima. It also pains to think that when the book will see the light, he will be no more to see it, and I shall miss his smiling presence. Mr. Sunil Pereira opened the Christian Communications Centre (Pratibeshi Library) for me. The library is situated in old Dhaka. Dr. Md. Aminul Islam Jewel helped me to understand the medical topic issue related to my book.

This research would not have seen the light of day without a generous support for type settings and publication-related expenditure from the Holy Cross Fathers and their Provincial in Bangladesh, Father James C. Cruze, CSC. I am always be grateful for their help. Thanks are also due to Fr. Tom McDermott, CSC and Fr. Patrick Gaffney, CSC for their taking huge pressure to read my entire manuscript and added their valuable suggestions at the very last stage of my work.

My special thanks are due to Fr. Joyanto Gomes and Fr. Rev. Bulbul Augustine Rebeiro for their unconditional help. They provided a huge number of photographic collections as well as documents from the archive of Christian Communication Centre, Luxmibazar, Dhaka. The director of the Province Archives Center is Rev. Christopher Kuhn, CSC, congregation of Holy Cross, U.S. Province of Priests and Brothers, Province Archives

Preface and Acknowledgments

Center, P.O. Box 568, Notre Dame, IN 46556, USA, help is beyond description. He sent me the most needed photographs to me through email.

My gratitude due to Mr. M M Zahidur Rahman Biplob and his photographic institution 'Studio Creation', both of them played a significant role as the old photos could get a proper shape as well as he invested a numerous time with me to collect photographs from different places.

Among fellow well-wishers and colleagues, my sincere thanks are due to Mr. Md. Muksodur Rahman Patwary, my maternal uncle, Additional Secretary, Cabinet Division, People's Republic of Bangladesh, Mr. Md. Jamal Uddin Ahmed, the then Deputy Commissioner of Dinajpur, Professor Mahfuza Khanam, former General Secretary of Asiatic Society of Bangladesh, and among other well-wishers and colleagues who were constant support for my research work.

My special thanks are due to my friends and well-wishers, who encouraged me during this arduous work; among them, Md. Jewel, Mehedial-Sakib, F. M. Masum, Mohammad Monzurul Hasan Riad, Md. Jayed Shahrear, Khandakar Nahid Hasano, Taufique Bin Islam, Delwar Hossain and many other friends.

Chapters 6 and 9 were read at the annual seminar of Bangladesh Itihas Sambiloni and Bangladesh Historical Association on 7 February 2015 and 15 May 2015, respectively. I am grateful to the authorities of the Associations where I received valuable criticism and advice on my essays.

In preparing this book I had to work in the Dhaka University Library, Moreau House, Banasree, Rampura, Dhaka, Christian Communication Centre (Pratibeshi Library), National Archives of Bangladesh, Holy Spirit Major Seminary Library, Banani, Dhaka, Caritas Bangladesh, Malibagh, Dhaka, Holy Rosary Church, Tejgaon, Dhaka, Rajshahi University Library, Rajshahi, Heritage: Archives of Bangladesh History, Rajshahi, the Liberation War Museum, Segun Bagicha, Dhaka. My thanks are due to the staffs, priests and sisters of these libraries, archives, museum and churches.

My special thanks are due to my mentor Professor David Burrell, CSC and Professor Fr. Stephen Bevans, S.V.D. for their great initiative so that my research could see the light of day in a form of a book. It is a great honor for me to have my book published from a top mark publication house like WIPF and Stock.

Finally, I want to express my gratitude to my family members for their unconditional support for my research work, especially my parents M. A. Sattar Miah and Begum Roushan Sattar. They are the sources of my all inspirations. The love, care, support and courage I have received from my three sisters Sumya Sattar, Tahmina Sattar and Humida Sattar Tanima is beyond description. My maternal uncle Mr. Najir Ullah Khan's support is well beyond any form of repayment. It is worth mentioning to show my gratitude to my wife, Nusrat Jahan Ahmed, who spent many sleepless nights beside me, while I was doing my research work from the very first day after our marriage.

S. M. Tanveer Ahmed
Assistant Professor
Department of History
Jagannath University, Dhaka.
25.04.2017.

Abbreviations

Bro.	Brother.
CSC	Congregatio a Sancta Croce [Latin]: Congregation of Holy Cross.
Fr.	Father.
OSB	Order of St. Benedict.
PIME	Pontifical Institute of Missions [Milano].
DD	Doctor of Divinity [for bishops].
Rev.	Reverend.
SJ	Society of Jesus.
SMRA	local congregation of sisters [Bangladesh].
Sr.	Sister.
SVD	Societas Verbi Divini [Society of Divine Word]—missionary group.
SX	Societas Xaveriena [Xaverian Fathers].

1

Introduction

AS A BENGALI ARCHBISHOP with a life spanning over three political regimes that Bangladesh went through, leading to socio-economic changes, the life and times of Archbishop Theotonius Amal Ganguly, CSC constitutes a significant chapter in the history of East Bengal.[1] My object of this research is not to describe his biography, but, rather to raise question why he is important from the context of history of East Bengal, and not simply because he was the first Bengalee Archbishop of this soil in the history of Catholic Church in the last four hundred years. To have a better understanding of his life and times, one should know the history of the missionaries' activities in this region. Hence, my question on the life and times of T. A. Ganguly is co-related with the progress of the missionaries' activities in East Bengal. No scholar has raised any question in this regard so far. Beyond a few PhD theses, some books were published at different times, mostly in the last century; but most of them dealt with the history of Protestant missionary activities. So, this would be the first attempt to fill in this gap and to address a long-felt need for the Catholic history of East Bengal. The literary review is divided into two parts. Firstly, an effort to investigate the missionary activities and later, examining the biographical books on Archbishop Theotonius Amal Ganguly, CSC.

---

1. The name of East Bengal was officially changed to East Pakistan on 23 March 1956 when the first Constitution of the Islamic Republic of Pakistan came into effect. Prior to that date, it was referred to both ways in official documents. After 1971, the same region became Bangladesh. I have used Bangladesh, East Bengal and East Pakistan interchangeably.

In 1908, Julius Richter, DD, published (Sydney H. Moore Translated), *A History of Missions in India,* which thoroughly covered early missionary activities in mid nineteenth century in India. He tried to investigate eight main aspects of the missionary activities in the region, and started his narratives from the landing of the Portuguese in India and spread of Roman Catholic activities here in the second half of the Sixteenth century, and how it declined within a short time. In addition, he described the activities of the Danish mission in India from 1706–1798. Consequently, he also pointed out that the development of Protestant missions' activities during the nineteenth century in the Indian sub-continent, in contrast, examined the religious problems of Indian missions within the framework of Indian society. Under such circumstance, how the missionary organizations had mitigated their problems, and continued their activities in such a difficult situation during that time, pointed out by the author. Furthermore, he recounted that the minor social and religious movements had attributed more or less directly to Christian influences observable in almost every part of India during the nineteenth century. Finally, it dealt with the success of the missions in India.[2]

In 1956, K. Ingham, published, *Reformers in India, 1793–1833: An account of the work of Christian missionaries on behalf of social reform,* which covered the work of Christian missionaries on behalf of social reform. It, however, hardly sheds any light upon the subject of the success or failure of the missionaries in gaining converts in India, which Ingham believes to be "beyond human assessment."[3]

In 1965, Muhammad Mohar Ali, published, *The Bengali Reaction to Christian Missionary Activities* 1833–1857, examining three main aspects of the reaction:

a. the reaction to evangelizing efforts in general,

b. the reaction to specific conversions to Christianity and

c. the reaction of the landed aristocracy in particular to the spread of Christianity in the *mufassal.*

He also investigated the three characteristics of the reaction to conversion to Christianity. Those are:

a. challenge to repossess the Christian converts to Hinduism;

---

2. Richter, D.D., *Missions in India.*
3. Ingham, *Reformers in India, 1793–1833.*

INTRODUCTION

b. challenge to put into effect caste disabilities upon converts;

c. violence upon missionaries and converts.⁴

In 1967, E. D. Potts, published, *British Baptist Missionaries in India, 1793–1837*, which dealt with "The History of Serampore and its Missions" where Dr. Potts endeavored to elaborately show the achievements of the Serampore Trio, viz. William Carey, Joshua Marshman, and William Ward. In his enthusiasm he made some rather wild charges against modern Indian historians, who are alleged to be "blind . . . to the role played by three remarkable men", and also "are reluctant to cite primary sources for their information."⁵

In 1971, Kanti Prasanna Sen Gupta, published, *The Christian Missionaries in Bengal, 1793–1833*, which dealt with the Protestant missionaries activities in Bengal. Dr. Sen tried to show the missionary attitude towards the people among whom they worked. He also tried to correlate between the missionary objectives and their achievements.⁶

In 1988, George Kottuppallil, S.D.P., published, *History of the Catholic Missions in Central Bengal, 1855–1886*. The author dealt with three aspects of the Catholic history of central Bengal. In the first part, he focused on the socio-economic and political conditions of central Bengal and on the condition of the Catholic Church in Bengal. The origin of the Protestant Bengali community was briefly alluded to and the search for a missionary society to look after the districts of central Bengal was described at length. The second part of the study refers to the period when central Bengal was *de jure* a mere mission territory under the jurisdiction of Calcutta, even though *de facto* it was autonomous. The third part describes the history of the territory of Central Bengal under the direction of Antonio Marietti (1870–79) and Francesco Pozzi (1879–86) until the establishment of the Diocese of Krisnagar.⁷

Antonio Marietti and Sir Man Mohan Ghose wrote the Catholics history of Jessore district. Under the title "*Jessorer Katholic Mondolir Itihas*" (The History of the Catholic Church in Jessore), it was added to the last of the three volumes of Marietti's, *Kristio Sobhar Sadharon Itihas*, (Church History), (Calcutta 1898). Even if inexact with regard to certain dates, Ghose's

---

4. Ali, *The Bengali Reaction to Christian Missionary Activities*.
5. Potts, *British Baptist Missionaries in India*.
6. Gupta, *The Christian Missionaries in Bengal*.
7. Kottuppallil, S.D.P., *History of the Catholic Missions in Central Bengal*.

3

work has provided several important insights regarding the Bengali's view of the Church and of the missionary apostolate. He also highlighted the importance of the role of the native catechist.[8]

Antonio Marietti is believed to have compiled a brief history of the early years of the Bengal mission, but unfortunately, he destroyed it after he resigned from the prefecture in 1879.[9]

In 1905, Francesco Rocca, one of the PIME missionaries stationed at Krisnagar, wrote a brief sketch of the earlier years of the mission, entitled *Cenni sulla Missione del Bengala Centrale*. As it was written several decades after the events, it contains certain inaccuracies. Gerardo Brambilla, in his book *"II PIME ele sue Missioni-Bengala"*, used the work of Rocca in its entirety. Brambilla's work, however, is in the nature of a popular narrative and poorly documented.

A truly valid contribution rendered to the historiography of central Bengal is that of Giovanni Battista Tragella who compiled a three-volume work, *Le Missioni Estere di Milano nel Quadro degli Avvenimenti Contemporanei*. Although he devoted only five brief chapters (roughly one tenth of the entire work) to Bengal, it is well documented with materials found in the archives of the PIME. As the title suggests, the work of Tragella is an example of the history of a young Church presented from the viewpoint of a missionary institute in Europe.[10]

In 2010, Zohra Sultana Runy's unpublished PhD dissertation, 'Rajshahi Bivage Christian Samproday: Akti Oitihasik Parjalochana' (The Christian Community in Rajshahi Division: A historical Observation),[11] dealt with the activities of the Christian community of the thirteen districts of Rajshahi Division from early settlement of Christianity to 2010. In her dissertation, she described that she could not find enough sources of the Protestant Christians.[12] On the other hand, to describe the situation of the

---

8. Ibid.

9. Ibid.

10. Ibid.

11. Runy, "Rajshahi Bivage Christian Samproday" (The Christian Community in Rajshahi Division).

12. It is to be noted that most of the Protestant sources are found at the archive of India office, London, School of Oriental African Studies (SOAS) and many other archives and libraries of London, England and different archives and libraries of the different countries in the world. On the other hand, Catholic sources are basically found in Rome, Portugal as well as different archives and libraries of the respective countries from where the missionaries came under the congregation. She did not use such type of archival

INTRODUCTION

Catholics, she used basically secondary sources on which her argument was developed. She tried to draw the picture of the activities of Christian community of the particular region. Her whole work was divided into eight chapters, where she tried to describe:

a. The origin and development of the Christian Community in Bangladesh,

b. The coming and the development of the Christian Community in Rajshahi Division,

c. The organizational structure of the Christian Community in Rajshahi Division,

d. The demographic discussion,

e. The socio-economic development work for Christian Community,

f. The social customs of the Christian Community of the division.[13]

All of her research works was descriptive; not analytical. Therefore, from the context of historical research,[14] it is a descriptive history where reader will get information only.

On the other hand, three books have been written on the Archbishop Theotonius Amal Ganguly, CSC till now, which are, basically, his biography. And they look at him from the religious point of view. These books lack the context of historical materialism and the proper way of using sources as well as the historical method. As far as historical method is concerned, it could be said that the books contained information only but failed to upgrade to become history. They can be considered as sources for writing history but cannot become a historical book itself.

In 1998, Bernard Sapon Gomes, published, *Bangladesh Mondolir Gourab-Archbishop Theotonius Amal Ganguly*, is a biography book. It included the reminiscences of the different personalities who were directly or indirectly connected with T. A. Ganguly. Even poems are also incorporated

materials for her dissertation. For an example, PIME priests had arrived from Italy as well as the early stage of the Christian missionaries in East Bengal had arrived from Portugal. Most of the documents they had sent to their own countries in their respective time. But she did not consult with the respective archival material for her research. Under the circumstances, it showed the limitation of the research, which was admitted by the researcher as well.

13. Runy, Ibid.

14. For an interesting discussion on historical research, see also my book, *Itihas Gabesona Paddhati* (History Research Methodology).

5

in this work. So the shape of the book failed to achieve to become a historical book. Besides that, it failed to raise any question about the importance of his life and times. It was full of stories and reminiscence and lacked the appropriate method of writing historical record as a work of research. The purpose of the book seemed to serve only a theological aspect. The author did not use any footnotes clarifying the sources used in writing the book.[15]

In 2009, Father Frank Quinlivan, CSC, published, *Strong in His Gentleness Servant of God Theotonius Amal Ganguly, C.S.C., Archbishop of Dhaka, Bangladesh*, also a descriptive biography of T. A. Ganguly. The author acknowledged that he had collected the information from different archives within the Congregation of Holy Cross, and the files, notes and memory of Fr. Timm, CSC, but he did not mention any note, footnote or reference in his writings. So, in this work too, the proper historical method was not followed in his writings. It also did not raise any question either. The perspective of the writing reflected a rather theological point of view instead of being historical.[16]

In 2011, Father Adam S. Pereira, CSC published, *Diba Loker Ujjal Nokhtra Theotonius Amal Ganguly, C.S.C.*, which also dealt with a description of his life. It can be presumed that the author took information basically from the archives of the University of Notre Dame, Indiana, USA, archives of the Holy Cross Fathers in Bangladesh and personal connection with the different priests and personalities. But he did not explicitly acknowledge this in his book. And he too, like many others, did not raise any question through his writings. The writing is based on description and, in several places, the author resorts to theological points of view to establish his argument, not in historical law of causation.[17]

It is under this circumstance that I attempt to show why the life and times of Archbishop T. A. Ganguly, CSC constituted a very important part within the context of the history of East Bengal. His appointment and responsibility as the Archbishop of Dhaka Archdiocese was a challenging one. The different types of difficulties he had faced in and outside of church, especially in the most important episode in the history of Bengal taking place during his tenure in 1971 triggers an important query. I try to investigate his role during the struggle for independence and the liberation war of Bangladesh and its aftermath as well as how he had initiated to reform

15. Gomes. *Archbishop Theotonius Amal Ganguly*.
16. Quinlivan, CSC, *Strong in His Gentleness*.
17. Pereira C.S.C., *Diba Loker Ujjal Nokhtra*.

INTRODUCTION

the Catholic Church after Vatican-II. I also try to examine his philosophical thoughts as well as activities through historical sources. I attempt to investigate these questions, through historical sources and materials, which have not yet been explored by any scholar so far. This investigation into the life and times of Archbishop T. A. Ganguly will certainly broaden the scope of the history of East Bengal.

PERIOD OF STUDY

In this book, I have mainly dealt with the events and issues in the life and times of Archbishop Theotonius Amal Ganguly, CSC from 1920–1977. But, at the same time, I have gone both forward and backward beyond these two points of time span as it influences his life and gives it a context. In order to go this, I have taken two chapters where firstly, I tried to investigate the social structure of East Bengal in the Colonial and Post-Colonial Period and then, very shortly, try to draw a picture of the background of the Catholic missionaries' activities on this soil (East Bengal). In an effort to put my sources in order, I have attempted to arrange the chronicles of issues and events in a linear fashion. In doing so, I believe, it will be easier for the readers to understand my arguments.

SOURCES

All types of published and unpublished documents from different archives and libraries of the missionaries, official documents, contemporary newspapers, journals, gazetteers, and declaration of court, interviews with the concerned personalities, published books, different websites, vernacular articles, reports, unpublished dissertations and all types of historical and literary sources have been very useful sources for this book. A numerous other primary sources have also been used to enrich the book.

However, the theme of the present study primarily remains an analysis of the life and times of Archbishop Theotonius Amal Ganguly, CSC and his activities. Therefore, I first try to sketch the social structure of this region and the background of the missionaries' activities and then merge them with my subject matter.

Finally, the categorization of chapters is required.

Chapter 2 deals with the social structure of East Bengal in the Colonial and Postcolonial period. In particular, it analyses the mode of production in British Colonial and Postcolonial period. A theoretical framework tries to take shape in the chapter.

Chapter 3 of this book provides a general picture of the background of the Catholic missionaries' activities in this region, providing a very short description from early activities to 1971 as the reader could easily be informed for the main discussion of this book.

Chapter 4 describes the family background of T. A. Ganguly and tries to explain how and why the family changed their surname from 'Gomes' into 'Ganguly'.

Chapter 5 discusses the educational career of T. A. Ganguly and sheds light on how he entered seminary life.

Chapter 6 examines the philosophical thoughts of T. A. Ganguly, and how he mixed the content of Christianity with the concept of local philosophy, tries to analyze his philosophy through his writings and uses other sources to clarify his arguments.

Chapter 7 discusses the question of the activities of T. A. Ganguly. It analyses how he went to the highest position of the Catholic Church in East Bengal through his activities.

Chapter 8 examines the role of Archbishop T. A. Ganguly in the Liberation War of Bangladesh and its aftermath. It analyses how he got involved in the war of independence through his works.

Chapter 9 deals with the religious reformation in the Catholic Church under the guidance of the Vatican-II. It also analyses the role of T. A. Ganguly, CSC in those reforms of the Catholic Church and how he acted during that time.

Chapter 10 describes his death and the aftermath of his life. It also describes the role of the local church for the process of canonizing him posthumously.

Chapter 11 is conclusion.

2

Social Structure of East Bengal in Colonial and Post-Colonial Period

To UNDERSTAND THE LIFE and times of Archbishop Theotonius Amal Ganguly, CSC it is very important to comprehend the social structure of East Bengal.[1] It would not be appropriate or even possible to de-link the argument of the social structure of the region from the continuing customs and structure of the greater Bengal, to give a context to the life and times of T. A. Ganguly. He was born and brought up in this soil. Hence, this chapter tries to portray a picture of the social structure of East Bengal.

SOCIAL STRUCTURE OF EAST BENGAL

The term social structure is not descriptive; rather it contains a theoretical framework. It would be worth mentioning that every society developed with different mode of production. When the new structure expanded further, it produced conflicts in social, political and economic arena as it continued to expand its sphere of authority in every arena. The result of the colonial rule in East Bengal produced the dynamics of such conflicts, catalyzing huge changes among those of the region.

Before the East India Company prevailed in the Battle of Plassey in 1757, Bengali society practiced a mode of production, which Karl Marx dubbed an "Asiatic Mode of Production."[2] Therefore, the social structure

---

1. For details see also, Mondal, 'Social Formation in Bangladesh," 343–66.
2. Islam, *Bangladesher Gram (Village of Bangladesh)*, 15. See also, Bhadra, "Marx's

9

was straight. The peculiar character of this system may be judged from the following description, contained in an old official report of the British House of Commons on Indian affairs, given by Karl Marx as follows verbatim:

> A village, geographically considered, is a tract of country comprising some hundred or thousand acres of arable and waste lands; politically viewed it resembles a corporation or township. Its proper establishment of officers and servants consists of the following descriptions: The *potail*, or head inhabitant, who has generally the superintendence of the affairs of the village, settles the disputes of the inhabitants attends to the police, and performs the duty of collecting the revenue within his village, a duty which his personal influence and minute acquaintance with the situation and concerns of the people render him the best qualified for this charge. The *kurnum* keeps the accounts of cultivation, and registers everything connected with it. The *tallier* and the *totie*, the duty of the former of which consists [. . .] in gaining information of crimes and offences, and in escorting and protecting persons travelling from one village to another; the province of the latter appearing to be more immediately confined to the village, consisting, among other duties, in guarding the crops and assisting in measuring them. The boundary-man, who preserves the limits of the village, or gives evidence respecting them in cases of dispute. The Superintendent of Tanks and Watercourses distributes the water [. . .] for the purposes of agriculture. The Brahmin, who performs the village worship. The schoolmaster, who is seen teaching the children in a village to read and write in the sand. The calendar-brahmin, or astrologer, etc. These officers and servants generally constitute the establishment of a village; but in some parts of the country it is of less extent, some of the duties and functions above described being united in the same person; in others it exceeds the above-named number of individuals. [. . .] Under this simple form of municipal government, the inhabitants of the country have lived from time immemorial. The boundaries of the villages have been but seldom altered; and though the villages themselves have been sometimes injured, and even desolated by war, famine or disease, the same name, the same limits, the same interests, and even the same families have continued for ages. The inhabitants gave themselves no trouble about the breaking up and divisions of kingdoms; while the village remains entire, they care not to what power it is transferred, or to what sovereign it devolves; its internal

views on India," 78–127. Umar, *The Indian National Movement*.

economy remains unchanged. The *potail* is still the head inhabitant, and still acts as the petty judge or magistrate, and collector or renter of the village.[3]

British trade and administration, for its own profit, completed a penetration of the social, economic and political status quo for the first time in the history of India. Karl Marx argued that:

> The British trade and commerce wrecked the structure of rural India which centered round the handlooms and the spinning wheels. Inter-relation between agriculture and cottage industry which formed the very basis of the old rural-economy was almost destroyed.[4]

Besides, the city-based industry also suffered because of the British colonial policy.

The East India Company had taken few initiatives to develop the infrastructure of the region as much as their military and commercial purpose could be fulfilled. The set-up of the railway system was one of the fundamental examples in the field of communication, which put an end to the loneliness of different remote parts of India. Bengal entered the era of rail communication system in 1854.[5] This also helped to develop modern industry. Giving such account of all these changes, Karl Marx pointed out in his famous essay on *The British Rule in India* in this way:

> England, it is true, in causing a social revolution in Hindostan, was actuated only by the vilest interests, and was stupid in her manner of enforcing them. But that is not the question. The question is, can mankind fulfill its destiny without a fundamental revolution in the social state of Asia? If not, whatever may have been the crimes of England she was the unconscious tool of history in bringing about that revolution.[6]

However, the intervention of East India Company as the state ruler introduced capitalism on land in the name of Permanent Settlement.[7] By

3. Marx, *The British Rule in India*. See also, Marx, *The Capital*; 337–39.

4. Marx, *Capital*, 492.

5. For detailed on Railway communication in Bengal see also, Islam, *An Economic History of Bengal*, 265–81.

6. Marx, Ibid., 493.

7. To further study on permanent Settlement, see also, Guha, *Chirastahi Bandobaster Sutrapat* (The preparatory of Permanent Settlement). See also, Islam, *The Permanent Settlement in Bengal*.

this arrangement, the power of tax-collection was given to the *Zamindars* (Landowners) and the revenue was fixed. The company had decided that nine-tenths of total collection of revenue should go to the company, and remaining money would be enjoyed by the ownership right on the land of the *Zamindars* class.[8]

The decision was basically motivated by political causes. However, the reality was different. Because after the proclamation of Permanent Settlement, the lowly subalterns are at the receiving, end and thus, are not the focus of this arrangement.[9] The proof is to be found behind the argument from a memorandum of the *Bongiya Pradeshik Krishak Sabha* (Bengal Provincial Peasants Association) put forward to the Floud Commission in 1939, which described the bad consequences of the Permanent Settlement in the industry and commerce of Bengal:

> The *Zamindears* of Bengal enjoy tax rebate on their income from agricultural product. Land revenue of Bengal accounts for half of the revenue collected from other classes than *Zamindears*. On the other hand, land revenue collection in Bombay is double of the income tax. That means more taxes have been wrongfully imposed on income from industry, trade etc. than on income from land. The mal-adjustment of tax-burden plays a vital role in hindering the growth of industry. If a man knows that by investing in land he can be assured of an almost tax free income, he would not invest his capital in industry which is comparatively risky. Thus it is seen that the Permanent Settlement is directly responsible for the backwardness of the province in industry and for the dangerous process of subdivision and fragmentation of land.[10]

Therefore, the Bengal society failed to develop as a capitalist society. A new type of mode of production was introduced here. New Marxist political economist Hamza Alavi pointed out this type of mode of production as the 'new colonial mode of production'. Although the mode of production seemed like capitalist mode of production, its main nature is central development. Therefore, the periphery failed to get any importance so far as development is concerned.[11]

8. Umar, Ibid., 6.

9. Guha, Ibid., 137–38.

10. Memorandum of the *Bongiya Pradeshik Krishak Sabha* (Bengal Provincial Peasants Association) *to the Floud Commission in* 1939, published by the Bengal Provincial Kisan Sava, 52; cited in Umar, Ibid., 8.

11. Alavi, 'India and the Colonial Mode of Production'. Cited from, Mamoon,

Social Structure of East Bengal

On the other hand, it was also true that a lot of false notions and inhibitions existed among the Bengalis, which also became an obstacle to the expansion of industry and commerce.[12] But these barriers would not have been critical if there were room in the society for the development or expansion of industry and commerce, as was the case in Bombay and Madras. The pressure was not built up in Bengal mainly because of the prevalence of the Permanent Settlement. When the guarantee was there to exist peacefully on what one earned from land, endeavor in commerce and industry was logically absent. Notions and shyness did not have any or not as much of an impact on other provinces. But the required endeavor in Bengal effortlessly went together with notions and shyness. So, both adjectives had stronger impact in Bengal than in other provinces in India. This became quite clearly apparent from the family history of Ramdulal Dey, Dwarakanath Tagore, Ramgopal Ghosh[13] and such other personalities. Although Dwarakanath Tagore spent but a fraction of his enormous earning from industrial and commercial activities in agreeable endeavors, the outstanding portion he spent on land. Dwarakanath Tagore was not prejudiced by any notions or shyness and he was one of the front-liners in commercial and industrial endeavor in the nineteenth century. In spite of his endeavor, Binoy Gosh has stated what a gigantic sum of money he had invested in buying lands:

> By investing in purchasing land than in industry, Dwarakanath buried lakhs of rupees under the ground. The history of Dwarakanath's purchasing landed property and becoming a *zaminder* will be available in the deeds and documents of the 'Board of Revenue.' By purchasing huge properties from North Bengal and East Bengal to West Bengal and Orissa he ultimately became a big *zemindar*. Dwarakanath could not understand that one could not be a *zemindar* and an industrial at the same time. One had to be both a *zemindar* and industrialist, land lordship which was firm and immovable survived, while industry being mobile would not last long. There was no exception to this rule in the case of Dwarakanath.[14]

Nineteenth Century East Bengal, 100.

12. Ghosh, *Banglar Samajik Itihaser Dhara*, 116–36.

13. For more details on the social change in Bengal, see also, Ahmed, *Social Ideas and Social Change in Bengal.*

14. Ghosh, Ibid., 141. Translated from, Umar, Ibid., 8.

That was the reality of Bengali society for its social structure. That is why the society failed to upgrade into as an industrial society. Therefore, it showed that the Bengali society developed based on land and government officials or any other job. In the long-run, the permanent settlement resulted in the Bengal society's failure to develop as an entrepreneurial society. Under the circumstances, a new type of social structure was developed here. So the Marxist discussion on the social structure does not address the East Bengal society. In the colonial period, a new mode of production was arisen here. Hamza Alavi pointed out a few features of the colonial mode of production:

a. Free labour, as in capitalism,
b. Economic compulsions on the primary producer, as in capitalism,
c. Separation between economic and political power as in capitalism,
d. Production of primary and capital goods, which acquire a distinctive colonial character.[15]

However, a different social structure was developed here since colonial period, where it might look like having a capitalist form, but in the reality society failed to achieve as a capitalist one. Under the proclamation of permanent settlement, the capital was invested in land. So the formation of villages took a new shape, while the land question remained unresolved. Who are the real owners of land? Because in Mughal and Nawabi period, peasants enjoyed cultivating the land, while its real owner was a king, appointed by God. Thus the permanent settlement brought a huge change in village structure. Now, as try to define the village structure of East Bengal, we must inquire into its structure.

VILLAGE STRUCTURE

How was the village structure formed in East Bengal? The village was a place where a Bengali peasant is associated with certain activities and others with his extended family all of which might or might not be coterminous with his "village." If a peasant was a Muslim, some of his activities were also associated with a mosque, whose devotees may or may not be coterminous with his "village." Political actions might occur for him inside the boundaries of both intra-village and extra-village alignment. Economic activities were

---

15. Alavi, Ibid., cited from, Mamoon, Ibid., 101.

also varied on different circumstances, depending on whether the villagers were tilling land of their own, or of another "village", or whether he was buying or selling in a nearby or far away market or town, and where, to or from whom, he had borrowed or lent land, money or rice.[16]

My question of concern on the social structure of a village was mainly related with two major phenomenons; class and power relation. So if any researcher wanted to analyze the social structure of East Bengal it would be seen as essentially Marxian. For the same analysis I resort to the discussion of Peter, J. Bertoci unpublished PhD thesis. In every society, we can see that it had a "material" foundation. The discussion of material foundation is very relevant to understand the social relations and political power in a human society. The material foundation of a society was built on the condition of different historical and cultural contexts; the opportunities for both choice and action for some individuals and groups are qualitatively and quantitatively constrained, while those of others are enhanced.

Under such circumstances, state endeavors always took place against the people's interests when it comes to its infrastructural development. The Indian people started their movements in different times in different ways against British colonial power.[17] At last, freedom came in India in 1947[18] and the sub-continent was divided into two parts based on two-nation theory.[19] By this time, the nature of the colonial mode of production had not changed. The newly born Pakistan and India brought about heightened hopes and aspirations stirred in the people's heart for a better future. East Bengal became the part of Pakistan, however, without any change in this post-colonial period; turning into a post-colonial mode of production. Moreover, East Pakistan was treated as the colony of West Pakistan, and the post-colonial mode of production was active in the region.

---

16. Bertoci, "Elusive Villages", 3.

17. In different times, the Indian people tried to build up the social, political and cultural movements against British colonial rule. For detailed discussions, see also, Bandyopadhyay, *From Palassey to Partition*.

18. For interesting discussion on Indian freedom Movement, see also, Lapierre and Collins, *Freedom At Midnight*.

19. For detail, see also, Wheeler, *The Politics of Pakistan*.

3

Background of Missionary Activities in East Bengal

CHRISTIANITY IS ONE OF the major religions of the world, deriving from Jesus Christ. It is a monotheistic religion through a differentiation initiated by Saint Paul's doctrine of 'Trinity',[1] experiencing Father, Son, and Holy Spirit as one God.

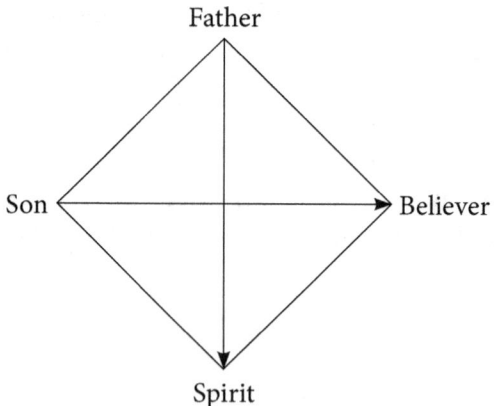

Source: Burrell, CSC, *Religious Understanding*, 228.

---

1. 'Trinity' is one of the most important issues in Christianity. For details see also, Burgh, *The Legacy*, 369–71.

Background of Missionary Activities in East Bengal

The source of the religion is the New Testament of the Bible. Christianity is divided into three branches—Roman Catholic,[2] Orthodox[3] and Protestant.[4] Their mission is essentially the same despite certain differences in structure. Their religious belief is 'Jesus is the son of God and savior'. However, there are different schools of missionaries, which play a significant role in preaching and in spreading Christianity throughout the World.[5] The discussion of this chapter is limited to the Catholic missionaries' activities in East Bengal.

The activities of Catholic missionaries in East Bengal from the early stage to 1971 constitute one of the most significant aspects in the history of East Bengal. The activities of the Catholic missionaries could be divided into four divisions according to the major administrative regions of the Catholic Church:[6]

Diocese and Archdiocese of Dhaka[7]

Diocese of Chittagong

Diocese of Dinajpur

Diocese of Khulna

---

2. Catholicism is a term, which in its broadest sense refers to the beliefs and practices of Christian denominations that describe themselves as catholic. It commonly reflects traditions of Catholic theology, doctrine, liturgy, ethics, and spirituality. For an interesting discussion on Catholicism, see also, McBrien, *Catholicism*.

3. It is to be noted that the Eastern Orthodox Church explains that it is the One, Holy, Catholic and Apostolic Church, which was established by Jesus Christ in his Great Commission to the apostles. It performs what it comprehends to be the actual Christian belief and upholds the holy custom approved down from the apostles.
For details on Orthodox Christianity, see also, Ware, *Orthodox Way*.

4. As we know from the history of Christianity, Protestantism is a method of Christian belief and rehearsal, which was instigated with the Protestant Reformation, a movement against what its followers considered to be errors in the Roman Catholic Church. For details on Protestantism, see also, Wylie, LL.D, *The History of Protestantism*.

5. Hannan, "Banglaya Christo Dharmer Prochar (The preaching of Christianity in Bengal)", 259.

6. Interview with the former Archbishop of Bangladesh the Most Rev. Paulinus Costa, DD at his present residing place at Holy Rosary Church, Tejgaon, Dhaka-1215 on 8 August 2014.

7. The Diocese of Dhaka turned into the Archdiocese in 1950.

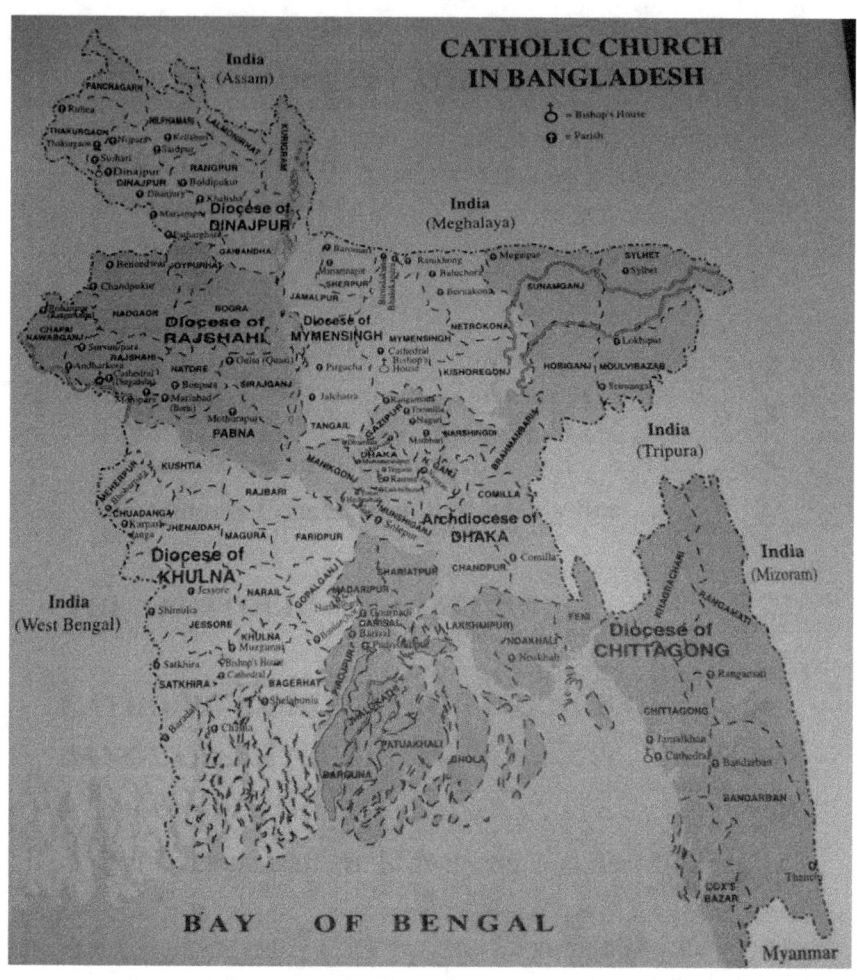

3.1 Map of Catholic Church in Bangladesh, Photo Courtesy: Catholic Directory 2011.

DIOCESE AND ARCHDIOCESE OF DHAKA

In the second half of the 16th century, there were Catholics in different parts of the province of East Bengal. Renowned among these early Christian settlements were Hussainpur of Mymensingh District and Shripur near Sonargaon,[8] the old capital of Eastern Bengal. When Mylapore (Madras,

8. For interesting discussion on the history of Sonargaon see also, Khan, *Thousand Years of Sonargaon*.

Background of Missionary Activities in East Bengal

India) was upgraded into a Diocese in 1606, the mission stations of Bengal were placed under its jurisdiction.[9]

Portuguese missionaries started their works in the East Bengal mission with two Jesuits[10] from Portugal in 1598. Francesco Fernandez and Father De Souza were assigned for this region. East Bengal covered a vast territory, which was situated in the northeast of India.[11] Its territory was more than 300 hundred miles long, together with Assam and the Arakan district of Burma as well as the two-third of the present-day Bangladesh.[12] Portuguese started the early missionaries' activities here around 1600 AD.[13]

However, the parishes which were under the jurisdiction of the Portuguese "Padroado" agreement were all turned over to the bishops of Dhaka (six parishes) and Chittagong (One parish Shibpur = Padrishibpur).[14]

There were two Roman Catholic missions had worked in Dhaka. The Portuguese, who were subject to the Bishop of Madras and the Congregation of Holy Cross,[15] who arrived here in 1853, an American religious order, whose chief filled the Roman Catholic See of Dhaka.[16] Holy Cross Missionaries are continuing their activities here still now.

In 1957, the last Portuguese priests left Dhaka. Portugal gave up jurisdiction of the Estates; the pastor of Nagori Parish continued to collect taxes in the estates until Bangladesh was independent in 1971.[17] According to the written answer by Fr. Joseph S. Peixotto, CSC on leaving, the region of Portuguese missionaries was as follows:

> "Padroado" Monsigner Da Costa, an old priest from Goa[18] was still in here, in Narayanganj, even during the independence struggle in 1971.

9. *Catholic Directories of Bangladesh* 2011, 68.
10. For Jesuit contribution in Bengal, see also, Raj. S. J., "Jesuit contribution."
11. Alonzo, C.S.C., Ph.D., *The Story of Fr. William Evans, C.S.C.*, 4.
12. Gomes, CSC, 'Preface,' v.
13. Campos, *Portuguese in Bengal*, 104.
14. Goedert, CSC, "Church in East Bengal 1497–1977," 29–30.
15. It is to be noted that Father Basil Anthony Mary Moreau, C.S.C. was the founder of the Congregation of Holy Cross. The list of the Holy Cross Priests in East Bengal see the Appendix I. For detailed discussion on the history of Holy Cross Mission in East Bengal, see also, Clancy, *The Congregation of Holy Cross in East Bengal, 1853–1953*.
16. Allen, *District Gazetteers: Dacca*, 69.
17. Goedert, CSC, Ibid., 38.
18. It is to be noted that Goa was a Portuguese colony since the 15th century, on the western coast of India, south of Mumbai. After 1947, when India and Pakistan got

Father Polycarp Alvares was the last Portuguese priest who served here in official capacity in charge of a parish or of the "Estate". When he departed from here, I presume that ended the involvement of the Portuguese government here.

Monsignor Da Costa was a very old Portuguese priest with a long beard, who was serving at the small church in Narayanganj, this church being a sub-center under Holy Cross (former cathedral) church in old Dhaka. He had chosen to remain here in this country and continue his service to the Christian people here, many of whom used to go to him for his blessing, especially in that period of great tension in the country. The church and priest's house are at the edge of the property adjacent to a main street in Narayanganj. One day during that 1971 nine months of independence struggle there was shooting on that main street Msgr. Da Costa was sitting in his second floor room of the building in which he lived, with the window overlooking that main street, and was praying from his "Office" prayer book, which was in the Portuguese language. A stray bullet hit one of the bars of the window next to him and broke the bar. That incident is well known, and verifies that he was still in the country during that year.[19]

In the question of the conversion of Eastern Bengal to Christianity, D. Antonio de Rosario (1643–1695) played a significant role. He came from a *Kshatriya*[20] Caste. He was the son of the king of the Busna. He was a local Bengali Augustinian priest. He converted a huge number of laymen. For this reason, he gained an out-standing position in the early history of Christianity in the region. In 1663, he was taken captive by the Maghs and taken to the Arakan, where an Augustinian Friar, Manoel de Rozario, purchased him and tried to convert him to Christianity, but in vain until St. Anthony was said to have 'miraculously' appeared in his dream and told him to embrace the Christian religion. Having thus turned into a Christian, he commenced to convert others with a favor and enthusiasm that puzzled

---

independence from British colonial rule, India took possession of that colony and made in a province of India. According to the note of Father Joseph S. Peixotto, CSC to the author through an email on 21 January 2017.

19. According to the written answer of the question that 'when Portuguese missionaries had left the country?' Father Joseph S. Peixotto, CSC replied the answer through email on 21 January 2017.

20. The tradition of *Kshatriya* class, from the context of Indian caste system, represents the second position in a society. They belonged to the ruling and military elites. Their role was to protect the society by fighting in wartime and governing in peacetime. For detailed on Indian Caste system see also, Zinkin, *Caste Today*.

Background of Missionary Activities in East Bengal

many missionaries. He composed conversations and a canticle, argued and sermonized in public about the faith of the Christian religion, elucidated his mission to the people of Eastern Bengal, and was accredited with having carried out miracles and conversion of thirty to forty thousand people.[21] After the death of D. Antonio this Christians were abandoning their homes, in the face of oppression by the Zemandar of Busna, and started living in Bhaoal Rajje (The Kingdom of Bhaoal)[22]

Among the Churches erected by the Augustinians at that time were those at Tejgaon, the church of Holy Rosary,[23] in 1677 and St. Nicholas Tolentino Church[24] in 1695 at Nagori, which is located thirty-five kilometers north-east from the capital city of Bangladesh, Dhaka.[25] In 1777, the Church of Hasnabad,[26] Dhaka was first built but later broken down after which the present Church was built in 1888. In 1894, the Church of

---

21. Campos, Ibid., 247–48; Bandyopadhyay, *Bangla Sahitter Itihas* (History of Bangla Literature), 109.

22. Bandyopadhyay, Ibid.,120; Tavernier, *Travels in India,* Vol. II, 140–41.

23. It is to be noted that Holy Rosary Church is considered one of the oldest churches in East Bengal. Portuguese Augustinian missionaries constructed Holy Rosary Church in 1677 at Tejkunipara of Tejgaon on the eastern side of present Holy Cross Girls' High School and College. The Church is locally known as 'the Church of Japamala Rani'. It is considered the second church of Dhaka. It is to be also noted that the church was refurbished three times. In 1714, 1940 and the last renovation was in 2000. Rahman, 'Holy Rosary Church'. See also, Mamoon, *Dhaka Shomogro* (in Bangla); Ahmed, *Discover the Monuments of Bangladesh.*

24. Here to be mentioned that St. Nicholas of Tolentino was constructed at Nagori in 1695, which is located 25 kilometers north-east of Dhaka (capital city of Bangladesh). Almost the whole church was accidently burnt on 8 April 1881. The current Nagori Church was renovated in 1888 on a location about 150 yards away from the place where the earlier one placed. Its foundation were consecrated on 24 August 1885 and the church itself being blessed on 22 February 1889. Campos, Ibid., 248.

25. Smith, *Creolization and Diaspora in the Portuguese Indies,* 129–30.

26. It is to be noted that Hasnabad Holy Rosary Church is considered as one of the ancient Christian churches of Dhaka among others and that was established by Portuguese Augustinian missionaries before the commence of British colonial rule in India. Merchants came to Bengal in 1579 after receiving farman (a majestic declaration) from Mughal Emperor Akbar (1556–1605) for business, evangelizing to Christianity and construction of churches there without any restrictions. By 1580, a Portuguese reimbursement counting business houses and dwellings of veneration was established in Dhaka City. Church of our Lady of Rosary was first established in 1777 at Hasnabad, which is forty kilometers south-west of Dhaka. But the Church was refurbished in 1888, because of its' broken down and present one founded there. http://offroadbangladesh.com/places/hasnabad-holy-rosary-church/

Campos, Ibid., 249–50.

Tuital,[27] Dhaka was built. The church of 'Our Lady of Piety' Dhaka was built in 1815.[28] But the number of the Augustinian Fathers were not more than thirty. So the number of priests were low against the needs of this region. To overcome this crisis, the Portuguese government and religious authorities decided to ask the Jesuits and Dominican priests to continue their works.[29]

Holy Rosary Church, Tejgaon, Dhaka, established in 1695. Photo: Internet.

27. Here to be mentioned that the Church of Tuital is comparatively modern one than the other churches of Dhaka. The church was established due to the difficulties of the villagers of Old Tuital, New Tuital and Sonabazar to attend their religious duties and for the parish priest as well. This was due to the distant of villages from Hasnabad Church. Under the circumstance, Bishop of Mylapore, Dom Henrique, ordered a decree of 25 May 1894 to erect the Church of Tuital; Campos, Ibid., 250.

28. Campos, Ibid., 247–50.

29. Sarkar, *Christianity and Christian Churches in Bengal* (1573–1960), 23; See also, Hambye, S.J., "Christianity in Bengal of the 17th & 18th Century."

St. Nicholas Tolentino Church, Nagori, Kaligonj, Gazipur, established in 1663.
Photo: Internet.

Holy Rosary Church, Hasnabad, Dhaka, 1777 (1+2),
Photo source: http://offroadbangladesh.com/places/hasnabad-holy-rosary-church/

The Vicariate Apostolic of Bengal came into being in 1834, under the authority of the Sacred Congregation for the Propagation of the Faith.[30] In 1850, this Vicariate was "de jure" separated into two, the Vicariates

30. The Catholic Directory of Bangladesh, 2011, 68.

Apostolic of Eastern and Western Bengal. In 1852, the Vicariate of Eastern Bengal, with headquarter in Dhaka, was entrusted with the newly established Congregation of Holy Cross. This Congregation still serves in this territory (East Bengal).[31]

The first Holy Cross Missionaries came in East Bengal in 1853. There was a story behind the screen to commence their activities here. The story is as follows:

> The founder of the Congregation of Holy Cross, Father Basil Anthony Moreau, was trying to get papal approval for his community which was not yet 20 years old. The Vatican was looking for a religious community that would undertake to serve and build up the church in the eastern part of the region of Bengal in India. Moreau agreed to send Holy Cross religious to East Bengal. The Vatican promised to look favorably upon his request for papal approval.[32]

Under the circumstance, after a long sea cruise, which took six months, the initial contingent of the Holy Cross Priests, Brothers and Sisters arrived in Bengal in the month of May in 1853. Among them, there was a priest, a seminarian, three Brothers and three Sisters. Four more missionaries had arrived by the end of the year. Most of them came from France but two of them had been taken from United States of America as they could communicate with the local people in English language.[33]

The first Vicar Apostolic was Rt. Rev. Msgr. Thomas Olliffe. He administered the vicariate from 1852 to 1853. The first Holy Cross missionaries landed in May 1853, which I mentioned earlier. 1855 to 1859, the Pro-Vicar Apostolic was Rev. Louis Verity, CSC. In 1860, Rev. Pierre Dufal, CSC was named Vicar Apostolic and was consecrated in France as the Titular Bishop of Delcon. He returned to Dhaka in 1861 and administered until 1876.[34]

From 1876 to 1889, when their superior in France recalled the Holy Cross missionaries, Benedictine monks of the Anglo-Belgian Province administered the Vicariate. Dom Cuthbert Downey, OSB was the Pro Vicar

---

31. Timm (ed.), *150 Years of Holy Cross in East Bengal Mission*, 3.

32. Connelly, Ebey, Ferguson, Marceau, Schlaver, Warner (Editorial Committee), *Holy Cross in Bengal*, 1853-1988, 3. It is to be noted that a committee was formed to publish the booklet on the commemoration for the Holy cross Missionaries, who worked in Bengal since 1853 to 1988.

33. Ibid., 3.

34. *The Catholic Directories of Bangladesh* 2011, 68; Connelly, Ebey, Ferguson, Marceau, Schlaver, Warner (Editorial Committee), Ibid., 3-4.

Background of Missionary Activities in East Bengal

Apostolic. Dom Gregory de Groote, OSB, as the Administrator, later succeeded him.

In 1889, the Holy Cross Missionaries returned to Eastern Bengal, under Rev. Michael Fallize, CSC. Earlier on 1 September 1886, the Diocese of Dhaka was canonically erected. The new Diocese was incorporated with the territories of the Diocese of Chittagong (Bangladesh), Silchar (Assam, India), and Prome (Myanmar). Chittagong was separated from the jurisdiction of Dhaka in 1927.[35]

Normally the Vicar Apostolic or Bishop was in addition the local superior of the Fathers and Brothers, up to the General Chapter of 1920. There were exemptions for a short time, e.g. Father Sorin was desired by the Chapter of 1852 as superior of the Dacca Mission,[36] but refused it. Father Voisin was named as the superior of the first group but did not depart until the second group. Father Vérité, the substitute Superior, did not become the first Holy Cross Pro-Vicar Apostolic until May 21, 1856, after Father Moreau established the Vicariate of Chittagong.[37]

The Canadian and American religious superiors were divided from 1923. Besides, subsequent to the Fathers and Brothers established separate authorities in 1946, every society had its own religious superior,[38] until 1984 when the Dhaka and Chittagong Districts turned into one.[39]

When independence came in India in 1947, after a long struggle against British Colonial rule,[40] the sub-continent was divided into two parts—India and Pakistan. East Bengal became a part of Pakistan.[41] Dhaka was still a suffragan of the Archdiocese of Calcutta (India). On 15 July 1950, a new Ecclesiastical Province was created, with the See of Dhaka raised to the archiepiscopal status. Most Rev. Lawrence Leo Graner, CSC became

---

35. *The Catholic Directories of Bangladesh* 2011, 69; R. W. Timm (ed.), Ibid., 19–28.

36. Clancy, C.S.C., *The Congregation of Holy Cross in Eastern Bengal, (1852–1876)*, 24.

37. R.W. Timm, CSC (ed.), Ibid., 87.

38. The lists of the Religious superiors see the Appendix II.

39. R.W. Timm, CSC (ed.), Ibid., 87, see also, Theodore, CSC, *Memories of Bengal*, 1939–40.

40. For details about Indian National Movement see also, Chand, *History of the Freedom Movement in India*; see also, Seal, *The Emergence of Indian Nationalism*.

41. For detailed about the partition of India in 1947, see also, Singh, A.I. *The Origins of the Partition of India, 1936–1947*.

the first Archbishop[42] of Dhaka Archdiocese.[43] Chittagong, Dinajpur, and Jessore (presently Khulna) were made the first suffragan Sees.[44]

Archbishop Lawrence Leo Graner, CSC (First Archbishop of Dhaka Archdiocese, 1947–1967), Photo Courtesy: Moreau House, Provincial Headquarter, Holy Cross Priests, Banashree Prokalpo, Rampura Dhaka 1219, Bangladesh.

In September 1960, His Holiness Pope John XXIII gave Dhaka (and in fact East Pakistan) its first Bangalee Bishop[45] in the person of the Most Rev. Theotonius Amal Ganguly CSC, naming him Titular Bishop of Oliva and Auxiliary Bishop of Dhaka. In November 1967, Bishop Ganguly became

---

42. The list of the Archbishops of Dhaka Archdiocese, see the Appendix III.

43. Gomes, 'Soaso Bacherer Siri Beya Dhaka Dharma Prodesh' (125 years of Dhaka Diocese), 17.

44. *The Catholic Directories of Bangladesh* 2011, 69.

45. See the list of Holy Cross Bishops in East Bengal Appendix IV.

BACKGROUND OF MISSIONARY ACTIVITIES IN EAST BENGAL

the first Bangalee Archbishop of Dhaka,[46] and the seventh prelate to grace the See of Dhaka. He died in 1977.[47]

DIOCESE OF CHITTAGONG

The early history of the Church goes back to 1537 AD. At that time, there were Catholics in the Portuguese settlements[48] in the regions, which became part of the Diocese of Chittagong. The first Churches were set up in 1600 (in what is now Diang and the city of Chittagong).[49] The cathedral of Our Lady of the Holy Rosary was built in Chittagong in 1600 and the following year, the Church of the Immaculate Conception, Jamal khan Parish also established there.[50]

Our Lady of the Holy Rosary Cathedral, P. O. Box-152, Bandel Road, Patherghata, Chittagong-4000, Bangladesh.
Photo Courtesy: www.ctgdiocese.com/parishes-of-chittagong-region/

46. *The Dacca Letter*, VOL. XVI, No. 4, Aug. 1965, 2, See also, Goedert, CSC, "Catholic Missions Among the Garos of Bengal, (1909–1959)," 40.

47. *The Herald*, September 16, 1977.

48. For details on Portuguese history in India, see also, Pearson, *The Portuguese in India*.

49. For interesting discussion on the history of missionary activities in Chittagong see also, Qanungo, *A History of Chittagong*, 515–21.

50. www.ctgdiocese.com/parishes-of-chittagong-region

Church of the Immaculate Conception,
Catholic Church, Jamal khan, 18, Jamal khan Road
Chittagong, Bangladesh.
Photo Courtesy: www.ctgdiocese.com/parishes-of-chittagong-region/

Father Francesco Fernandez, SJ, who arrived to Chittagong in 1598, was rendered blind, tormented, and died in imprisonment on November 14, 1602, and became Bengal's first martyr in the history of Catholic Christianity.[51]

Later, the Augustinian priests broadened their activities in Chittagong in the year of 1621. They had taken the place of Jesuits who had been residing there with many dilemmas. In 1598, there were 2,500 Portuguese and their children in Chittagong and Arakan; in addition, there were Indian Christians. In the slaughter of Dianga, which followed Brito e Nicote demand of the harbor, all the Churches of the Jesuits were destroyed and some of the missionaries were murdered. There were some who absconded to Swandip and established the Catholic religion there, afterwards Fateh Khan launched an expedition for military conquest there. When the Augustinians instigated themselves there in 1821, a reinforcement of Christianity took place. They had constructed a Church and dwelling in Angaracale, and a chapel in Arakan, enthusiastically to 'Our Lady of Success'. It must be kept in mind that this was the time when the Portuguese were in the service of the King of Arakan and together with the Maghs were carrying out

---

51. *The Catholic Directories of Bangladesh* 2011, 128.

Background of Missionary Activities in East Bengal

appalling depredations from the very beginning on the banks of the rivers in the Sunderbunds, transporting Muslims and Hindus to be imprisoned. Between 1621 and 1624, the Portuguese conveyed 42,000 slaves to Chittagong, 28,000 of whom the Augustinians baptized. In addition to these, they converted 5,000 Arakanese or Maghs.[52] On the other hand, according to the narratives of the *East Pakistan District Gazetteers: Chittagong*, the conversion story is as follows:

> Manrique has reported that on an average 3,400 persons were annually kidnapped and brought to Dianga and of these he could baptize 2,000 annually. It was easier to convert these wretched beings than local residents, converts from whom were not more than 400 annually.[53]

In 1640, the Augustinians extended to Balasore where they constructed a Church devoted to our Lady of the Rosary. They also established a Church in Ossampur and two Churches in Rangamati dedicated to Our Lady of the Rosary and Our Lady of Guadeloupe.[54] Jesuit priests had visited Sripur, Bakala and many other regions in the period.[55]

In 1845, Chittagong became the residence of the first Vicar Apostolic of Eastern Bengal, and later the administration was transferred to Dhaka in 1845.[56] Anthony Beniot Mercier was the first ordination to the sub diaconate in East Bengal, at Chittagong on 13 January 1854. He was the first Holy Cross person ordained as a priest-in Nazareth Convent in Dhaka on 10 September 1854. The Vicar General Fr. Augustus Goiran and Father Vérié, "the edifying and zealous incumbent of Noakhali", helped Bishop Olliffe at the ceremony.[57] Noakhali was also the first community to receive the Holy Cross missionaries, who disembarked there in June 1853.[58] The first church of Noakhali, Church of Our Lady of Lourdes, was established in 1843.[59]

---

52. Campos, Ibid., 104–5.
53. Rizvi, MA, *East Pakistan District Gazetteers: Chittagong*, 112.
54. Campos, Ibid., 104–5.
55. Thekkedath, *History of Christianity in India,* 458; Runy, Ibid., 26.
56. *The Catholic Directories of Bangladesh* 2011, 128.
57. R. W. Timm (ed.), *Ibid*, 11.
58. *The Catholic Directories of Bangladesh* 2011, 128.
59. www.ctgdiocese.com/parishes-of-chittagong-region

Church of Our Lady of Lourdes, Catholic Church, Noakhali, P. O. Sonapur, Noakhali-3802, Bangladesh.
Photo Courtesy: www.ctgdiocese.com/parishes-of-chittagong-region/

The Diocese of Chittagong was canonically erected on 25 May 1927, comprising a good half of the region that encompassed the then Diocese of Dhaka. The Diocese then included Chittagong, Noakhali, Barisal, Gournadi, Narikelbari, Haflong, Badarpur, Akyab, Sandoway, Gyeithaw and Chaugtha. Akyab, Sandoway, etc. were relinquished to the *La Salette* Fathers in the Diocese of Akyab in 1937–38.[60] Most. Rev. Alfred Le Pailleur, CSC became the first bishop of Chittagong Diocese and worked there from 1927 to 1951.[61]

---

60. *The Catholic Directories of Bangladesh* 2011, 128.
61. Ibid, 129.

Background of Missionary Activities in East Bengal

Most Rev. Alfred Le Pailleur, C.S.C., D.D., (First Bishop of Chittagong Diocese, 1927–1951), Photo Source: www.ctgdiocese.com/former-bishops

The newly established Diocese of Chittagong in 1927 was handed over to the Canadian Province of the Congregation of Holy Cross. When the new ecclesiastical province of Dhaka was created in July 1950, Chittagong turned into a suffragan of Dhaka. Later in 1952, fragments of the Diocese of Chittagong that were located in Assam (India) became a separate ecclesiastical entity, called the region of Haflong, and afterward the Diocese of Silchar, which was later identified as the Diocese of Agartola and the Diocese of Aijwal.[62]

DIOCESE OF DINAJPUR

Carmelite missionaries first evangelized the region including the Diocese of Dinajpur in the 17th century. Since the mid-19th century, the region

62. *The Catholic Directories of Bangladesh* 2011, 128.

turned into a part of the Mission of Krishnagar (at the moment the Diocese of Krishanagar in West Bengal, India). The PIME Missionaries[63] initially came to work in the area in 1855 from Italy and they are working there still now.[64]

The diocese of Dinajpur in Bangladesh relates to the region usually named North Bengal, which encompasses the districts of Dinajpur, Rangpur, Bogra, Rajshahi, and Pabna.[65]

The manifestation of the Roman Catholics in North Bengal can be outlined back to nearly a century year back. With the inauguration of railway communication between Calcutta-Siliguri (accomplished in 1885), accommodation was organized for a Catholic chaplain at the railway center of Saidpur and a beautiful church was established there in 1893. This was the most ancient church in the history of North Bengal. On November 21, 1887, the first Mass documented for Saidpur was on the occasion of a wedding ceremony.[66]

Fr. F. Rocca, PIME, was appointed as the first chaplain of Saidpur in 1893.[67] Before his appointment Bishop F. Pozzi, PIME of Krishnagar was himself doing the job. Fr. Rocca used to come visiting from his residence in Pakuria (Kushtia) and came to reside enduringly in the newly-built rectory of Saidpur from 1906. At the end of the same year, he got a companion of Fr. O. Pedrotti, PIME. He resided in Saidpur for most of the 45 years of his missionary life, and never got back to his homeland, Italy. During Fr. Pedrotti's tenancy, the number of Catholics touched a maximum of about

---

63. The PIME Missionaries are Catholic priests and brothers who commit themselves to lifelong missionary service, especially to non-Christians. (PIME stands for the Pontifical Institute for Foreign Missions in Latin.) Founded in Italy in 1850, PIME is an International Society of Apostolic Life with about 500 members in 17 countries. PIME's priority is the proclamation of the Gospel. 'We are actively involved in human development and the promotion of justice and peace. Our ministries include the foundation of schools, hospitals and clinics, orphanages, and the pastoral care of newly founded Catholic communities.' www.pimeusa.org/ For an interesting discussion on PIME missionaries in India and Bangladesh, see also, Gheddo, *Missione Bengala*. The list of the PIME missionaries in the diocese of Dinajpur, see the Appendix V.

64. *The Catholic Directories of Bangladesh* 2011, 157, for detail, see also, Kottuppallil, S.D.P., *History of the Catholic Missions in Central Bengal* 1855–1886.

65. Pinos, PIME, *Uttar Bonge Catholic Mondolir Shuvo Suchona* (Catholic Beginnings in North Bengal), 1; Garello, SX, (edited), *Bangladeshe PIME Missionarygon*, (PIME Missionaries in Bangladesh), 33.

66. Pinos, PIME, Ibid., 1; Garello, SX, edited, Ibid., 33–34.

67. Pinos, PIME, Ibid., 1.

800. They were residing scattered in 10 railway stations, from Lalmonirhat to Amnura, from Paksey to Siliguri.[68]

The chaplaincy of Saidpur was measured a complete parish, regardless the circumstance that both the church and the rectory were constructed on railway land, and that the congregation had grown up mainly on the basis of temporary residents, Englishmen and Anglo-Indians.[69] According to the description of the *Eastern Bengal District Gazetteers Dinajpur*, the number of the population of Christians is as follows:

> With the exception of a few officials and railway employees there are no European residents in the district. The Christian population consists mostly of Sāntāl converts, the majority of whom live in the Patirām thānā. The Christians of mixed descent are Roman Catholics, while those of purely Indian origin are Baptists.[70]

By the year of 1916, Fr. Rocca had gone back to Italy.[71] In 1927, the Diocese of Dinajpur was canonically established, encompassing the whole of north Bengal. The new Diocese was handed over to the PIME Missionaries, and Rt. Rev. Santino Taveggia, PIME, until then Bishop of Krishnagar, became the first Bishop of Dinajpur. Their main associates were the Sisters of Charity (Maria Bambina). In 1952, late Bishop Rt. Rev. Joseph Obert (PIME) founded the Diocesan Congregation of the Catechist Sisters of the Immaculate Heart of Mary the Queen of Angels (CIC). The Missionary Sisters of the Immaculate (PIME) disembarked in the diocese in 1953.[72]

---

68. Pinos, PIME, Ibid., 1; Garello, SX, edited, Ibid., 33–34.
69. Pinos, PIME, Ibid.,1; Garello, SX, edited, Ibid., 33–34.
70. Strong, *Eastern Bengal District Gazetteers: Dinajpur*, 39.
71. Pinos, PIME, *Catholic Beginnings in North Bengal*, 33.
72. *The Catholic Directories of Bangladesh* 2011, 157.

Most Rev. Santino Taveggia, PIME (First Bishop of Dinajpur Diocese, 1927–1928 [Formerly of Krishnagar 1906–1927]), Photo Courtesy: Father Luigi Pinos, P.I.M.E., Catholic Beginnings in North Bengal, Saidpur: Catholic Church, 1984.

In 1952, after partition of India in 1947, the areas of the Dioceses in India, now the Dioceses of Dumka, Raiganj and part of Jalpaiguri, were separated from the Diocese of Dinajpur. In January 1976, the District of Pabna, along with St. Rita's Parish, Mathurapur, was transferred from the jurisdiction of the Archdiocese of Dhaka to the diocese of Dinajpur, so the diocese comprised the whole of North Bengal (Rajshahi Division), across the rivers Jamuna and Ganges.[73]

---

73. *Ibid*, the list of the Bishop of Dinajpur Diocese is given the Appendix VI.

Background of Missionary Activities in East Bengal

DIOCESE OF KHULNA

The Diocese of Khulna was canonically set up on 3 January 1952 as Diocese of Jessore, with constituents acquired from the Archdiocese of Calcutta and the Diocese of Krishnagar, both in India now. In this area, the Foreign Missionaries of Milan (PIME) had commenced their apostolate in 1855. In fact, in 1856, Fr. Antonio Marietti, PIME, disembarked in Jessore. From 1927 to 1952, the Salesian Missionaries vacationed in this area. On the other hand, Satkhira Parish was under the Jesuits from Calcutta during 1918–1952.[74]

Xaverian missionaries arrived in East Bengal in 1952. They have been working in Jessore and Khulna region of Bangladesh since they arrived. More than hundred priests have been working here during the last fifty years.[75] Of those who are working here most of them come from Italy, Spain, USA, UK, Brazil and Indonesia.[76]

On June 14, 1956, the Episcopal See was shifted from Jessore to the larger city of Khulna and as such has been called the Diocese of Khulna. The newly created Diocese was handed over to the St. Francis Mission Society (S.X.), popularly known as the "Xaverian Fathers".[77] To come into East Bengal, the Xaverians already had a history. According to the unpublished *diary of Father Rigon S.X.*, in the middle of twentieth century, the Xaverian society went to the Pope Pius XII seeking permission to go to Africa for missionary activities. Pope told the society that he could grant the permission if they would agree to come in East Pakistan. As a result, Bishop Battaglierin arrived in East Bengal on 19th August 1952 as Apostolic Vicar and Fathr Rigon[78] arrived in Calcutta on 6th and then in Jessore on 7th January 1953. He arrived in the mission compound of Jessore, one of the early missionary of the Xaverian Society.[79]

---

74. *The Catholic Directories of Bangladesh* 2011, 188.
75. The list of Xaverian missionaries in the diocese of Khulna, see the Appendix VII.
76. Garello, SX, "Introduction," ii-iii.
77. *The Catholic Directories of Bangladesh* 2011, 188.
78. It is to be noted that Fr. Marino Rigon, SX is one of the early Xaverian priests, who arrived in East Bengal from Italy. To know his life and times see also his memoirs, Rigon, S.X., *Villaverla Theke Shelabunia*, (From Villaverla to Shelabunia).
79. The unpublished Diary of Rigion, S.X., which was provided by Father himself to the researcher at *Xaverian* House, Asad Ghate, Muhammadpur, Dhaka on 25.08.2012.

Most Rev. Dante C. Battaglierin, SX, DD (First Bishop of Khulna Diocese, 1952–1969), Photo Source: Father Silvano Garello, S.X., Bangladesher Tin Bandhu, (Three Friends of Bangladesh), Xaverian publisher, Dhaka, Bangladesh, 2nd Edition, 1993.

Iswaripur, fifty miles south of Satkhira town was of special historical attention. The first ever Christian Church structure was located at the place that was contributed by the Jesuits on 1 January 1600 AD beneath the title of "The Church of the Holy name of Jesus"; though nothing of this Church remains now. There was no other Christian Church in the locale, not even the present Khulna Diocese[80] until the entrance of the PIME Missionaries in 1856. Then, the first Church was built at Jessore (1856). Other early Churches are those at Shimulia (1859), Bhabarpara (1866), Malgazi of Shelabunia Parish (1870) and Khulna City (1873).[81]

80. The list of the Bishop of Khulna Diocese is given the Appendix VIII.
81. *The Catholic Directories of Bangladesh* 2011, 188, For detail, see also, Mondal, *Raro Samotota Christ Dharmo*.

Background of Missionary Activities in East Bengal

Catholic missionaries arrived in East Bengal in the later part of 16th century through the hands of Portuguese traders and missionaries. At present, they are the less than 1% (0.3%) of total population of Bangladesh.[82] During the 16th century, the Portuguese advanced in the surrounding area of Chittagong, where they were believed to be active both in piracy and in business. In the 17th century, some Portuguese entered Dhaka. They played a significant role for the development of East Bengal in the field of education, health, social activities as well as NGOs activities since they have arrived.

---

82. Bangladesh Bureau of Statistics, July 2003; the demographic situation of Christian people in Bangladesh is given the Appendix IX.

4

Family Background of Theotonius Amal Ganguly

THEOTONIUS AMAL GANGULY WAS born on February 18, 1920 in the village of Hasnabad 25 miles south of under the district of Dhaka during the British Indian province of East Bengal.[1] The Bengali name "Amal" means "spotless" or "innocent".[2] His father called him "Theton" while his grandmother called him as "Teton". The meaning of Teton is "intelligent" or "sparkling". These days, the word means "smart".[3] He was baptized on 26 February in 1920 at Hasnabad Church.[4] According to one of his family members, this gentle, good-natured man was born during a raging thunderstorm; making them wonder what that might portend.[5]

1. *Weekly Pratibeshi*, 2 September, 1977.
2. Quinlivan, CSC, Ibid., 1.
3. Pereira, CSC, Ibid., 9.
4. Ibid., 9.
5. Quinlivan, CSC, Ibid., 1.

Family Background of Theotonius Amal Ganguly

Archbishop Ganguly as a boy at Hashnabad, Dist. Dhaka, Bangladesh.
Photo Courtesy: Province Review (October, 1977), published by Priests of Holy Cross, Indiana Province, Notre Dame, USA. Source: Internet.

His father's name was Nicholas Kamal Ganguly and mother's name was Ramona Costa. His father worked in Calcutta and died on May 7, 1957.[6] It's worthwhile mentioning that according to the statement of Pius Ganguly (Nicholas Kamal Ganguly's grandson), his grandfather went missing from Calcutta leaving everyone concerned whether he was alive or not.[7] His mother died on January 1, 1965.[8] He had two brothers. His elder brother's name was Xavier and the younger named Bimal.[9]

DEBATE ON FAMILY SURNAME

Previously Ganguly's family title was 'Gomes.'[10] According to the description of Fr. Adam S. Pereira C.S.C., when T. A. Gangugly's father went from

---

6. Ibid., 1.

7. Interview with Mr. Pius Ganguly at his residence at Indira Road, Dhaka on August 1, 2014. It is to be noted that Mr. Pius Ganguly is nephew of Archbishop Theotonius Amal Ganguly, CSC.

8. Frank Quinlivan, CSC, Ibid., 1.

9. Interview with Pius Ganguly at his residence at Indira Road, Dhaka on 1 August 2014.

10. It is to be noted that the Bengali people who were converted by the Portuguese missionaries, they had taken Portuguese surnames. Such as: Ascensao (Ascension of Jesus), Costa (coast), Corraya or Correia (belt; strap), Cruz (the cross of Christ), da Costa or D'Costa (of or from the coast), da Cruz or D'Cruz (of or from the cross), da Rosario (da Rozario) or D'Rosario or D'Rozario (of or from the rosary—of the Virgin Mary), da Sa or D'Sa (of or from the manor house; da Silva or D'Silva (of or from the forest), da Sousa (da Souza) or D'Sousa (D'Souza) (of or from the salt-marsh), Dias (days), Dores

East Bengal to Calcutta, in 1930, looking for work, he had decided himself to change his family surname. So, it was later that he took 'Ganguly' title as his family surname.[11]

However, a declaration of the court of the Chief Presidency Magistrate, Calcutta on 19 February 1938, provided a different picture in front of us, which is as follows:

> I, Xavier Gomes, son of Nicholas Kamal Gomes, of village Hasnabad, P.S. Nawabganj, Dist. Dacca, at present residing at No. 44 D, Taltala Bazar Street, Calcutta, aged about 24, by provision Medical Student, do hereby solemnly affirm and declare as follows:
> 1. That I am a Bengalee Christian and am called Xavier Gomes. That I am a Bengalee and was born at Hasnabad in the District of Dacca and hence I wish to hold and assume a Bengalee Surname in place of a foreign Surname.
> 2. That henceforth I intend to call myself and intend to be called and known by all as Xavier Ganguly instead of as Xavier Gomes.
> 3. That I do hereby change my name, Xavier Gomes into Xavier Ganguly.
> 4. That from this day I shall call myself and shall be called and known by all as Xavier Ganguly and that I do hereby relinquish my foreign Surname "Gomes" and hold, assume and take the Bengalee Surname "Ganguly" instead.
> 5. That the statements and declarations made above are true to my knowledge and that this day I have changed my Surname "Gomes" into "Ganguly" of my own accord and will.
>
> Explained and identified by me
> Sd/-Hiralal Das, Sd/-Xavier Gomes.
> Pleadr.
> 19.2.38.[12]

So, under the circumstance, the declaration of court provided affirms that his family surname was changed in 1938 (not in 1930) and it was changed by his elder brother Xavier Ganguly. Now the question could be

(sorrows), Gomes (a man; a male) and so on. Therefore, it may be argued that T. A. Ganguly's ancestors might be converted by the Portuguese missionaries.

11. . Pereira, CSC, Ibid., 9–10.

12. Declared before the Magistrate of Calcutta on 19th February 1938, Sd/-S. Wajid Ali, Presidency Magistrate. No.1493 of 1938.True copy to the Secretary, State Medical Faculty of Bengal, 11.08.1938.

raised whether he belonged to Christianity and then why he had changed his foreign family surname as well as taking a Bengalee surname.

To find out the answer to this question, Fr. Adam S. Pereira, CSC—a biographer of T. A. Ganguly, put forward that it was a wish of God. To explain his argument he had brought few examples under the light of Bible that it was not the first example in the history of Christianity and the entire incident was taken place because of the wish of God so that they could do a greater job in their time.[13] From the context of historical method and law of causation,[14] the argument cannot be acceptable. To get the answer why and how the decision was taken, several pictures could be found:

Firstly, Ganguly surname had never belonged to Christianity; it belonged to the *Brahmin*[15] class in the Hinduism. It has to be mentioned that *Brahmin* is the highest hierarchy in the caste system of Hindu religion. According to Romila Thapar, the myth of Purusha Sukta, a Rigveda chant, *Brahmins* were born from the mouth of *Purusha*, a life form, the fraction of the corpse from which words materialize.[16] Therefore, it could be socio-psychological causes working behind the screen to take such a decision.

Secondly, it could be said that the decision was taken by Xavier Ganguly. Because if anybody could critically look into his family structure, he could see that during the time, Xavier Ganguly was a student of Medical College. His father belonged to the peasant class of East Bengal,[17] who later went to Calcutta, all the way from Hasnabad of Dhaka, to get a job. So, the change of surname could not have been his 'headache'. On one hand, in the year of 1938, Archbishop T. A. Ganguly studied at class eight and had just entered the seminary a few months before. So he was not in a position to take such a big decision. On the other hand, he stayed in East Bengal. If anybody could look into the communication system of East Bengal with West Bengal, it was not possible to provide his decision to Xavier Ganguly to change the surname from East Bengal to West Bengal. No documents

---

13. Pereira, CSC, Ibid., 10.

14. For detail, see also, Bloch, *Historian's Craft*, 138–97.

15. For detail on 'Brahmin', see also, Chattopadhyay, *Bharatiya Darsan*, (Indian Philosophy), 109–11.

16. Thapar, *Early India*, 125.

17. For an interesting discussion on the situation of peasant class in East Bengal during the last three decades in British colonial era, see also, Hashmi, *Peasant Utopia*.

could be found yet to prove this argument. Bimal Ganguly was just at the age of nine to ten.[18] So, he was not mature enough to take the decision.

Under the circumstance, it could be argued that according to the declaration of the court, the decision was taken by Xavier Ganguly himself and he was capable and mature enough to take the decision and implement it for the other members of his family. This is showed later when his whole family changed their surnames from Gomes to Ganguly. It was the social structure of colonial Bengal that gave him such an authority, where he could take and implement his decision over his other family members. For although still just a student of medical college, he was the first educated one among his family members. All this enabled him to take the decision and implement it.

Now, let us portray the socio-psychological background that instigated him to take the decision to change his surname. To argue on this matter, it is necessary to examine between the social histories of Bengal in the context of the trend of changing surnames of Christian families during that time in Bengal. Changing of surnames among many native Christians was quite 'a la mode' at that time. And, they took surname as *Bannerjee, Chatterjee, Das Gupta* and as such, as was the trend of changing surnames. Most of the cases, the surnames basically belonged to 'Brahmin' class. Most converted Christians came from the lower caste and they might have thought that the change of surnames could upgrade themselves into a higher social stature from the lower class.[19] This practice took place in the nineteenth and twentieth centuries in Bengal and mainly in Calcutta[20] based on Bengali 'bhadralok' society, who were gradually disconnected from their rural connections in the late colonial era.[21] So, the change of surnames in Christian families in the Bengali society was not a new phenomenon. The scenario also showed that it was the year of 1938; the last phase of the British Empire.[22] Within a short time later, India became in-

18. Interview with Pius Ganguly (son of Bimol Ganguly) at his residence at Indira Road, Dhaka on 1 August 2014.

19. For an interesting discussion on the social background of the converts in Bengal, see also, Gupta, Ibid., 143–46.

20. Interview with Dr. James Tejosh S. Das at Eskaton Garden Road, Ramna, Dhaka-1000 on 13 August 2014 and Interview with Brother Jarlath D'Souza C.S.C. at his office Muhammadpur Zakir Hossain Road, Dhaka-1207 on 13 August 2014.

21. For an interesting discussion on Bengali 'Bhadralok' (gentleman) see also, Iqbal, *The Bengal Delta*, 93–116.

22. For detail about the history of Modern India, see also, Sarkar, *Modern India*.

dependent in 1947. Between these times, the world witnessed the Second World War, 1939–45.[23] The ninetieth and twentieth centuries were full of reformation movements in the history of India and Bengal like Muslim Reformation,[24] Hindu revivalism and reformation movements.[25] The center of it was Calcutta being the capital city of India until 1911. These events of reformations might have had an impact in his (Xavier Ganguly) mind and, especially the Hindu reformation[26] movements. Besides, the conservatives and reformers in Bengal in Hindu religion in the nineteenth and twentieth century[27] probably instigated him into his decision although he resided in the city of Calcutta where Hindu class was advanced with Western education and Muslim society was backward compared to the Hindus.[28] We can surmise that his decision to change his surname and that of his family was because of the background of the social structure of Calcutta during that time. Therefore, it may be argued that 'a man can be converted from his religion but he cannot abandon his age-old traditions'[29], which is connected with their social formation and that may be also true for the Ganguly family as well as other Christian families who had changed their foreign surname into a 'local' surname. Moreover, as we know, they adopted the surname of upper caste of Hindu society, i.e. the 'Brahmin'.

---

23. For detail about the history of Second World War: 1939–45, see also, Keegan, John, *The Second World War*.

24. For detail about the history of Muslim religious reformation movements see also, Khan, "Muslim Reform Movements," 187–214.

25. For detail about the history of Hindu revivalism movements, see also Jones, *Socio-Religious Reform Movements in British India*, 30–47.

26. For detail about the history of Hindu religious reformation movements, see also, Farquhar, J. N., *Modern Religious Movements in India*, 29–80.

27. For detail about the history of conservatives and reformers in Hindu religion in Bengal see also, Ahmed, *Social Ideas*, 29–59.

28. For detail about the history of Bengali Society and Western Impact see also, Ahmed, Ibid., 6–28.

29. Samanta (Director), *Anand Ashram*. It is to be noted that the dialogue was delivered by the Father of Asha (heroine) in the film named as Dinesh Mukherjee, who converted into Christianity from Hindu religion. See also, Kazi Nazrul Islam, *Mrittu khuda* (Novel), Mowla Brothers, Dhaka, Eight editions, 2012.

5

Educational Career

THEOTONIUS AMAL GANGULY ATTENDED primary school in his home parish, Hasnabad. Later he was admitted at the Holy Cross High School in Bandhura.[1] While in Class VIII in high school, he entered the Little Flower Seminary,[2] also at Bandhura, as a seminarian for the Diocese of Dhaka.[3] At home, he used to play 'Mass' with his mates by using a wooden stool as an altar, a towel as a vestment, and leaves as Holy Communion.

At the seminary, he began his studies in earnest. On holidays, he would go to his village, help the parish priest by teaching hymns to some youths, and prepare them for both Christmas and Easter Masses. He was also the only Bangali (Bengali) in the locality who could play an organ at the time.[4]

In 1940, he passed the Matriculation (now known as Secondary School Certificate Examination or S.S.C.) Examination in grade 10, held under the University of Calcutta and secured a First Division—gaining the third place winning a special scholarship.[5]

1. Bandura Holy Cross High School is a Catholic secondary school founded in 1912 by the Congregation of Holy Cross at Bandura in Nababgonj Thana of the Dhaka district of Bangladesh.

2. It is to be noted that Little Flower Seminary established in 1925. Fr. Joseph Legrand, CSC (the forth bishop of Dhaka diocese, 1916–29) had given a responsibility to Fr. John Baptist Delaunay, CSC as he built a seminary at Bandhura, Nawabgonj, Dhaka. Later, he was the first director of the seminary. *Souvenir, 125th Anniversary of the naming of the Diocese of Dhaka,* 2012, 60.

3. *Weekly Pratibeshi,* 2 September 1977, 2–3; Quinlivan, CSC, Ibid., 1.

4. Pereira C.S.C., Ibid., 11–12.

5. *Weekly Pratibeshi,* 2 September 1977, 2–3.

EDUCATIONAL CAREER

Bandhura Holy Cross High School, Bandhura, Nababgonj, Dhaka, established in 1912.
Photo Courtesy: Internet.
(Archbishop Ganguly, CSC was the former student of this school).

He was sent to study philosophy and theology at St. Albert's Seminary, Ranchi,[6] and Bihar State in India, which was run by the Jesuit Fathers. He studied there for six years from 1940 to 1946, successfully completing two years of philosophy and four years of theology studies at the seminary. He was ordained to priesthood on June 6, 1946, at the seminary in Ranchi by Oscar Severin, SJ,[7] and Bishop of Ranchi, when he was 26 years old.[8]

He had come back to East Bengal from Ranchi after his ordination. Then he was assigned as a teacher of Little Flower Seminary where he

---

6. It is to be noted that as early as 1907 six candidates for the priesthood, hailing from Chotanagpur, were studying philosophy at Kandy Seminary, Sri Lanka. To get an advanced training, more modified to local conditions and requirements, a philosophy course was launched at Ranchi Apostolic School in 1911 with six students on its revolves. Under the name of St. Albert a Major Seminary was commenced at Bankuli, some sixteen miles south-west of Ranchi, in January 1914. Later, in 1916, it was transferred to its present location. It was established by the Jesuits Fathers of Belgium. The vision of the seminary to build the Kingdom of God on earth: a just and humane society based on the values of the Gospel.www.stalbertsranchi.org.

7. It is to be noted that Fr. Oscar Severin, SJ, was the bishop in Ranchi mission from 1934 to 1957. He established a church of the poor among the tribal population; Camps, *Studies in Asian Mission History*, 308–11.

8. *Weekly Pratibeshi*, 2 September 1977, 2–3; Pereira, CSC, Ibid., 13–15.

taught religion and Latin Language to the young seminarians. His working place was his birthplace Bandhura. Therefore, he had to live there for one year from 1946–1947.[9]

A newly consecrated Bishop Lawrence Leo Graner, CSC, of the Diocese of Dhaka, sent Father Ganguly to the University of Notre Dame in the United States of America,[10] On July 28, 1947, to pursue higher study in Philosophy.[11] He completed his graduation Degree from there. Later he completed his M.A. Degree on 31 January 1949. He also completed his PhD degree from the same institution in 1951.[12]

He wrote his M.A. thesis on "St. Thomas (Aquinas) and the human body", in which he argued the basic goodness and dignity of the human body. He contrasted this with the Hindu philosophy that seeks to escape the human body.[13] His doctoral dissertation, called *Purush and Prakriti (Self and Nature): A Philosophical Appraisal of Patanjali-Samkhya-Yoga.* Patanjali was an ancient Hindu philosopher who introduced yoga for inner contemplation, and was born in India in about 250 B.C. Father Ganguly was the first Bangali Christian to obtain a PhD degree.[14] His doctoral dissertation was on "Yoga Philosophy". He wrote to inform Father Albert Cousineau, CSC, Superior General of the Congregation of Holy Cross and a very close friend, about his studies. Fr. Cousineau replied, "Your degree will not change your approach so charming by conquering simplicity."[15]

---

9. *The Dacca Letter*, Vol. XVI, No. 4, August, 1965, 2; Quinlivan, CSC, Ibid., 1.

10. The University of Notre Dame du Lac (or simply Notre Dame) is a Catholic research situated close to South Bend, Indiana, in the United States. In French, *Notre Dame du Lac* means "Our Lady of the Lake" and refers to the university's patron saint, the Virgin Mary.

The school was established by Father Edward Sorin, CSC, who was also its first president. Many Holy Cross priests carry on to work for the university, including its president. From the initial stage, it was established as an all-male institution on November 26, 1842, on a piece of land donated by the Bishop of Vincennes. The university first enrolled women undergraduates in 1972. As of 2013 about 48 percent of the student body was female. Notre Dame's Catholic character is reproduced in its overt dedication to the Catholic faith, abundant ministries funded by the school, and the architecture around campus. www.en.wikipedia.org/wiki/University_of_Notre_Dame

11. Pereira C.S.C., Ibid., 16–17.

12. *The Dacca Letter*, Vol. XVI, No. 4, August 1965, 2.

13. Ganguly, "ST. Thomas and the Human Body."

14. Ganguly, M. A., "Purusa and Prakrti (Self and nature): A Philosophical Appraisal of Pātañjala-Samkhya-yoga."

15. Quinlivan, CSC, Ibid., 2.

Educational Career

The Congregation of Holy Cross had been working in Bengal, Burma and Assam since 1853, as I described in my preceding chapter. But for two exceptions in their history, Holy Cross had taken no vocations to the priesthood in order to fully build up the diocesan clergy.[16] The two exceptional cases in the history of Holy Cross Congregation were related with Fr. T. A. Ganguly and Fr. Micheal D Rosario. They had started their lives as a diocesan priests but later changed their minds and became Holy Cross priests.[17] As Father Ganguly was interested in entering the Congregation of Holy Cross, he was sent to the Novitiate of the Fathers of Holy Cross in Jordan, Minnesota, USA. One year later, on August 16, 1952, he made his Religious Profession and in October, he returned to Dhaka.[18]

Archbishop Ganguly as a young priest, (Date and place unknown), Photo Courtesy: Province Review (Oct., 1977), published by Priests of Holy Cross, Indiana Province, Notre Dame, USA. Source: Internet.

---

16. For detail, see also, Timm, CSC (Edited), 150 *Years of Holy Cross*.

17. Interviewed with Former Archbishop of Dhaka Archdiocese the Most Rev. Paulinus Costa, DD at his present residing place at Holy Rosary Church, Tejgaon, Dhaka-1215 on 14 December 2014.

18. *The Dacca Letter*, November 1, 1952.

DEPARTURE CEREMONY

While studying at the University of Notre dame, Father Ganguly, who had been residing there for five years, petitioned to join the Congregation. On August 15, 1951 he was accepted, and entered the novitiate. He took first vows in the Congregation in the United States on August 16, 1952.[19] Then he renewed his vows on those dates in 1953, 1954 and 1955, and took final vows in the Congregation in Dhaka on October 26, 1955, a little over nine years after his ordination.[20]

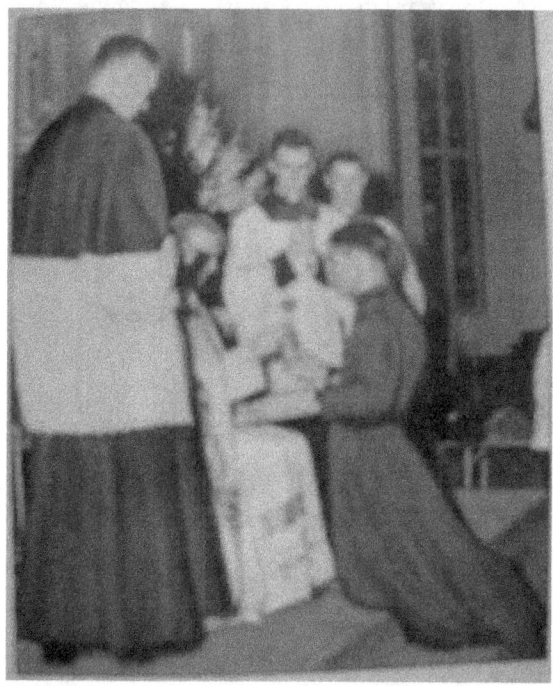

Fr. Theotonius Amal Ganguly, CSC took his first vows in the Congregation in the United States on August 16, 1952, Photo Courtesy: https://www.holycrossusa.org/spirituality/holy-cross-causes-for-sainthood/servant-of-god-theotonius-ganguly/

After completing his doctorate degree he was assigned to join Notre Dame College, as a teacher, once he came back to East Bengal. Notre Dame College was established in 1949, just a few years earlier by the Holy Cross

---

19. *The Dacca Letter*, October 1, 1952.
20. Quinlivan, CSC, Ibid., 2–3.

Congregation.[21] There was always a "departure ceremony" each year for newly assigned or inveterate missionaries to Bengal, a special commissioning, sending, and blessing of the missionaries. The one held in 1952 marked one hundred years since the first band of Holy Cross people had left for Bengal.[22] The Holy Cross Congregation was founded by Father Basil Anthony Mary Moreau, CSC. East Bengal was one of the early missions of Holy Cross, exterior to France. The missionaries came here in 1853. Before that, the founder sent the Holy Cross Missionaries to Canada in 1847, to Louisiana in1848, and to Italy in 1850.[23]

A letter from Father Arnold "Gus" Fell to the editor of *The Dacca Letter*, Fr. James Martin, CSC (DL Oct.1, 1952, P.3) brought the community up-to-date on the preparation to Father Theotonius Amal Ganguly's departure.

> The Departure Ceremony, Which we are listing as Centennial one, is slated here at the Foreign Mission Seminary [in Washington, DC] for October 5th. The plans call for all the men going to be in for it [all those due to leave for Dhaka]. They are Fathers Ray Massart, Voorde, Ste, Marie, Croce, Timm, and Gaunguly, together with Brothers Charles Hill, John O'Laughlin, and Richard Cunningham. The last time I asked Fr. Fitzpatrick when the sailing date was to be, he said he was planning to get them off during the week following Departure [ceremony]. The radiogram from Fr. Rick came in this past week saying Fr. Ganguly would be needed for the beginning of classes on October 18th, which means that he would have to fly. Since that is so, Fr. Fitz may decide now that one or others will fly too.
>
> We have word that here will be a ship leaving for Chittagong on Nov. 10th, and there is likelihood that the freight may be shipped on that, unless we hear of another ship leaving before that. There seems to be a mountain of the stuff downstairs, overflowing the storage room and lining the walls in the corridor of the basement. It is going to be a job to pack that for overseas shipment. And all indications are that more will be coming in every day.

---

21. For detail, see also, Gillespie, CSC and Peixotto, CSC, *The Spirit of Notre Dame*.

22. Quinlivan, CSC, Ibid., 3.

23. Rev. R.W. Timm CSC (Edited), "150 Years of Holy Cross in East Bengal Mission," 3; See also, Clancy, Raymond J. *Holy Cross in East Bengal*, 1853-1953, 2 Volumes.

The Superior General Fr. Christopher O'Toole, CSC, has been asked to give the sermon or talk at the Departure and has accepted.[24]

The November 1, 1952 issue of *The Dacca*[25] *Letter* described the arrival of Father Ganguly in Bombay[26] from USA.[27]

Photograph of the Holy Cross Missionaries who sailed for East Bengal in 1952. (L-R) Fr. Joseph F. Voorde, Albert A. Croce, Bro. John O'Laughlin, Fr. James Connerton, Fr. Aldrian Ste Marie, Fr. Chris O'Toole, Fr. Theotonius Ganguly, Bro. Ephrem O'Dwver, Fr. R.W. Timm, Rector Michael Mathis, Fr. Mike Mathis, Fr. Ray Massart, Bro. Richard Cunninghum, Br. Charles Hill and Fr. Chris O'Toole (sat on the chair in middle of among priests). Photo Courtesy: Holy Cross Archives, Notre Dame, Indiana, USA.

But Fr. Theotonius was delayed a bit in Bombay—India transit visa difficulties-which held him up for four days. He stayed with the Salesians[28]

24. *The Dacca Letter*, October 1, 1952, 3.
25. In 1982, Dacca is spelling changed to Dhaka.
26. The city was renamed Mumbai in 1996. www.wikipedia.com
27. *The Dacca Letter*, November 1, 1952.
28. The Salesians of Don Bosco (or the Salesian Society, officially recognized as the Society of St. Francis de Sales) is a Roman Catholic religious institute founded in the late nineteenth century by Saint John Bosco in sequence, throughout works of charity, to assist the youthful and underprivileged offspring of the industrial revolution. The

in Bombay, got a plane on the 20th and proceeded to Dhaka via Calcutta. He had to go with Ray Massart on the 18th. His family met with him at Calcutta airport at 2 AM. They hadn't seen him since August of 1947 when he left for the USA. He spent the day with his family before proceeding to Dhaka on the 21st, arriving about 6 PM.[29]

On October 21, at 6 pm, devotions (prayers and other religious practices) were on at the Cathedral when he arrived at Ramna Archbishop House. He had supper with the Brothers and came down to the college[30] escorted by Fathers Harrington, Wetzel, Askins, Jacob, Clement and Brother Jude. At the college, classes were called off for the night and Catholic hostel boys greeted him with Bengali songs of welcome in a hurriedly arranged program, climaxed by the traditional garlanding ceremony. He took up residence at St. Lawrence Hostel. He was appointed as a logic teacher. The post was vacant because of the departure of Fr. McMahan, who left there on October 2nd for home leave. He had taken the classes in the day and night shift.[31] A ceremonial greeting was held for Fr. Ganguly. On November 2, 1952 Kamal Hossain,[32] who was the student of Intermediate 1st year, in

---

Salesians' charter portrayed the society's mission as "the Christian perfection of its associates obtained by the exercise of spiritual and corporal works of charity towards the young, especially the poor, and the education of boys to the priesthood". The institute is named after St. Francis de Sales, an early-modern bishop of Geneva. St. John Bosco died on the 31st January 1888. "The Salesian Society", www.newadvent.org › Catholic Encyclopedia ›

29. *The Dacca Letter*, November 1, 1952.

30. According to the official Website of Notre Dame College, Dhaka stated that it is a degree college affiliated with the National University of Bangladesh. Shortly after the formation of Pakistan, the then Archbishop of Dhaka, His Grace Lawrence L Graner, CSC, invited the Priest Society of the Congregation of Holy Cross to establish a college in Dhaka. Accordingly, the priests assigned to this task obtained permission from the Religious Brothers of Holy Cross and in November 1949 started a college on the campus of St. Gregory School, Luxmibazar, giving it the name St. Gregory College. Though the initial institution was humble, the aim was lofty: to spread the light of education in the eastern part of the newly born country, Pakistan. Since its inception, the priests of the Congregation of Holy Cross have administered the college.

In 1955, the college was relocated to its present site in the Motijheel area of Dhaka and renamed "Notre Dame College." See also, Gillespie, CSC and Peixotto, CSC, Ibid., 16–22.

31. *The Dacca Letter*, November 1, 1952.

32. Kamal Hossain secured the first place at the HSC (Higher Secondary School Certificate) examination from humanities group in that year. He was given a community scholarship to get his BA at the University of Notre Dame, which he accomplished in two years. He then got a doctorate in law at Oxford University, became the first foreign minister of Bangladesh and was one of the main architect of the nation's constitution

humanities group, gave the address on behalf of the students.[33] The following year, on September 21, Father Ganguly was appointed to set an examination in Latin.[34] Two of the first students of St. Gregory's College were seminarians and eventually went on to be ordained (by Fathers Paul Gomes and Urban Corraya). The seminarians began their study of Latin in the minor seminary (Little Flower Seminary) in Bandhura and continued it in college. The examination was not held under the government education department, since Latin as a government-approved course for Intermediate students was only introduced later at Notre Dame College. Because of his tremendous academic background, Father Ganguly could help also as an examiner for the junior clergy examinations.[35]

On January 12, 1956, Fr. Ganguly was appointed as 'Prefect of Studies'. In this capacity, he looked after the students' studies.[36] He was also designated as the assistant director of studies at Notre Dame College on October 26, 1956 and later became a full director of the studies. Having assumed this position, he dealt with the Spiritual Legion of Mary, became the producer of "Mukur", a religious bulletin in Bengali, and also a Member of the House Council on January 8, 1957.[37] He also took responsibility as a diocesan consultant from 1956–59 and was appointed as a member of the diocesan council of the administration.[38]

---

in 1972, according to the description of Quinlivan, CSC, Ibid., 5; Gillespie, CSC and Peixotto, CSC, Ibid., 19–20.

33. Quinlivan, CSC, Ibid., 5.
34. *Chronicles of Notre Dame College*, Vol. I, September 21, 1953.
35. Quinlivan, CSC, Ibid., 5–6.
36. *Chronicles of Notre Dame College*, Vol. I, January 12, 1956.
37. *Chronicles of Notre Dame College*, Vol. 1, January 8, 1957.
38. Pereira, CSC, Ibid., 30–32.

6

The Philosophical Thoughts of Father T. A. Ganguly, CSC

IN ORDER TO UNDERSTAND the philosophical thoughts of T. A. Ganguly, a researcher should depend on his three major writings. The writings of T. A. Ganguly contained his philosophical thoughts, which are found in his Master Degree level dissertation and another one for his PhD thesis, which have not been published. To clarify my arguments, I have paraphrased and quoted from his dissertations. Later on, he wrote articles from time to time and published in the *Weekly Pratibeshi*—Dhaka based Catholic newspaper. Eventually, all his articles in *Pratibeshi* were compiled and published as a book titled 'Jibon Ahban' *(Vocation[1] of Life)*.

Basically, these are three resources that would help in understanding the philosophical thoughts of Archbishop T. A. Ganguly. These are the follows:

'*St. Thomas and the Human Body*', Unpublished M.A. Dissertation, Department of Philosophy, Notre Dame Indiana, January, 1949.

'*Purusa and Prakrti* (Self and nature): A Philosophical Appraisal of Pātan_jala-Sāmkhya-Yoga,' Unpublished PhD Dissertation, Department of Philosophy, Notre Dame Indiana, January, 1951.

Jibon Ahban (Vocation of Life), Pratibeshi, Dhaka, March, 2011.

---

1. The Bengali Word 'Ahban' is translated as 'Vocation', which is taken from Garello, S.X., (edited), *Christo Dharmio Sabdaratho*, 43.

The philosophical thoughts of T. A. Ganguly, CSC will be examined according to his three major writings.²

ST. THOMAS AND THE HUMAN BODY

The principle reason behind his study in the philosophy of St. Thomas was to acquire a fuller realization of the rightful place and dignity of the human body. He mentioned that he wrote his dissertation in the age of materialistic philosophy.³ It is evident that he tried to revisit through the centuries and examine the significance of the human body as envisaged by St. Thomas in his enormous works. Since man was so grossly trapped in the bodily activities, it was well-nigh impractical for him to turn out to be ignorant of the authenticity of his material elements. A human being can be so attentive to the material side of his nature that he tends to ignore the spiritual self in him—his soul. As a result, his bodily existence gains predominance. His principal concern was to look to the sense of happiness in the human body. The soul, as it were, retreats to the background. This is deformed viewpoint has achieved its peak in the western Civilization, which is, above all, materialistic. The spiritual and the supernatural has vanished earlier than the highly developed industrial civilization. Hence, a study of the material surface of man, exclusive of his spiritual counterpart, would be a substantiation of this materialistic position. From a historical point of view, however, it would not be entirely futile. T. A. Ganguly supposed to examine St Thomas's philosophy about the true self-respect and importance of the human body and the source from which it originated; and in his research he attempted to carry out St. Thomas' opposition to the views of some of his ancestors and contemporaries, and as well as some recent philosophers of that time. As for the later class, T. A. Ganguly had in mind predominantly the oriental philosophers of the *Vedantic School.*⁴

He argued in his dissertation that the so-called Humanists of the 16th century boastfully claimed to have brought man back to his senses. The medieval philosophers and priests emphasized the spirit of man and left the material content of the humans by the roadside for the humanists to come

---

2. Please note that I have extensively cited, sometimes verbatim, from the dissertation papers as well as his book of T. A .Ganguly, CSC to clarify his philosophical thoughts.

3. The twentieth century visualized as the age of materialism. However, the thinker and philosopher pointed out the 21st century as the age of mechanical materialism.

4. Ganguly, "ST. Thomas and the Human Body," 1–2.

and pick it up. This approach towards the medieval philosophy definitely betrays required understanding of the Thomistic spirit.[5]

He also pointed out that:

> Those who accuse the Catholic of disregarding the human body are, as a rule, misinformed of the Catholic doctrine of the high dignity of the human body. They are shocked by the details of the excesses of Christian ascetics, especially of some of the Fathers of the Desert. The New Testament and the Catholic Church, they say, lauds virginity and celibacy to the sky and advocates penance and mortification; hence Catholics seem to consider sex as an evil in itself. Such is also, in the main, the retort of some of the Hindu philosophers when accused by Christians of belittling the human body as if it were something evil in itself.
>
> It is therefore not inopportune to go back to the Angelic Doctor and study his views on the human body under the light of the Christian interpreters, for his was no Manichean attitude towards matter. Thomism is out-and-out optimism, because it gives even the devil his due.[6]

The philosophy of T. A. Ganguly did not consider St. Thomas' doctrine of the human body from the biological point of view, but rather from the psychological and metaphysical perspective. Although St. Thomas, following Aristotle, whom Dawson so aptly calls 'the divinely appointed hierophant of the mysteries of nature' wrote extensively on the biological and psychological functions of human body, which would be outside the scope of his paper to treat them at any leangth. He had given his argument on the positive and optimistic standpoint of St. Thomas philosophy.[7]

In fine, T. A. Ganguly argued that the human body in itself is so real, that a human has no need of a microscope to realize its value and dignity, in spite of its perishability, in spite of its imperfections and miseries. Every human has a body which appeared physically and it was comparatively required a divine method to maintain it. On the other hand, the human soul contain with its natural deficiency in the order of intellectual material. So the soul had to be integrated to a human body to be perfect. Thus, the body and soul could be purified. At last, he produced his argument on the view that if after death the body were to be completely destroyed, never to rise again, the bridge between the material and the spiritual world would be

5. Ibid., 2.
6. Ibid., 2–3.
7. Ibid., 3.

broken for good. For "the lower world is in some sense dependent on him (man) for its spiritualization and its integration in the universal order." If man were not to rise again, i.e. if there were no resurrection of the body the connection between the two worlds would be out of order from the whole chain of reality. The ultimate fate of a human life consequently must be found in a future resurrection after death. The human body must share in the eternal beatitude in the measure of actuality. The human being could not be considered by a Catholic Philosopher as something evil in itself but he must bow his head in reverence of the Creator's goodness and glory, He, who has created everything to participate in His infinite Being and Goodness. Moreover, the human body is incorporated in the kingdom of those created beings. Far from despising the human body, God has hoisted it to the inimitable dignity of being Hypostatically united with the planet, the second person of the Blessed Trinity.[8]

PURUSA AND PRAKRTI (SELF AND NATURE): A PHILOSOPHICAL APPRAISAL OF PATANJALA-SAMKHYA-YOGA

The purpose of T. A. Ganguly's dissertation was to explore *Patanjali's Yoga* philosophy with special reference to its dogma on the relation between the soul and the body. The technical details of the yogic practices had been carefully left out of consideration, because they were outside the scope of his research, the central concern of which was to shape an assessment of the philosophical basis of the methods.[9]

Since Yoga philosophy was, in the main, a re-statement of *Samkhya* doctrines, it was necessary to take into account the *Samkhya-Karika*, the most ancient textbook of *Samkhya* school, and commentaries on it.[10]

Yoga relied upon individual experience and intuition as the most clinching contention for all philosophic verities and aimed to acquire the release of the *self* from the bondage of substance by means of mystic trance prolific of discriminative knowledge. It was; consequently, appropriate to settle on the limits of the mystical experience of yoga in the introductory deliberations.[11]

8. Ibid., 72–75.
9. Ganguly, M. A., "Purusa and Prakrti (Self and nature)," i.
10. Ibid., i.
11. Ibid., i.

T. A. Ganguly had divided his dissertation into three parts. The first part was divided into two chapters, which provided the historical background of *Samkhya-yoga* philosophy, outlining the religio-philosophic literature of the Hindus and the six orthodox systems of Indian philosophy. The second part was devoted to an expose of *Samkhya-yoga* philosophy. It was subdivided into three chapters, treating respectively *Samkhya-yoga* cosmology and psychology and the yogic ideal release. The third part purported an evaluation of *Samkhya-yoga* philosophy of nature in two chapters: the first dealing with cosmology and *Samkhya-yoga* dualism of spirit and matter, and the second attempt was an objective estimate of *Samkhya-yoga* 'angelism', i.e., the dichotomy between the soul and the body.[12]

Purusa and *Prakrity* were the terms, which are used in the Indian philosophy to authorize 'self' (or soul) and 'nature'. The connotation attributed to these terms, however, differs significantly from that of Thomistic classification, as they have been distinguished in the course of his paper. There is an enormous dissimilarity between Thomism and Hindu philosophy with view to their particular dogmas on the recurrent dilemma of the soul-body affiliation.[13]

He also pointed out that the *Samkhya* and the *Yoga* were considered between the six conventional structures of Indian philosophy. Because of the resemblance of their dogmas, they are frequently referred to as *Samkhya-Yoga Darsana* (Samkhya-Yoga philosophy). In other words, yoga cosmology and psychology are nothing but *Samkhya* philosophy under different names. *Patanjali* (200 B.C. - ?), the originator of the Yoga school of philosophy, only accumulated and systemized the popular yoga practices obtainable at the time under the name of *Yoganuśānam* (Yoga recension), which is also recognized as *Ptanjala-Yoga* or Yoga of Patanjali.[14]

Although orientalists and historians treated these two schools of philosophy together as *Samkhya-Yoga Darsana*, given their almost identical teachings on cosmology and psychology, T. A. Ganguly showed that the difference between the two schools might be conveniently resolved as follows:

---

12. For detailed see also, Ibid., i-186.
13. Ibid., iii.
14. Ibid., iii, 58–59.

a. while the *Samkhya* is considered to be atheistic or rather agonistic, the yoga admits a personal God and assigns Him a role, though very precarious, in the process of the *purasa's* release;

b. whereas the *Samkhya* insists on the discriminative knowledge alone as a means of liberation, the Yoga advocates physical exercises and specially mental control as indispensable to acquiring the discriminative and liberative knowledge.[15]

So, the traditional procedure treated the two systems together as *Samkhya-Yoga*. Patanjali was the founder of the *Samkhya School* of thought. T. A. Ganguly did his dissertation on *Patanjali-Samkhya-yoga*, where he tried to put his argument that the cause of the dogma of the nature of the *Purasa* and *Prakrti* was only a restatement of the *Samkhya philosophy* of Nature. Actually, Yoga philosophy formulated wisdom only when one could realize the *Samkhya* investigation of spirit and matter.[16]

In his research work, T. A. Ganguly tried to find out a philosophical and critical assessment of the *Samkhya-Yoga* cosmology and psychology with particular reference to the theory of the nature of the soul and body and their relation to each other. He argued on *Samkhya-Yoga philosophy* that both were rejecting as it could play the considerable unity of the soul and body. The causes of the ideas failed to explain the essence of the unity of man.[17] Later, he had provided his own explanation on the failure of the idea in such way as follows:

> ... it seems to me, is its tenacious adherence to and absolute reliance upon the unconceptualizable data of a direct and immediate experience of the soul, which within its proper limits seems to be an authentic experience; but taking this experience as its point of departure, the Sāmkhya-Yoga was bound to wind up in a dichotomy between the soul and the body, comparable to the platonic or cartesian 'angelism'.[18]

T.A. Ganguly's philosophical thoughts defines the dichotomy between the Cartesian 'angelism' and what might be called the *samkhya-Yoga* angelism. The *purusas* of the *Samkhya-Yoga* were not *Paulo minores angelis*, but in a sagacity, they were envisaged as being better to the angels of Catholic

15. Ibid, iv.
16. Ibid, iv., 59–85.
17. Ibid., v; 85–103.
18. Ibid., v–vi; 85–103.

theology; for, unlike the angels, the *purusas* were theoreticals to be uncaused, spiritual entities.[19]

He tried to examine the physical and mental practices in detail. Because the entire *Yoga Darsana* (yoga Philosophy) is confessedly oriented to obtaining the release of *purusa* (self) from the bondage of the *prakṛti* (matter or body) by means of *samādhi* (contemplative trance). Release was the comprehension of loneliness and self-abidance (Kaivalya) of the *purusa* in entire thought from the body. Therefore, his thoughts did disapprove the value of physical exercises and breath-control in asceticism. The control of the body, the intelligence actions, the mind and its activities, might certainly be an advantage to an ascetic who aspires to attain higher excellence in spiritual life—at that inexpressible spiritual amalgamation with the Divine—in the Christian sense. An adequate understanding of the ultimate aim of these techniques, however, is of paramount importance if we would form an objective critique of the *Sāmkhya-Yoga* philosophy in its entirety.[20]

He concludes, in his dissertation, as follows:

a. Although supernatural mystical experience transcends all techniques, a certain amount of physico-mental control might be a help in discursive meditation, acquired contemplation, and thus dispose the soul for the reception of infused contemplation. Hence the possibility of a Christian Yoga.

b. Samkhya-yoga dualism (or pluralism) cannot be a rational explanation of the universe. In general, the Hindu view of God, souls and nature has been colored by the failure to arrive at the fundamental doctrine of creation. The theories of *Karma* and immanent teleology in nature only increase the problem of the one and the many instead of solving it.

c. By taking the mystical experience of the unlimited act of existence of the soul as the point of departure Patanjali and the yogins had eventually to wind up in the dichotomy between the soul and the body. They conceived souls as pure spirits, eternal, infinite and uncaused and thus failed to explain man as unit.

d. The problem of knowledge in Samkhya-yoga is naively solved by deducing mind from matter and by postulating a transcendental influence of the *selves* by which matter becomes conscious and intelligent.

---

19. Ibid, vi; 104–24.
20. Ibid., vi-vii; 125–47.

e. Despite the aberrations and the limited success of their metaphysical and psychological adventures, the ancient Hindus deserve our admiration and sympathetic study if we consider the data and the means of research at their disposal at that early stage of human history.[21]

JIBON AHBAN (VOCATION OF LIFE)

It is already mentioned that this book is a compilation of T. A. Ganguly's articles previously published in *Weekly Pratibeshi*, at different times. The book is very important in order to understand the meaning of life as Father Kamal Corraya described in his introductory words.[22] Now I am trying to find out his philosophical thoughts, which came forward to us through his articles.

T. A. Ganguly tried to portray his philosophical thoughts through the book where he not only explained the ideals of a priest's life but also explained the other aspects of human life in general. He argued that every life has a call and everybody should understand the meaning of that life where there is a call. Therefore, he did not underestimate any way of life. He pointed out that every life has a call, which is connected with his way of life. As he tried to argue that every life has to bear different stages and the life's story of an individual is different due to the places and situations of life. From this perspective, he explained the meaning of life from psychological, familiar, social and spiritual point of view as well as its effects and development. He gave importance to the diversity of human life. He also shed light on how to discover the call of human life, how we could understand the call of God, and how the call of life can help parents, teachers as well as others to develop their life to lead a better life in an appropriate time.[23]

T. A. Ganguly also pointed out how to lead the life in priesthood with its objectives and purposes defined. He delineated the virtues that are to be practiced, in one's daily life, in priesthood. The virtues are mainly: the state of bachelorhood and virginity, abiding the rules and regulations and poverty among many others. These are also the teaching of Jesus Christ.[24]

---

21. Ibid., ii-iii; 173–86.
22. Ganguly, CSC, *Jibon Ahban*, IV.
23. Ibid.
24. Ibid.

By practicing those, Jesus himself stood in the middle of death and life where he put forward the question as:

> 25 Jesus said to her, "I am the resurrection and the life. He who believes in Me, though he may die, he shall live. 26 And whoever lives and believes in Me shall never die. Do you believe this?"[25]

He also pointed out the importance of marriage and how one can have a conjugal partnership leading to a happy life.[26] To find an answer to this question, he had taken the concept from Christianity and analyzed it in local context. Therefore, when we explained his philosophy on human life, we found the similarity with the *Vedic* (Chatur Ashram)[27] system. Under the system of Ashram, the human life was divided into four periods. The goal of each period was the ideal fulfillment of each of the four consecutive stages of life. According to Professor Patrick Olivelle, an eminent scholar on Indian theology and philosophy, he who describes the system is as follows:[28]

The Ashram System

Ashram or stage	Age (years)	Description	Rituals of transition
Brahmacharya (student life)	Till 24	The male child would live with his family till the age of 5. He would then be sent to a Gurukul (house of the guru) and typically would live with a Guru (teacher), acquiring knowledge of science, philosophy, scriptures and logic, practicing self-discipline and evangelicalism, learning to live a life of *dharma* (righteousness).	Upanayana at entry.
Grhastha (household life)	24–48	The ideal householder life is spent in enjoying family life, carrying out one's duties to family and society, and gainful labor. The man in this ashram has to shoulder responsibilities of the other three ashrams.	Samavartana at entry. Other rituals of Hindu marriage later.

---

25. Bible: John 11:25–26 New King James Version (NKJV).
26. For detail, see also, Ganguly, CSC, *Jibon Ahban*.
27. For detail, see also, Thapar, *A History of India*: Volume 1.
28. Olivelle, *The Āśrama System*, 1–29, 84–111.

Ashram or stage	Age (years)	Description	Rituals of transition
Vanaprastha (retired life)	48–72	After the completion of one's householder duties, one gradually withdraws from the world, freely shares wisdom with others, and prepares for the complete renunciation of the final stage.	
Sanyasa (renounced life)	72-demise	One completely withdraws from the world and starts spiritual pursuits, the seeking of *moksha* (freedom from the cycle of rebirth), and practicing meditation to that end.	

Archbishop T. A. Ganguly also placed his philosophy trying to show a path which belonged to belief on the loved of Christ. He tried to put his point in the view of Christianity along with the reconciliation of locality. He gave the examples in the light of Bible but it shadow were local, where his local identity came to the surface. His philosophical thoughts on religion and spirituality were both inimitable and cooperative.

In conclusion, it could be said that the philosophy of T. A. Ganguly was related with humanism. To define humanism, he had taken the concept from Christianity but its content was local. We can see that he had taken the topic initially for his MA dissertation from the Catholic Christian concept but, later, he had written on the Indian philosophy as his PhD dissertation, where he reconciled the Indian philosophy with Christianity. So, his philosophy basically is a synthesis of Christianity and the local philosophy. It could be argued that his philosophy belonged to a *synthetic* Christianity, which is purportedly blended with local philosophy. Thus, his conscious mind was prepared to play a significant role for the localization of the Catholic Christianity when he became the first Bengali Archbishop for the East Pakistan. It also could be said that his philosophy was reconciliation and reconstruction of Catholicism with the local philosophical thoughts, where human being is the main character in writings and the vocation of life is the source of development in human life. He could be compared with the nineteenth century Hindu religious reformer in Bengal—Ramakrishna Paramahamsa. Whose great philosophy was:

Jato mat tata Path (there are as many ways as there are views)[29]

29. Mitra, "Hindu Reform Movements", 234.

However, the goal is essentially the same. This simply connoted that the avenues showed by different religions lead to the same spiritual goal. T. A. Ganguly showed the combination of Christianity with the local culture[30] in the name of synthesis through his philosophical writings.

---

30. For details on Local Culture see also, Murshid, *Hajar Bachhorer Bangla Samskriti.*

7

The Activities of T. A. Ganguly

THE PROFESSIONAL RESPONSIBILITIES OF Father Theotonius Amal Ganguly, CSC, were delineated after his return from the United States of America, where he had received higher degree. As a professional priest, Father Ganguly's first assignment, after having returned from the USA, completing his PhD and ordination, was to set an examination in Latin in September 1953.[1] Two of the first students, Fathers Paul Gomes and Urban Corraya, of St. Gregory's College were seminarians and eventually went on to be ordained. The seminarians began their study of Latin in the minor seminary (Little Flower Seminary) in Bandhura and continued the same in to college. The examination was not under the government education department, since Latin as a government-approved course for Intermediate students was only introduced later at Notre Dame College. Because of his commendable academic background, Father Ganguly, CSC, also helped as an examiner for Junior Clergy examinations.[2]

On January 12, 1956, Fr. Ganguly was appointed as 'Prefect of Studies'. In this capacity, he looked after the students' studies[3] and, additionally was designated Assistant Director of Studies at Notre Dame College on October 26, 1956.[4] He later became the full director of studies on January 8, 1957.[5]

---

1. *The Chronicles of Notre Dame College*, 21 September 1953.
2. Quinlivan, CSC, Ibid., 5–6.
3. *The Chronicles of Notre Dame College*, 12 January 1956.
4. *The Chronicles of Notre Dame College*, 26 October 1956.
5. *The Chronicles of Notre Dame College*, 8 January 1957.

He also took the responsibility of a diocesan consultant from 1956–59 and was appointed as a member of the diocesan council of the administration.⁶

Notre Dame College, Dhaka, Holy Cross teaching and non-teaching staffs, 1957–58.
Source: Files of Notre Dame College, Dhaka.

THE ACCIDENT

On February 1, 1957, one winter morning he was going from the college, between 5:30 and 5:45 am, to Narinda to hear First Friday confessions and say Mass for the Brothers. On his way, Father Ganguly fell into a newly excavated ditch which was 10–12 feet deep. The ditch was dug by the municipality across Hatkhola Road to repair sewer lines. The details of the accident would be as follows:

Because of the excavations and bamboo barricades along the road, he was forced to get off his bicycle and walk cautiously while pushing it. The

6. Quinlivan, CSC, Ibid., 6–7.

weather was heavy with an unusually dense fog, making it difficult to see the way ahead of him. He stepped forward on to what he thought was solid ground, but fell some ten feet or more deep into a ditch, which had been excavated across the road. He landed on his left thigh in a pool of muddy water and broken bricks. His bicycle landed right on top of him. He lay in the bottom of the ditch in the muddy water, partly stunned, but conscious enough to realize that his left thighbone was broken—causing terrible pain. A passerby, also a jogger out for early morning exercise, heard Father's groans and came to his rescue. The man (could not find out his name from any sources) went to nearby Paramount Press to get others to help him lift Father out of the ditch. Father Ganguly was carried to the verandah of Paramount Press, where he was laid out on a bench and wrapped in a blanket until the college van arrived and took him to Holy Family Hospital.[7]

At the hospital, he was X-rayed at once by the Medical Mission Sisters. It was soon known that his left thighbone (femur) was fractured.[8] It was a simple horizontal fracture, as they said, but the ends of the bone overlapped by 3 inches.[9] On February 2, Sister Benedict attached a traction apparatus to his leg just below the knee joint to hold the broken ends in alignment.[10] He was in great pain and couldn't sleep for five nights, despite taking pain killer and sedatives. He was allowed no visitors and unable to walk. His pain decreased but it was still intolerable until February 5.[11] He could not even put his foot down. Father Ganguly was still in great pain, both in the knee and thigh, until February 19. On February 25, the broken bone ends were almost touching as seen by X-ray. Sr. Benedict made an initial effort for a perfect lineup of the broken bones. On March 7, it was close to perfect. On March 11, he again made a major attempt by doctors to make it even closer to perfection; she (Sr. Benedict) made the second major attempt for the upper part of his leg. On May 29, the supporting piece of equipment was removed from his leg. On July 9, Father Ganguly was able to get out of bed and stand on his leg but only for a few minutes. He gradually got "small

---

7. *The Dacca Letter*, Vol. VII. NO. 7, January Issue, 1957, 1; Quinlivan, CSC, Ibid., 6–7.

8. Thighbone (femur) is the longest and strongest bone in human body. Because the femur is so strong, it usually takes a lot of force to break it. For details see also, www.orthoinfo.aaos.org/topic.cfm?topic=A00521

9. *The Dacca Letter, Ibid.*

10. *The Dacca Letter*, Vol. VII. NO. 11, May, 1957, 1.

11. *The Dacca Letter*, Vol. VII. NO. 7, January Issue, 1957, 1; Quinlivan, CSC, Ibid., 6–7.

treats" as a morale booster, like sitting in a chair for a while or going for a wheelchair ride.[12]

On July 21, he was able to attend Mass for the first time—a great consolation for him—but he felt "tired and weak." By the end of the month, he graduated onto crutches but was allowed to walk only a short distance. In early August, it was deemed best for him to go to Karachi, West Pakistan, for consultation with an orthopedist. He got a jolt when that doctor advised to send him to the United States of America as soon as possible, as the condition was beyond his capabilities to handle.[13] A local Catholic Doctor, named Sr. Benedict, told him that he may not need the trip and advised more exercise. They would see after a month if an operation was necessary. It was not. And on September 3, Father McKee brought him back to Dhaka. The recovery was going well but the bone was somewhat curved and he could not put full pressure on his leg while standing. However, he could participate in Mass, using altar for support. By September 10, he taught his first logic class. By the end of the month, he drove himself to the hospital in "Tilly"—the college Morris utility van. There, he received heat therapy and mobility exercises for his stiffened knee. By October 25, Father Ganguly was able to set aside his cane with some degree of tremor and discomfort while walking. In December, he joined some Christian hostel students for a picnic in Joydeypur. On December 18; the last hurdle was vaulted when he traveled to Karachi for his final checkup. He returned to Dhaka on December 23 in 1957 with a satisfactory medical report.[14]

RECOVERY AND WORKING TIME AT NOTRE DAME COLLEGE

After full recovery of his health, he came back to Notre Dame College, Dhaka and, on January 8, 1958, assumed his responsibilities as director of studies, prefect of religion, spiritual director of the Legion of Mary, a producer of a religious bulletin in Bengali named "Mukur", and a member

---

12. *Ibid.*
13. *The Dacca Letter*, Vol. VIII. NO. 2, July, 1957, 1; Quinlivan, CSC, Ibid., 7–11.
14. *The Dacca Letter*, Vol. VIII. NO. 2, July, 1957, 1; *The Dacca Letter*, Vol. VIII. NO. 4, September, 1957, 2; According to Archbishop the Most Rev. Paulinus Costa (ret.), DD, in an interview with the researcher, he corroborated what I described in my text. The interview was taken by the researcher at his present residential place at Tejgaon Dharmapalli, Dhaka on 28.04.2012.

of the house council.[15] In the same year on November 1, he was made acting vice principal and acting assistant house superior. Then on the 14th, he was made prefect of discipline for the college.[16] Fr. Martin was getting ready to go off for home leave early in the year of 1959. During that time, Fr. Ganguly was appointed as vice principle of the college on March 29.[17] He also took the responsibility to direct the writing and publication of the periodical, "Harvest" on 1 May 1959.[18]

His final teaching assignment at Notre Dame College, Dhaka was in January 1960 when he was appointed to teach a course in morality to the intermediate level for the Science group students.[19] About that time, Fr. Jim Martin's infirmity and early demise at the age of 42 brought about a dilemma to the college and to the professional life of Fr. Ganguly. Fr. Ganguly took over the responsibility of the college, when Fr. Martin was admitted to Holy Family Hospital in a critical condition subsequent to a deterioration of his typhoid. After Fr. Martin's passing away on February 21, 1960, and entombment the following day at Tejgaon cemetery, Fr. Ganguly was named Acting Principal on April 12. Later he took full responsibility as Principal, by the decision of the governing body of the college on August 30, 1960.[20]

He was the first Bangali to hold this position. Students and other professors alike loved him and appreciated his skills. Previously, Fr. Martin, with the college from its establishment, had undertaken excessive burdens on his own shoulders; filling up a vacuum for a capable person. Ultimately, the college Fathers realized that there was an outstanding priest teacher with such capabilities. In their midst was an exceedingly skilled and respected priest teacher, Fr. Theotonius Ganguly, CSC. He had taught and worked in the college for eight years and had proved himself to be a competent, hardworking teacher. He was very appreciated by all who knew him. Fr. Ganguly became the third principal in the history of Notre Dame College.[21]

15. *Chronicles of Notre Dame College*, Dhaka, East Pakistan, 8 January 1958.

16. *Chronicles of Notre Dame College*, Dhaka, East Pakistan, vol. 1, 14 November 1958.

17. *Chronicles of Notre Dame College*, Dhaka, East Pakistan, 29 March 1959.

18. *Chronicles of Notre Dame College*, Dhaka, East Pakistan, 1 May 1959; Pereira, CSC, Ibid., 34.

19. Quinlivan, CSC, Ibid., 4.

20. *The Dacca Letter, Vol. XI, No. 3*, September 1960, 1; *Chronicles of Notre Dame College*, Dhaka, East Pakistan, February-August 1960; Pereira, CSC, Ibid., 34–35.

21. Gillespie, CSC and Peixotto, CSC, Ibid., 56–57.

The Activities of T. A. Ganguly

Rev. Theotonius A. Ganguly, CSC, Principal, Notre Dame College, Dhaka. Source: Files of Notre Dame College, Dhaka.

SCHOLARLY ACTIVITIES

Because of his focus and scholarly capabilities as an intellectual and orator, he was frequently asked for consultations on diverse issues under discussion, or to attend conferences on a series of issues. He presented an article on Catholic youth problems in the archdiocese at the annual congregation of the pastors in the Archbishop's House on December 15, 1954.[22] He attended a meeting of the educational commission on September 17 in 1956 at the Archbishop's House to discuss the catechism syllabus for teaching religion in the schools.[23] He submitted an article on 'young leadership' at the monthly clergy conference held at the Archbishop's house on December 4, 1956.[24] As a philosopher, he was invited to the seventh All-Pakistan Philosophy Congress at Curzon Hall, Dhaka University from January 9–11, 1960.[25] Later, on September 29, 1960 he flew to Lahore, West Pakistan to attend the All-Pakistan Education Conference.[26]

AS A BISHOP

About six months after becoming Principal of the college, he was designated the Auxiliary Bishop of Dhaka on September 13, 1960, by Pope John XXIII. At that time, Most Rev. Lawrence Leo Graner, CSC, was the Archbishop of newly formed Dhaka archdiocese after independence of India and Pakistan from British colonial rule in 1947. He took *Deus Adjutor Meus* (God is my helper) as his motto. On October 7, 1960, Cardinal Gregory Peter Agaginian, Prefect of the Congregation for the Propagation of the Faith in the Vatican, consecrated Father Ganguly as the first Bengali local bishop. Hundreds of priests, religious people, and thousands of Catholic faithful were present at the ceremony at St. Mary's Cathedral in Dhaka. It was a watershed event in the history of the Catholic Church in East Pakistan in the last 400 hundred years.[27]

At a public reception following his consecration, Archbishop Lawrence Graner, CSC, said about his newly appointed auxiliary bishop that

22. *Chronicles of Notre Dame College*, Dhaka, 15 December 1954; Quinlivan, CSC, Ibid.,11.

23. *Chronicles of Notre Dame College*, Dhaka, East Pakistan, 17 September 1956; Quinlivan, CSC, Ibid., 11.

24. *Chronicles of Notre Dame College*, Dhaka, East Pakistan, 4 December 1956; Quinlivan, CSC, Ibid., 11.

25. *Chronicles of Notre Dame College*, Dhaka, East Pakistan, 9 January 1960; 1; Hamid (editor), *The Blue and Gold*: 1960, page number did not mention; Quinlivan, CSC, Ibid., 11.

26. Quinlivan, CSC, Ibid., 11.

27. Gillespie, CSC and Peixotto, CSC, Ibid., 57.

he was a "day-star." The Archbishop explained why he portrayed him as a "day-star" in a such way that many stars are visible at night, but that a star that stands out even in daylight is truly outstanding, a bright star indeed. Archbishop Graner referred to his "zeal and quiet piety."[28]

On September 14, 1960, the Archbishop's House published a schedule to receive the new bishop with a program. For this reason, the leaders of different congregations and lay organizations in Dhaka called off a meeting to map out their plans for the program. Fr. Houser, CSC became coordinator of the committee and different groups were appointed to handle different type of tasks, like: accommodations, transportations, invitations, decorations for the cathedral, and many other tasks to make the event a success. Since the time was extremely short, everyone had to work hard. Invitations were printed and sent out to all the corners. Brother Martinan at St. Gregory's was in charge of accommodations for all those who were coming from outside of Dhaka. He did a magnificent job on such a short notice in getting everyone set up some way or other. Many Archbishops and bishops also came to Dhaka to attend the program. Some of the visiting Archbishops and bishops were accommodated in Archbishop's House, Karail, Ramna, Dhaka,[29] some of them at Holy Family Hospital, and the rest of them at Notre Dame College, Motijheel, Dhaka. Father McKee, at Moreau House, took care of Religious Superiors, while St. Gregory's took care of the remaining large number of priests and Brothers from their own diocese as well as from other dioceses of East Pakistan. All the sisters were put up at Holy Cross College,[30] the Orphanage or at Holy Family Hospital, as well as St. Francis Xavier's Convent, Mohammadpur, Dhaka.[31] During

---

28. Quinlivan, CSC, Ibid., 12.

29. It is to be noted that up until 1922 the only establishment of the Church in Dhaka was at St. Gregory's which was the Bishop's residence, the rectory for the parish priest, hotel for missionaries and school. When Bishop Legrand returned from a trip home in 1922, he decided to relive the congestion at St. Gregory's by building a separate Bishops House. Property was acquired in Ramna and the present Bishop's House was completed and occupied in late 1923, Goedert, CSC, 'History of the Church in East Bengal: 1497–1977', 25.

30. Holy Cross College (HCC) is a Catholic higher secondary school for girls, which is located at Tejgaon in Dhaka, Bangladesh. It serves students in class 11 and class 12. Sister Augustine Marie, Sisters of the Holy Cross, founded the institution in 1951, which is near the Holy Rosary Church, Tejgaon, Dhaka. The college is well known as one of the renowned educational institutions in Bangladesh for girls. Gomej, 'Holy Cross Girls' High School'.

31. *The Dacca Letter,* Vol. XI, No. 4, October 1960, 2.

the hectic time, the Holy Cross Priests and Brothers Retreat took place at St. Gregory's from Sept 27th until October 4th, 1960. After the Retreat, most of the Holy Cross Fathers had to get back to their posts so that the Diocesan Fathers might be able to come in for the Consecration and for their own Retreat. Gradually things began to shape up and as the big day approached, excitement increased.[32]

THE CARDINAL ARRIVED

Finally, the big and eventful day arrived in the history of Catholic Church in East Bengal on October 7, 1960. The weather was very clear, sunny and hot. The Cardinal was due to arrive by plane from Calcutta about 9 o'clock in the morning. The highest bodies of the Catholic Church in East and West Pakistan were waiting for the reception of Cardinal Gregory Peter Agaginian at Dhaka airport. Many bishops from the two wings of Pakistan had arrived earlier a day before on October 6 to attend the inaugural ceremony of newly appointed Auxiliary Bishop. In addition, just about every priest, Brother and Sister were present in Dhaka at the time, as well as a large number of the Catholic people from Dhaka, Tejgaon and Narayangonj, gathered in the airport to welcome the cardinal. There were over a thousand Catholics people also present outside airport to welcome Cardinal Gregory Peter Agaginian. When the cardinal stepped out of the plane, the waiting crowd burst into applause. Soon after, the little orphans from Bottomley House placed a garland around the cardinal's neck. The cardinal was accompanied from Calcutta by the Most Rev. James Knox, Apostolic Internuncio in India, Archbishop Cordeiro of Karachi, Msgr. Francis Lally, Editor of the Boston 'Pilot' and Msgr. Borgna. These latter two were acting as secretaries to the Cardinal on his tour. To welcome the Cardinal there were also present at the airport: the Most Rev. Emmanuel Clarizio, Apostolic Nuncio in Pakistan, Archbishop Lawrence Graner, CSC of East Pakistan, Archbishop Von Miltenburg of Hyderabad, West Pakistan, Bishop Hettinga of Rawalpindi, Bishop Sherer of Multan, Bishop Obert of Dinajpur, Bishop La Rose of Chittagong, Bishop Bataglierin of Khulna and the Vicar General from Lahore. It was certainly the biggest assembly of the Hierarchy of the Catholic Church that Dhaka airport ever witnessed in its history. There

32. Ibid.

were even a group of American Christians from Dhaka there to greet the Cardinal in his own language.[33]

CARDINAL ADDRESSES TO THE SISTERS

From the airport, the cardinal drove down Mymensingh Road for about five minutes to the Bottomley House orphanage—the venue for the Sister's Conference. There, about eighty Sisters representing the entire Sister's communities in East Pakistan had assembled to greet him. The Cardinal spoke to the Sisters briefly and met them afterwards for a short time before embarking on his way to attend other programs in his crowded schedule.[34]

CARDINAL OPENED THE PAKISTAN BISHOPS CONFERENCE

From Tejgaon, his Eminence proceeded to Archbishop House at Ramna where he opened the Bishops' Meeting. It was an extremely hot day and all were beginning to wonder how the Cardinal would be able to hold up during the rest of the busy day, since he had experienced some sickness earlier in the previous evening. As it all turned out, he managed magnificently well and no one would have guessed what an ordeal it was for him.[35]

Even though the Consecration was not due to begin until 4 pm Friday afternoon, people began pouring into the new Cathedral from about 1 O'clock. Every Bengali Catholic, who could possibly make it, wanted to be there. Several launches were hired to bring in large delegations from Hasnabad, the new Bishop's home village. A number of representatives came from every parish. There was even a large delegation of Garo Christians all the way from Biroidakuni and other points. Bishop Ganguly's mother and brother came up from Calcutta to join other members of the family in Dhaka. By the time four o'clock came around, every seat was taken and the people filled the wide spacious verandas around the perimeter of the new Church at Ramna Archbishop House.[36]

---

33. Ibid.
34. Ibid.
35. Ibid.
36. *The Dacca Letter*, VOL. XI, No. 4, October, 1960, 3.

During the previous weeks, non-stop activities had been underway to get the new Church in shape for this occasion. Just a few days before, the lighting system was installed and the white terrazzo altar bases completed. Temporary altars were set up for the Consecration.[37]

The front section of seats on the Epistle Side was reserved for distinguished guests. Among those present were many high Government officials of the East Pakistan Government, Judges of the high Court of Dhaka, members of the Diplomatic Corps. Mr. Nat King, the American consul General, attended and stayed for the entire ceremony. In addition, there were a large number of foreign Catholics present. Large delegations of priests, Brothers and Sisters had come from all the other dioceses of East Pakistan, from Chittagong, Khulna as well as Dinajpur.[38]

THE CONSECRATION

Right at four o'clock, the long, solemn procession started out from the Archbishop's House, preceded to the back of the cathedral and up the middle aisle. First came the long line of priests, including all the local clergy and visitors, next the Cordeiro Monsignori, the Bishops, the co-consecrators, Archbishop Graner and Archbishop Cordeiro, Bishop Ganguly and finally Cardinal Agagianian in his flowing red robes.[39]

The choir for the occasion was formed of the priests and Brothers and with a big assist from the visiting Fathers and Brothers from Chittagong, Khulna and Dinajpur. The congregation, getting its strongest support from the large number of Sisters present, sang the Mass itself. The whole congregation took part during the singing of the Litany. Even the old Bengali women were responding wholeheartedly to the Latin refrains. All the visitors present seemed to be very impressed with this group singing. Somewhere in the middle of the ceremony, during a lull, someone started a Bengali hymn in which all joined.[40]

Due to the extreme heat and hot weather and the fact that the Cardinal was not feeling too well, the ceremonies were shortened, lasting altogether just over two hours. The most solemn moment came when the Cardinal, standing before the kneeling Bishop Elect placed the open book

37. Ibid.
38. Ibid.
39. Ibid.
40. Ibid.

of the Gospels upon the neck and shoulders of the Bishop Elect, then together with the Assistant Consecrators, placed his hands on the head of the Bishop-to-be and said, 'Receive the Holy Ghost'. This was followed soon after by anointing of the new Bishop. The climax of the ceremony came towards the end when the new Bishop, clad with miter and full Episcopal vestments, holding his crozier, proceeded down the middle aisle to give the people his first Episcopal blessing. As one of the local papers described it, the Bengali people were so filled with joy and pride that many were in tears. For he was the first Bengali bishop in the history of Catholic Church in the last four hundred years in East Bengal. The excitement of people knew no bounds. After the ceremony was completed, Archbishop Graner, CSC went to the pulpit, and delivered a short but stirring sermon both in Bengali and English, thanking the Cardinal for his great kindness in coming to perform the ceremony and expressing the joy and happiness that all felt on this great occasion, when the first son of the soil in East Bengal was raised to the highest dignity of the Catholic Church in their history of the last four hundred years.[41]

---

41. Ibid.

Episcopal ordination of newly appointed Auxiliary Bishop T. A. Ganguly, Cardinal Peter Gregory Peter Agaginian, Apostolic Dologato from Rome to Pakistan on 7 October 1960. (Source: Moreau House, Provincial Headquarter, Holy Cross Priests, Banashree Prokalpo , Rampura Dhaka 1219, Bangladesh.)

(L-R) Archbishop Lawrence Leo Graner, CSC, Father John VandenBosche, CSC, Father George Pope, CSC, consecrator Cardinal Agaginian, and newly-consecrated Bishop Theotonius A. Ganguly, CSC, imparting his special blessing at St. Mary's Cathedral, Ramna, Dhaka (October 7, 1960). Photo Courtesy: Moreau House, Rampura, Dhaka.

(L-R) Archbishop Lawrence Leo Graner, CSC, Father John VandenBosche, CSC, Father George Pope, CSC, consecrator Cardinal Agaginian, and newly-consecrated Bishop Theotonius A. Ganguly, CSC, at the ordination program of newly appointed Bishop T. A. Ganguly. Photo Courtesy: https://www.holycrossusa.org/spirituality/holy-cross-causes-for-sainthood/servant-of-god-theotonius-ganguly/

Ordination program of newly appointed Bishop T. A. Ganguly.
Photo Courtesy: https://www.holycrossusa.org/spirituality/holy-cross-causes-for-sainthood/servant-of-god-theotonius-ganguly/

THE BANQUET AFTERWARDS

Later in the evening, the Hierarchy, Clergy and religious crossed Dhaka town to St. Gregory's school hall, which was beautifully decked out for the occasion. A beautiful picture of the new Bishop with his Coat of Arms was placed behind the head table. The decorating work was carried out by the Sisters and girls of St. Francis Xavier's Convent. The hall was just big enough to accommodate sitting 125 Bishops, priests and Brothers.[42]

When Cardinal Agagianian arrived, he received a big ovation from the audience. Then followed a delicious meal, furnished by the Medical Mission Sisters, ably assisted by Brothers Aloysius and Martinian. At the end of the meal, there were short but excellent speeches. Archbishop Graner started off in a humorous voice, mentioning how he had become fifteen years younger in the last few days. He then went on to thank the Cardinal again for his great kindness in taking the trouble to come to Dhaka, sacrificing one of his rest days in doing so. Then the Archbishop asked Bishop Theotonius to say a few words. The new Bishop, handling himself like an old veteran gave a fine little speech, expressing his thanks to one and all

42. Ibid.

for the great honor bestowed on him. He was particularly grateful to the congregation of Holy Cross, to the Brothers for his early training and the shaping of his Vocation at Bandhura, and to the Fathers for his University training and for the help and cooperation he had received in his work in the community. Then, the Cardinal rounded off the evening with a really wonderful talk. He congratulated the new Bishop, Archbishop Graner and the Congregation. He then went on, addressing himself to all the missionaries, on the theme, "you must increase, I must decrease," showing how mission work progressed, gradually missionaries themselves fade into the background. When this happened, he said, 'this is sure sign that the Church is coming of age in that particular mission field.' The Cardinal's evident holiness and humility could not but impress all who most him and as he left the hall that evening, he got another big ovation.[43]

The next morning, the Cardinal journeyed over to Amputty to say mass for the Cloistered Adoration Nuns. At the end of Mass, the Cardinal delivered another inspiring message to the Sisters. About nine o'clock that same morning of October 8th, Cardinal Agagianian, with his party, departed by air for Calcutta, having given the Archdiocese of Dhaka the most memorable twenty four hours in its history.[44]

(L-R) Mr. Brian Kenneth Good, newly-consecrated Bishop T. A. Ganguly, C.S.C., and Professor Robert Gomes at a reception in Dhaka Archbishop is given reception in St. Mary's Cathedral, Ramna (Photo Courtesy: Holy Cross Archives, Notre Dame, Indiana, USA; Source: Christian Communication Centre, Luxmibazar, Dhaka.)

43. Ibid.
44. Ibid.

BISHOP GANGULY AT VATICAN COUNCIL II

Subsequently appointed auxiliary Bishop by Pope John XXIII, Ganguly recalled that going to Rome, prior to his consecration, to be "outfitted," he was granted a private audience with the Pope. On seeing the very young looking forty-year-old Bishop Elect, Pope John XXIII, in greeting asked him, "How old are you? Are you only 18?"[45] During his time as Auxiliary Bishop, he traveled throughout the vast archdiocese serving the pastoral needs of the people. At the same time, he was, for a while, a pastor himself (an experience he had not had before), and was the treasurer of the archdiocese. He attended all four sessions of Vatican Council II held in the autumn months of 1962, 1963, 1964, and 1965.[46]

A TIME OF TENSION FOR THE CATHOLIC CHURCH AND THE CIRCUMSTANCE, THAT LED TO A NEW ARCHBISHOP

A time of tension for the Catholic Church in East Pakistan surfaced in the early 1960s, during a riot situation in the Northern districts of the East Pakistan (now Bangladesh) between Bangali localities and ethnic Garos (Mandis) and Hajongs. Due to land grabs and other forms of persecution, backed by provincial and local administrations, thousands of these minorities, mostly Christians, left their homesteads and became refugees in the Meghalaya State of India.[47]

Many Mandis left Madhupur, under the district of Tangail, for India in February 1964, when war broke out between Pakistan and India. Mandi villages and homes were looted, houses burnt. Many died en route or were

---

45. Here to be mentioned that according to the report of *Dacca Letter* that where Archbishop T. A. Ganguly pointed out in his Address reception on January 21, 1968 as an Archbishop told that Pope John XXIII asked him "How old are you? Are you only 13?" On the other hand, one of his biographer Quinlivan, CSC, wrote in his book on the page number 12 that "How old are you? .Are you only 18?" For details see also, *The Dacca Letter*, VOL. XIX, No.1, January 1968, 4; Quinlivan, CSC, Ibid., 12.

46. *The Dacca Letter*, Vol. XIV, No.5, October 1963; Quinlivan, CSC, Ibid., 12–13.

47. *Chronicles of Jalchatra Mission*, Pirgacha, Madhupur, Tangail, 1965, 41.

shot by the E.P.R (East Pakistan Rifles). Father Rev. Eugene E. Homrich, CSC[48] wrote, "We defended the village with bows and arrows."[49]

On September 8, 1965, the Pakistan Army took over the Jalchatra Mission and Fr. Homrich, CSC lived with them (Pakistan Army) as communal conflict continued at that time. During the conflict between Muslims and Hindus, many Hindus left Pakistan and went to India. The Garos were neither Muslims nor Hindus, but they were attacked and some of them residing near the border, left for India for a very temporary period after which they returned to their homes. But as they left for India even for a short time, their lands had been recorded capriciously under the Vested Property Act.[50]

Over 25 villages had disappeared or moved to new areas in the deep forest. The Pakistan government refused to recognize registration of the lands and collect taxes, saying that the Zemindars' lands were "Enemy Property".[51]

The Leprosarium tabernacle was stolen on May 12, 1964. It was found without the sacred hosts in the jungle near Gachabari. Fr. Alex Costa was Assistant and had a stroke on May 14, 1964. September 3, 1964 Fr. Urban Corrayia taught the children the Bengali Mass and Archbishop Graner gave permission to have the Mass in Bengali.[52]

In the war of 1965 between India and Pakistan, the Pakistan Army took over the Jalchatra Mission on September 8. Colonel Cordaro, a Catholic, was in charge of the area. There were 3,000 Pakistan Army in the area to stop the invasion of the Indian tanks. The Indian tanks never went there.[53]

Archbishop Lawrence Leo Graner, CSC, who was an American, had personally visited the affected areas at the initial stage and requested the government to take immediate action, before the situation got worse. However, the government failed to take appropriate action.[54] The Archbishop

---

48. For details on Fr. Eugene E. Homrich, CSC see also, my article, 'Father Eugene E. Homrich and His Role in the Liberation War of Bangladesh', *Bangladesh Historical Association*, Vol. XXIII, 2012–2014, 231–50.

49. Homrich, CSC, "Pirgacha ST. Paul's Church", May 15, 2010, 1. (The unpublished official documents were given by Fr. Homrich to the researcher at St. Paul's Church, Pirgacha, Madhupur, Tangail, on 28.05.2011.)

50. Ibid., 1.

51. Ibid., 1.

52. *Chronicles of Jalchatra Mission*, Pirgacha, Madhupur, Tangail, 1965, 41.

53. Ibid.

54. Pereira, CSC, Ibid., 85–86.

was forced to take recourse and publicize the sad plight of these ethnic groups in his Easter letter in the *Pratibeshi,* the diocesan Catholic newspaper published from Dhaka.[55] He wrote in his 'Easter Message' that almost 30,000 Christians were fled from Garo area into India.[56] Consequently, the local leader in Mymensingh district, who was the secretary of the Muslim League, sent resentment to the press at the objectionable Easter message.[57]

On the other hand, the Easter letter drew the attention of the world, a number of news stories were published from India about the Archbishop's 'Easter Message.' The issue was even discussed in the United Nations in New York. For that reason, the Pakistan government was unhappy with Archbishop Graner, CSC. As a result, he was denied renewal of his visa. The government told him that he could leave the country, but he could not return.[58]

Archbishop Leo Graner, CSC made clear his position to the government as well as the people through a pastoral letter in *the Pratibeshi* on 27 July 1964, which is as follows:

> ... Recently I spent a month in several of parishes in Mymensingh District. I had occasion to encourage our Garo Catholics who have been returned to their homes, and I myself was pleased to see them settle down again. A great deal has been done by the authorities, and more will be done, to make this possible. There is much that we also can do, as I mentioned in my Easter Message.
>
> My Easter Letter was written to comfort those who had suffered and reassure all of you, by recalling the suffering of Christ and the joy that followed on Easter Sunday. Unfortunately, my words of encouragement were overlooked by some who quoted out of context only that part of my message which referred to suffering, in order to prove their claim, not mine, that Pakistan persecutes Christians. In the bitter controversy that followed, the Government of Pakistan and I myself were both blamed.
>
> Now the controversy has subsided, let me remove from your minds any doubts you may have had. Contrary to reports, I did not go abroad, foreign press. My only message was directed to you, as this one is. I did not speak of persecution. And you yourselves

55. *The Pratibeshi*, Vol. XXIV, No. 11, 29 March 1964.

56. *The Pratibeshi*, Vol. XXIV, No. 11, 29 March 1964. For detail Easter Message of Archbishop Lawrence Leo Graner, CSC, see the Appendix X.

57. *Morning News*, April 6, 1964.

58. Pereira, CSC, Ibid., 85–86.

know, dearly beloved, that Christians in Pakistan enjoy religious freedom. No one can deny that.

This very freedom means that you, as loyal citizens, must play your part in the tremendous progress that is taking place. Along with the rights and privileges, you must also share in the responsibilities that are common to all citizens. Opportunities are plentiful, provided you are prepared, by study and hard work, to make use them.

Let this thought be the subject of the usual essay contests held in our schools for Independence Day, and I ask headmasters and teachers to emphasize the need for education and the opportunities that await those who are well trained for their life's work.[59]

In such a suffocating situation, on July 6, 1965, Bishop Ganguly was appointed by Pope Paul VI as the Coadjutor Archbishop with the right to succeed the Archbishop of Dhaka.[60]

The Government was unhappy and soon made it clear that the Archbishop was persona-non-grata. In private talks with him, officials admitted that the Easter Message contained nothing new or untrue, but they were unhappy about it and were determined that he had to go. The Archbishop was planning to go Rome for the Council. The Government gave him permission to leave, but no visa to return. They would not force him out, since this would be more bad publicity. But if he left on his own, he would not be allowed back. So Archbishop Graner chose to skip the Council.[61]

The Government continued the campaign of silence against Archbishop Graner. Then in August 1965, he was informed that he had violated the laws of the foreigners' registration in the country. Finally, in the month of October, he was told to come Rome for the Council. Thus, Rome had settled the matter. On November 3, 1965, Archbishop Graner left the country.[62]

He had worked in the Bengal delta for 37 years.[63] He played a significant role in the socio-economic development for the poor, development of education, such as establishment of Notre Dame College, Dhaka, Holy Cross College. Both institutions have been playing a wonderful role in the social developments of East Bengal since their establishment and they

---

59. *The Pratibeshi*, Vol. XXIV, No. 27, July 26, 1964. For detail Pastoral Letter of Archbishop Lawrence Leo Graner, CSC see the Appendix XI.
60. *The Dacca Letter*, VOL. XVI, No. 4, Aug.1965, 1, Quinlivan, CSC, Ibid., 15.
61. Pereira, CSC, Ibid., 85–88.
62. Pereira, CSC, Ibid., 87–88.
63. Timm, 150 *years of Holy Cross in East Bengal Mission*, 80.

are on the front line of educational institutions here. He had to leave the country due to his protest against the discrimination of Garos in form of his Easter Message, which I described, earlier in this chapter.⁶⁴

Archbishop Graner, CSC remained as the Archbishop of Dhaka until on November 23, 1967; when Bishop Ganguly, CSC became the Archbishop of the Archdiocese of Dhaka as the first Bengalee Archbishop in the history of Catholic Church for the last four hundred years in East Bengal and south Asia.⁶⁵

AS AN ARCHBISHOP

The incredibly placid, intellectual Archbishop experienced in quick succession events that were not only related with the history of Catholic Church in East Bengal but also touched the life of the people of this region. So, discussion of these events can be discussed in five parts, according to the narratives of Frank Quinlivan, CSC.⁶⁶ These are:

a. The execution of Vatican II;

b. A cyclone of such a large scale that it was possibly the solitary largest natural disaster in conditions of loss of lives in the history of East Bengal (1970);

c. A brutal and cruel nine-month struggle for independence of Bangladesh in 1971;

d. A larger scale requirement for relief and rehabilitation program for the overwhelmed newly born country Bangladesh as well as the recognition from Vatican City; and

e. The religious necessity to generate the Church organizations, particularly seminaries, in a newly born country (Bangladesh), which was no longer ingredient of the church in Pakistan.⁶⁷

---

64. Pereira, CSC, Ibid., 88.
65. Quinlivan, CSC, Ibid., 16–17.
66. Quinlivan, CSC, Ibid., 22.
67. Ibid.

Archbishop Theotonius Amal Ganguly, CSC
(Source: Christian Communication Centre, Luxmibazar, Dhaka.)

ARCHBISHOP GANGULY'S JURISDICTION

As the Archbishop of Dhaka, his Excellency directed the activities of the Catholic Church in five Districts of East Pakistan: Dhaka, Sylhet, Comilla, Mymensingh and Pabna. Under his jurisdiction, there were 111 Primary schools, 10 High schools, 2 colleges and also a Technical school, as well as three hospitals and another for lepers, and 11 dispensaries helped to bring relief to thousands of sick people. An orphanage of Tejgaon cared for children. These and other activities and institutions in the Archdiocese of Dhaka came under the Archbishop's jurisdiction.[68]

The Catholic Community in Dhaka held a reception program for newly appointed Archbishop Ganguly, CSC at Archbishop's House on January 21, 1968. There were talks by laymen, with Fr. Mullahy and Archbishop

---

68. *The Dacca Letter*, Vol. XIX, No. 1, January 1968, 4.

Ganguly representing the Congregation. These were followed by a variety program and at 6 p.m. 35 Priests concelebrated with the Archbishop in the Cathedral. There were two other bishops in the sanctuary, Bishop Dante Battaglierin of Khulna and bishop Blair, Anglican bishop of Dhaka.[69] During the reception program, the new Archbishop gave a speech.[70] Another function for government officials was held in February.[71]

Archbishop T. A. Ganguly, CSC is speaking in Suridh Songha Club, Luxmibazar (Source: Christian Communication Centre, Luxmibazar, Dhaka.)

---

69. Ibid.
70. For detail of the speech see also, Appendix XII.
71. *The Dacca Letter*, VOL XIX, No. 1, January 1968, 3.

The Activities of T. A. Ganguly

Archbishop T. A. Ganguly, CSC presented a speech in Notre Dame College, Dhaka (date and event unknown).
(Photo Courtesy: Christian Communication Centre, Luxmibazar, Dhaka.)

(L-R) Father Benjamin Costa, CSC (former, Principal of Notre Dame College, Dhaka and current Vice Chancellor of Notre Dame University, Bangladesh); Father (later, Bishop) Joachim Rozario, CSC; Father Dominic Rozario, CSC; Archbishop T. A. Ganguly, CSC; and an American Holy Cross priest (date, place and occasion unknown).
(Photo Courtesy: Christian Communication Centre, Luxmibazar, Dhaka.)

VATICAN II AND ARCHBISHOP GANGULY

T. A. Ganguly was just 47 years old when he became the Archbishop. He had faced the most important challenging period in his tenure: to implement the mission of Vatican II in East Pakistan. That was the most challenging reform of Catholic Church in their history since the Protestant reformation.[72] The modification and renewal of Vatican II were in East Bengal, as in many places, a time of ecstasy and enthusiasm, pain and dispute. This was the starting point of the local church, which begun its transformation from a "missionary" to an "indigenous" church, that modification insisted it was not to appear "foreign" in a country where Christians were only a modest portion of one percent of the whole population, in a country with a strong and urbanized culture. When the local hierarchy was recognized by 1970, there was a huge modification in the local church and vocations abounded. People not only welcomed the local church but also were respectful of it. They felt that the church was "their church."[73]

The new Bengali Archbishop was himself permeated with Vatican II. He documented the apostolate of the laity. He wanted good relations with the Protestant denominations and all people of benevolence. He wanted to carry his priests collectively. He wanted a Bengali liturgy that would be culturally responsive.[74]

THE DEVASTATING CYCLONE OF 1970 AND ARRANGING FOR FUNDING AND THE ROLE OF ARCHBISHOP GANGULY

While a devastating cyclone and tidal surge of November 12, 1970 struck the coastal area, a lesser cyclone struck Dhaka. The next morning's newspaper informed that the wind blew at 120 mph. and the tidal surge was 20 feet high. However, there was no inkling of the magnitude of the tragedy. Three days had passed, BBC, London, speculated that as many as 500,000 people had been killed in this disaster. Immediately there was a great rush to the affected area.[75] The coastal areas of the districts of Chittagong, Noakhali, Barisal, Patuakhali and Khulna were entirely devastated. The most affected

---

72. For details on Protestant Reformation see also, MacCulloch, *The Reformation*.
73. Most of the lines are verbatim from, Quinlivan, CSC, Ibid., 22–23.
74. Ibid., For details on 'the religious reformation in East Bengal' see also chapter-9.
75. Timm, CSC, *Forty years in Bangladesh*, 136.

areas were Cox's Bazaar, Sandweep, Moheskhali, Kutubdia, Hatia, Ramgati as well the larger Char areas of Noakhali Sadar thana. These regions were completely disconnected from the rest of the country.[76] According to the description of by R. J. Liberatore Jr, is as follows:

> A 115-mph cyclone devastated the low-lying areas of an Asian country, East Pakistan (now called Bangladesh) killing an estimated 500,000 people on Nov. 12, 1970.
>
> A tropical cyclone that formed over the South China Sea gained new life when it reached the Indian Ocean and headed toward East Pakistan in early November 1970. Then everything became horribly worse for the people of East Pakistan, which is now called Bangladesh. The 1970 Bhola Cyclone grew in intensity to a massive 115-mph Category 3 storm with a killer storm surge.
>
> The storm made landfall on Nov. 12 and wiped many villages off the map. In Tazumuddin, more than 45 percent of the area's 167,000 people were killed by the Bhola cyclone. Most of people who were killed were living in the low-lying areas of the country and could not escape the storm's killer waves.
>
> Because emergency services were slow to arrive, East Pakistan and international political leaders criticized the way the East Pakistan junta leader General Yahya Khan handled the disaster. Resentment against Khan eventually led to the Bangladesh Liberation War and the creation of the country of Bangladesh.[77]

There was a severe crisis of drinking pure water, food, medicine, clothes, and particularly warm clothes in the affected areas. The government apparatus was exceedingly sluggish, and the assistance prepared was insignificant compared to the crucial needs.[78] As a result, even two to three weeks after the tragedy, there were an immense number of locales with no relief either from the government or from any political and non-political charitable relief association.[79] Under these circumstances, according to Fr. R. W. Timm, CSC, the Church was among the first to rush aid to the victims of the 1970 cyclone.[80] The first Church personnel to visit the coastal areas and big offshore islands made their own personnel arrangements to

---

76. Umar, *The Emergence of Bangladesh*, vol. 2, 265.

77. According to the unpublished written narratives of R. J. Liberatore Jr., Tuesday, November 12, 2013.

78. *Ganashakti,* 22 and 29 November 1970; Umar, Ibid., 265–66.

79. Umar, Ibid., 266.

80. Interview with Father Richard William Timm, CSC at the Caritas office of Dhaka on 21 March 2011.

form relief parties and procure relief goods.[81] Pope Paul VI touched down at Dhaka Airport on his way to Manila on November 27, 1970. He donated $100,000 to the government for cyclone rehabilitation and an equal amount to the church for the same purpose.[82] Archbishop Theotonius Amal Ganguly, CSC also sent a telegram to Father Charles J. Young, CSC to return from Rome to East Pakistan to help the relief work due to his experience in disaster situations.[83]

The Bishops Conference met in Dhaka on 12–13 January 1971 and decided that CORR upgraded to a perpetual national organization of the Church as a whole, instead of Caritas. Archbishop Theotonius Amal Ganguly, CSC, as the President, was chosen Fr. Benjamin Labbé and appointed him as National Director in the place of Bishop Joachim Rozario. The General body of CORR were later confirmed the appointments. Fr. Paulinus Costa was named Director of CORR Mymensingh.[84]

On the other hand, Andy Koval arrived in Dhaka, East Pakistan in January 1971. Msgr. Andrew Landi, the Deputy Executive Director of CRS arrived in Dhaka three days later to conduct on-site visits with Andy Koval. He then met with Archbishop Ganguly and Andy to inform them that he would be returning to Rome to present to an Emergency Meeting of Caritas Internationalis, CI, two to three proposals (each requiring about $1 million) to finance comprehensive Cyclone Rehabilitation projects to assist the victims of the November 12, 1970 disaster. Andy visited the sites, met the priests, brothers and nuns of the Chittagong and Dhaka Dioceses, worked with the leadership of Notre Dame College to collaboratively finalize three Cyclone Rehabilitation projects and submit them in time for the C.I. meeting in Rome. At the Rome meetings, full funding for three projects was approved.[85]

---

81. Timm, CSC, *Master of Disaster*, It is to be noted that written communication from Jeffrey Pereira on May 10, 2011. The document was provided by Fr. R. W. Timm to the author at Caritas on November 25, 2011.

82. Timm, CSC, *Forty years in Bangladesh*, 137.

83. For detailed about Father Charles J. Young see also, Timm, CSC, *Father Charles J. Young, C.S.C.*, 112–36.

84. Timm, CSC, *Master of Disaster*, 23–24.

85. Extensive use has been made in the description of Andy Koval's unpublished paper from page no. 4–5, almost verbatim, it is to be noted that Andy Koval worked with Fr. R. W. Timm, CSC in Bangladesh from 1971 to 1974. He arrived here along with his family on January 9, 1971 as the CRS (Catholic Relief Service) country representative. Andy also worked closely with Father Labbé for the planning the cyclone recovery program in the early phase of CORR. He was mainly associated with all the cyclone projects

The Activities of T. A. Ganguly

Once the funding was announced, Archbishop Ganguly asked Andy to set up and guide a Catholic organization for the modified design, funding, initiation and implementation of the three major Cyclone Rehabilitation projects to assist the victims of the 115-mph cyclone that devastated the low-lying areas of East Pakistan killing an estimated 500,000 people on Nov. 12, 1970.[86]

During the struggle for the independence of Bangladesh, Andy Koval was honored by Archbishop Ganguly to represent the Catholic Church of Bangladesh in the 1971 launching of the Pontifical Council COR UNUM, which at the first major launch meeting at the Vatican was focused on the conflict between Pakistan and India and to the resolution that would lead to the independence of Bangladesh. As a result of Andy's presentation before the full Pontifical Council COR UNUM assembly of the devastations, atrocities, tortures and displacements imposed on millions of innocent Bengali men, women and children during the Liberation War of Bangladesh, major donor commitments were made and hundreds of thousands of dollars of private donor funds were awarded by those attending the COR UNUM launch at the Vatican to fund the expanding program of CORR and CRS during the last months of the War of Liberation of Bangladesh. After the Independence of Bangladesh, the funding from those groups who attended the inaugural meeting of COR UNUM plus increasing numbers of European and American NGOs and donors and the full membership of Caritas Internationalis increased funding to over $40 million to assist the country-wide relief and rehabilitation programs of CRS and CORR, the Christian Organization for Relief and Rehabilitation.[87]

During the time, as an Archbishop of East Pakistan, T. A. Ganguly was deeply involved with this rehabilitation program, as well as guided it properly, ensuring that the subalterns and affected people get help in a proper way.[88]

---

in Bangladesh.
  86. Ibid.
  87. Ibid.
  88. Interview with former Archbishop of Bangladesh the Most Rev. Paulinus Costa, DD, at the Holy Rosary Tejgaon Church of Dhaka on 20 September 2011.

HOLY FAMILY HOSPITAL AND ARCHBISHOP T. A. GANGULY

Sisters of the 'Society of Catholic Medical Missionary' had established Holy Family Hospital. This was an institution of Catholic Church. But the question arose: why had Archbishop T. A. Ganguly taken the decision to hand over the hospital to other organization after the liberation war of Bangladesh? To explain the matter, Father Adam S. Pereira, CSC pointed out five causes.

> Firstly, the first cause was economic. The hospital failed to achieve its budget according to its need.
>
> Secondly, the administrator of the hospital Mr. Lonni proposed that the economic crisis meant that the activities of hospital would have to be closed. But from the context of staffs and labors of the hospital, the authority thought that if such a type of decision would be implemented here, the staffs and laborers would face a very critical situation with their family members. So he also proposed that the hospital could be handed over to the government Directorate of Health or International Red Cross.
>
> Thirdly, the number of Sisters was reduced until 1970, when there were only three sisters working at the hospital.
>
> Fourthly, the situation of work became very tough in March 1971. Labor agitation also arose in the hospital. They had made procession in hospital compound. The workers-owner relation turned into a critical situation.
>
> Fifthly, under the circumstance, the Catholic Church failed to get a good administrator under whose leadership the hospital could run.
>
> Under the circumstances, the Holy Family Governing Body, the members of Registrade Society, the chief of Dhaka Archdiocese and Archbishop had taken the decision to handover the hospital to the other organization.[89]

On the other hand, Dr. James Tejosh S. Das pointed out the matter as follows:

> Though all the doctors were foreigners, and had to leave the country during the liberation war of Bangladesh in 1971, the local Church failed to get such type of educated people from the

---

89. Pereira C.S.C., Ibid., 101–3.

The Activities of T. A. Ganguly

localities who could run the hospital, so the Church had decided to hand over it to Red Cross.[90]

But the former Archbishop of Dhaka Archdiocese, Paulinus Costa, DD, pointed out the problem in different way. He argued that though he was working with Archbishop during that time, he got a different picture. So, as an eyewitness of the episode he argued that:

> There was a severe labor problem in the hospital, which made it very difficult for the Sisters to run it. Archbishop Ganguly approached the 'Society of Catholic Medical Missionary' in Ireland to help him run the hospital. Unfortunately, decision had already been taken by the sisters to hand over the hospital to the Red Cross in Dhaka. Consequently, the Irish sisters declined to accept the new assignment. Archbishop Ganguly was unable to keep the administration of the hospital within the jurisdiction of the Church.[91]

Under the circumstance, it could be said that all the causes might have played significant role behind the screen to abandon the right of Holy Family Hospital from the Catholic Church in Bangladesh.

---

90. Interview with Dr. James Tejosh S. Das at Eskaton Garden Road, Ramna, Dhaka-1000 on 13 August 2014.

91. Interview with the former Archbishop of Bangladesh the Most Rev. Paulinus Costa, , DD, at his present residing place at Holy Rosary Church, Tejgaon, Dhaka-1215, on 16 August 2014.

8

The Role of Archbishop T. A. Ganguly in the Liberation War of Bangladesh and the Aftermath

THE MOST IMPORTANT CHAPTER in the history of Bangladesh as well as the Catholic Church on this soil was the struggle for independence of Bangladesh.[1] But what was the role of Archbishop T. A. Ganguly, CSC during that time? As an Archbishop he was the central figure of Catholic Church. Along with his bishops' decisions, his own would prove very significant in the context of this history. Did he take a stance in favor of people or against them? To find out the answer, this writing resorts to several written official documents of Catholic Church, vernacular reports, articles, memoirs, writings as well as interviews of the relevant persons.

To explain his position in the liberation war, the background of the war needs to be described, more so to clarify the law of causation of history. Why was such situation created within twenty three years after Pakistan's gaining independence from British colonial power in 1947? Following is an effort to briefly describe the background of the liberation war of Bangladesh; the description might help readers to understand the political situation of East Pakistan. Then it analyze his personal role—[2] how Archbishop

---

1. For details on the role of Christian missions and missionaries in the liberation war of Bangladesh see my forthcoming article, "Bangladesher Muktijuddhe Missionarider Bhumika" (The Role of missionaries in the Liberation War of Bangladesh).

2. Here to be mentioned that as a personal point of view he was a priest, as Archbishop, he was in effect the institution of the Catholic Church and for his people. So his decisions could not remain his own but would invariably be considered as institutional

T. A. Ganguly, CSC, as a priest, gradually became involved with the political issues. With this goal in mind, I have tried to portray a brief scenario of the political background of the struggle for independence of the country. Then I explore his role during the liberation war of Bangladesh and its aftermath.

BACKGROUND OF THE LIBERATION WAR OF BANGLADESH

It is known to all that Pakistan was created on the basis of two-nation theory.[3] Even though there was no cultural relation between the wings of Pakistan, they were joined together only by their overwhelming majority as followers of Islam. Although the majority population were Bengali, they could not attain any way to rule themselves. Under the circumstances, after the end of British raj those in East Bengal entered a new era of new colonization in the state of Pakistan.[4]

PAKISTAN MOVEMENT AND THE ROLE OF BENGALIS

At the midnight of 14 August 1947, the eastern part of the Indian province of Bengal became the part of Pakistan.[5] (Here I am trying to give a brief background.) The election of 1946, the authenticity of the Muslim League's claim to speak for the Muslims, especially in Bengal where they constitute the majority, was proved beyond doubt. The League captured 113 seats out of 121 reserved (Muslim) seats polling 20,36,775 out of 24,34,100 Muslim votes. Eighty percent of the Muslim voters had cast their votes.[6] The election functioned as a plebiscite on Pakistan, so the activists underplayed the excellence and merit of entity candidates.[7] Muslim youths of universities and colleges, professionals and mullahs, peasants and community leaders

---

decisions of the Catholic Church of this region. So a political background is needed before describing his role in the liberation war of Bangladesh.
    3. For details see also, Pirzada, ed. *Foundations of Pakistan*.
    4. Ahmad, *A Socio-Political History of Bengal*, 43–91.
    5. Kamal, *State Against The Nation*, 11.
    6. Ibid., 2.
    7. 'Vote for a Muslim Leaguer even if he be a Lamp Post', see Weeks, *Pakistan*, 86. Cited from Kamal, Ibid., 2.

all combined their efforts to win the election.⁸ A huge popularity brought the Muslim League to power in Bengal in 1946.⁹

In this state of affairs, most Muslims wanted a separate state under the leadership of Muslim League. A small number of Bengali leaders wanted a third state for the Bengal region, but that demand could not make a dent against the popular politics of the Muslim League.¹⁰ During that time, Muslim League came forward as the symbol of the Muslims aspiration. This situation as described by a Pakistani historian:

> It started its career in the new State with all the advantages that a party could wish for . . . The country looked to it not only with respect and gratitude, but also with a passion and affection not usually associated with a political group.¹¹

Just before the independence, Mohammad Ali Jinnah Gave his historic speech to the nation on 11 August 1947 at the Constituent Assembly of Pakistan.¹²

In Dhaka, Maulana Abdul Hamid Khan Bhashani, a Muslim Nationalist, also expressed the similar expectations on the floor of the Legislative Assembly.¹³

DEMOGRAPHIC DIFFERENCES BETWEEN THE TWO WINGS OF PAKISTAN

According to considerations of the political science's theoretical perspective, a national integration problem is treated as a border problem. But in the case of Pakistan, there were also many problems; political, economic, cultural, and many other differences of the both sides.¹⁴ Clifford Geertz called this problem: 'old societies and new states.'¹⁵ According to Myron

---

8. Kamal, Ibid., 2.

9. Ibid., 2–3.

10. For detail, see also, Rashid, "A Move for United Independent Bengal," 386–406. For a very interesting debate on the divide of Bengal see also, Chatterji, *Bengal Divided*.

11. Aziz, *Party Politics in Pakistan*, 78. Cited from, Kamal, Ibid., 1.

12. *Dawn*, Independence Day Supplement, August 14, 1999. See the full Speech of Md. Ali Jinnah in Appendix XIII.

13. Kamal, Ibid., 16.

14. Jahan, *Pakistan: failure in national integration*, 4–5.

15. Clifford Geertz, *Old Societies*, cited, Jahan, Ibid., 5.

Weiner, national integration depends on five tasks: 1) the creation of a sense of territorial nationality; 2) establishing of a national central authority; 3) bridging of the elite-mass gap; 4) creation of a "minimum" value consensus; and 5) devising of integrative institutions and behavior. In this context, we should consider the plural society of Pakistan, with ethno-cultural group conflict from very beginning.[16] Many historians pointed out it as a double state. The total area of Pakistan was 365,529 square miles, which was made up of two unequal regions (East Pakistan: 55,126 square miles and West Pakistan: 310.403 square miles) separated from each other by thousands of miles. West Pakistan is mainly a scorched land, where average rainfall is less than twenty inches. On the other hand, East Pakistan is situated in one of the largest and most heavily watered deltas of the world. The average rainfall in the monsoon season here is one hundred inches. The relation between two wings of Pakistan was very tense and costly one in many ways, even the mobility of the population between the two wings was also difficult. Naturally, people-to-people relation between two wings was not very strong either. West Pakistan was closer to the Middle East, and East Pakistan nearer to Southeast Asia. Therefore, the strategic interest between two wings was also divergent. Even the density of population between the two wings of Pakistan was very dissimilar.[17]

LANGUAGE CONTROVERSY

The debate on what would be the state language started at the very beginning of formation of Pakistan in 1948. Mohammad Ali Jinnah—a respected leader of Pakistan, died on 11 September 1948. He visited East Pakistan and declared that Urdu shall be the state language of Pakistan. Later the leaders of Pakistan also took the same stand.[18] Professor Serajul Islam Choudhury looked at this decision critically from both a political and economic point of view.[19] Hence, the people of the eastern part of Pakistan thought that it was an unjust decision to be imposed on them. So, they demanded equal

---

16. Weiner, 'Political Integration," 52–64, Cited, Jahan, Ibid., 3.

17. Jahan, Ibid., 10. The demographic difference is given in the Appendix XIV.

18. Umar, *The Emergence of Bangladesh*, vol.1, 191. For further study on Language Movement, see also, Umar, *Purba Banglar Bhasha Andolon*, (Language Movement in East Bengal) vol.1. And Umar, *Purba Banglar Bhasha Andolon*, (Language Movement in East Bengal) vol.2.

19. See also, Choudhury, "The Language Movement."

status for Bengali language. Even the Pakistani leaders tried to establish new script for Bengali language. The debate on language created a new national feeling for Bengali natives, which later gained momentum as Bengali nationalism.[20]

THE ELECTION OF 1954 AND FALL OF MUSLIM LEAGUE

Then history unraveled very fast. Seven years later, the Muslim League had a test on its popularity in the First General Election of East Pakistan on 8 March 1954. By this time, Awami Muslim League had been formed on 23 June 1949,[21] and under their leadership, United Front was formed. They had participated in the election based on 21-point program[22] as their election manifesto and the first program was "To make Bengali as one of the State Language of Pakistan." The result was absolute disaster for the ruling party (Muslim League), which won only ten seats out of the 237 Muslim seats in the Provincial Assembly. Even the Prime Minister also defeated by an unknown student leader. The party had secured only 16.29 percent of total cast vote.[23] Why did Muslim League fail in the election? To answer this question many scholars tried to point out that the charismatic leaders and the activists who played a significant role for Pakistan movement became the opposition leaders: Maulana Abdul Hamid Khan Bhasani[24], Fazlul Haq, Husen Shaheed Suhrawardy, Ataur Rahman, Abul Musnsur Ahmed, and Sheikh Mujibur Rahman,[25] to name a few.[26]

---

20. Jabeen, Chandio, Qasim, "Language Controversy," 99–124.

21. For further study Please see, Ghosh, *The Awami League*. The frequency of languages is common spoken given Appendix XV.

22. The 21 point is given Appendix XVI.

23. Kamal, Ibid., 3.

24. To brief study on uncompromising character of Moulana Abdul Hamid Khan Bhashani, see, Kabir, *The Red Moulana*.

25. For an interesting discussion on the politics of Pakistan see also the unfinished memoirs of the father of the nation of Bengali people, Rahman, *Oshomapto Atmo jiboni*, (Unfinished Memoirs).

26. Ahmed, *Amar Dekha Rajnitir Panchas Bachar*, 331. For detail see, Kamal, Ibid., 3.

AYUB IN POWER

In the course of time, the politics of Pakistan took a new shape. The government declared the date of proposed election on 15 February 1959. Nevertheless, it failed to continue the democratic process of Pakistan. Rather Iskander Mirza abrogated the constitution and proclaimed the Martial Law on October 7, 1958. Just 20 days later, the history of Pakistan fell into a black hole for a decade and five months. For by this time Iskander Mirza had been compelled to abandon power to General Ayub Khan on 27 October and leave the country. Mirza and his wife were sent in exile to London. As soon as Ayub Khan assumed power, he proclaimed the martial law and banned all types of political activities in Pakistan from 1958–1962.[27]

SIX-POINT FORMULA

Forward for East Pakistan acquired a more definite form in 1966. The question was raised by Sheikh Mujibur Rahman under his 'six point formula', and an opportunity was created for the opposition party because of the Tashkent Declaration.[28] A conference was called at the house of Chaudhury Mohammad Ali to which Sheikh Mujibur Rahman was invited as an opposition party leader of East Pakistan. Presumably, the intention was to creature pressure on the Ayub regime.[29]

In February of 1966, in the Council meeting of the Awami League held at Dacca,[30] the 'six point Formula'[31] for the autonomy of East Pakistan was adopted. In the same meeting, Sheikh Mujibur Rahman was elected president of the party. Then he went to Lahore to participate the program as one of the opposition party leaders. The formula, with an explanatory note, was circulated with a sub-title 'our right to live' in the name of the president of East Pakistan Awami League, Sheikh Mujibur Rahman.[32]

---

27. Kamal, *Unosouttorer Gono Aovuttthan (People's Upsurge of 1969)*, 30.
28. For details on Tashkent Declaration see also, Amin, *The Tashkent declaration*.
29. Khan, *Constitutional and Political History of Pakistan*, 179.
30. The Romanized spelling of the Bengali name was changed from Dacca to Dhaka in 1982; by then President Lieutenant General Hussein Muhammad Ershad who thought the spelling did not reflect the true pronunciation of the word as it is said in Bangla.
31. For details of Six Point formula is given the Appendix XVII.
32. Ahmed, *Bangladesh: Constitutional Quest For Autonomy 1950–1971*, 87. For details to understand the six points formula from the context of Bangabandhu Sheikh Mujib's point of view see also, Rahman, *6-points Formula*. It was later printed at Hossen,

ECONOMIC DISPARITY BETWEEN TWO WINGS

At this juncture, some very important questions surfaced regarding the political and economic situation of both the wings of the state. Because of the Indo-Pakistan war of 1965, the Army was starkly divided into two factions, even Ayub Khan gradually lost his luster. However, because of his overall authority, the circumstances did not get out of control,[33] although few developments could be shown in different sectors during his time. In this context Megasthenes wrote that:

> Impressive strides were made in infrastructure and private sector development, agriculture was modernized through better use of irrigation, and there was industrial growth effected through liberal tax benefits. GNP rose by close to 45% in 10 years. Ayub Khan enacted land reforms, emphasized family planning, brought about important and welcome changes in Muslim personal law and the country's foreign policy and also achieved understanding with India on the complex Indus water sharing issue. A "certain orderliness and predictability" characterized "Government practices and policies". Pakistan was even cited by some foreign visitors "as a model for the Third World". There are thus people who tend to look to his years of power as the halcyon period of Pakistan's history, particularly in the context of what followed. There was, to be sure, a downside to all this, but more on that later. In the last decade or so, information—in the shape of memoirs, declassified papers and diaries—has come to light that afford insights into, and add to the understanding of, the man, his regime and his times.[34]

However, the reality was different, because this huge growth of GNP was artificial and there was incongruity between upper class and masses in terms of their livelihood. That '22 patronage families' at the controlled the wealth of Ayub's administration only proved that gross injustice took place in the distribution of national wealth. Moreover, all '22 families' were belonged to West Pakistan, so the response in East Pakistan to such disparity of wealth inevitably took an astringent form.[35]

Unasattorer Ganoandolon, 44–63.

33. Ahmed, Ibid., 133.
34. Megasthenes, "The Field Marshal."
35. Ahmed, Ibid., 133.

Besides the economic disparity between two wings, discrimination was obvious in the educational sector as well.[36]

The same was reflected in the representation of East Pakistan in the army; it was no more than 5 percent of the East Pakistan region.[37]

Bengalis, moreover, had only 30 percent representation in the civil bureaucracy of Pakistan. The imbalance had been created due to historical factors. Prior to the partition of Bengal in 1947, Calcutta was formed as a capital city of India. Even East Bengal had grown up as the hinterland of Calcutta. Pakistan inherited 133 ICS-IPS officers during the period of partition. Amongst them, only one was a Bengali Muslim. The initial difference between two wings of Pakistan created an overwhelming scenario of discrimination.[38]

Under these circumstances, the government spent approximately 100 million (10 crores) rupees in 1968 to celebrate the 'Decade of Reforms' and 'Decade of Development,' but the year-long promotional campaign attracted more criticism than appreciation. Particularly in East Pakistan, the campaign became counter-productive as it invoked further antipathy against 'Punjabi' exploitation. This substantial propaganda program was initiated to publicize Ayub's attainments prior to the presidential election scheduled in 1969.[39]

PRESIDENTIAL ELECTION UNDER BASIC DEMOCRACY

When the question of election came forward, public opinion favored direct election. The historical experience of the election of 1964–65 was also helped people take such a decision. Only excepting Ayub's own convention of Muslim League, all the political parties of the two wings had developed a common issue on the ground of universal adult franchise and this feeling was very strong even in Punjab. By this time in the middle of 1968, after recovering from his illness, Ayub Khan decided to hold presidential elections on the merit of his 5 years tenure, so political parties decided to boycott the election and mobilize the public opinion based on universal adult franchise. Ayub ignored the demand of the politicians and went ahead with his

---

36. The economic disparities can be shown in chart, which is given in Appendix XVIII.
37. Chowdhury, *Pakistan,* 50. The chart is given in Appendix XIX.
38. Chowdhury, Ibid., 50.
39. Ahmed, Ibid., 133.

own strategy, mainly at the advice of some civil servants like Altaf Gauhar and Fida Hasan.[40]

START STUDENT AGITATION

By this time, two important issues were resurrected the political activities in the both wings of Pakistan. The issues are reflected in the Agartola Conspiracy trial and the Tashkent agreement. The case had a direct impact on the political thought-processes of the leaders of all shades, and as a response to the trial, political agitation began to form at a fast pace. Secondly, since having been renamed by Ayub Khan after the Tashkent agreement, Zulfikar Ali Bhutto came forward with his slogan 'thousand year war' against India. With that poster, Bhutto could link with the Army barracks that did not like Ayub's conciliation with India, and gain considerable support from Punjab. If Ayub Khan brought him into the politics and he served him eight years, Bhutto was waiting for an opportune moment to finish his previous chief. During this time, Bhutto attracted a large number of urban elites with his socialistic promises for the workers and peasants, and very soon gained support from students and masses because of his rhetorical and erudite approach.[41]

On the other hand, East Pakistan was already in a sweltering condition with the proceeding of the conspiracy case ongoing on a daily basis. The leaders of Awami League being in jail, the leaders of the opposition either indirectly supported the Ayub regime or failed to organize their party to sustain as an opposition party against government. Many of the leaders were in fact only individuals without any party affiliation. During the time, only one sustaining group who could mobilize the movement, the students. The entire responsibility to mobilize the movement depended on student leaders of Dacca University. They started a three-month long movement against Ayub regime. At last, the Ayub regime came to end in the month of March, 1969 after a great mass upsurge in the history of Pakistan.[42]

The reality of the two wings was hardly the same. Rather, people had participated in the mass upsurge due to their own class interest. The 'reality' for the middle class people of the urban area and peasants from villages was

40. Ahmed, Ibid., 134.
41. Ahmed, Ibid., 134.
42. Ahmed, Ibid, 136; for details about the mass upsurge of 1969 see also, Kamal, Ibid.

not the same. The people wanted free from the political, socio-economic, cultural exploitation by the Pakistani rulers. They tried to break the colonial mode of production, which was sustained in the Pakistan era also. The people fought for multi-party representative democracy, where all the public interests will be discussed without any fear. The people of the Eastern wing of Pakistan had the dream to establish a classless economic system devoted to evenhanded allocation of the 'national resources'. They also wanted separation of religion and politics, because Pakistani ruler used religion 'Islam and Pakistan' in a synonymous connotation. The people wanted freedom from these bitter experiences.[43] Given all these circumstances, East Pakistan was boiling under the ground and when a proper time came, the society burst into the mass upsurge in 1969. As the result of mass upsurge, field marshal Ayub Khan was compelled to abandon power, and the politics of Pakistan turned into a new era, now linked with the struggle for the independence of East Pakistan with a new hope.

1970 ELECTION AND AFTERMATH:

The 1970 election was held but the Pakistani ruler did not agree to handover the power of the majority party of Pakistan. Therefore, the Awami League under the leadership of Bangabandhu Sheikh Mujibur Rahman began a constitutional movement, but they failed to gain power because of the West Pakistani's martial rulers. After the election of 1970, Awami League became the majority Party of Pakistan Constitutional Assembly. Nevertheless, Pakistani martial rulers did not want to hand over the power to the leader of the people.

Under these circumstances, Bangabandhu Sheikh Mujibur Rahman carried the constitutional movement for East Pakistan's regional autonomy to its utmost limit. Regional autonomy, as visualized and demanded by the Awami League, could not really be achieved within the framework of the Pakistan state, the movement for its achievement reached a heightened stage in the month of March when it was no longer possible to push it further on the constitutional path. Or, in other words, there was a breakdown and collapse of the Awami League's constitutional movement for self-determination and autonomy.[44] But the well-equipped Pakistani occupation force cracked down on 25 March 1971—with 'operation searchlight'.

43. Kabir, Ibid., 20.
44. For details about the history of Bangladesh see also, Umar, Ibid., (Vol. I & II).

The peace-loving unarmed Bengalees did not know how to respond to the sudden crackdown. Under such circumstance, Bangabandhu Sheikh Mujibur Rahman was arrested on the night of 25 March and restrained at Dhaka Cantonment until he was taken to West Pakistan to stand trial for 'sedition' and provocative insurgency. Before his arrest, Bangabandhu Sheikh Mujibur Rahman, sent a wireless message to Chittagong over the ex-EPR transmitter declaring the independence of Bangladesh.[45]

ROLE OF T. A. GANGULY IN THE LIBERATION WAR OF BANGLADESH

During the Liberation War of Bangladesh, Catholic Missionaries played significant and powerful roles in country's liberation, mostly in a peaceful and silent manner from behind the scene. Some of them were Catholic Christian missionaries. Amongst them, the name of Archbishop Theotonius Amal Ganguly, CSC resonates strongly in Bangladesh's history. As an eyewitness of the brutalities of the Pakistani occupation force, he became part of the living history of the Liberation War of Bangladesh. Though my chapter's theme is on the role of Archbishop T. A. Ganguly during the Liberation War in 1971, this part of my chapter is based on interviews, the unpublished documents of the Catholic Church, chronicles of the Mission, vernacular etc as I earlier mentioned.

The struggle for Liberation of Banglees was a story of sacrifice. During that time of overall melancholy, the Archbishop reported that one-third of the Catholics in the Dhaka Archdiocese and one-half of those in Khulna and Dinajpur had been dislodged.

During the liberation war, the Catholic Church in East Bengal felt that they had to take their position against the brutal massacre by the Pakistani Army. To be on the safe side before committing themselves, the Catholic Bishops' Conference met to discuss whether or not to make some kind of public statement about the war, especially the genocide and its atrocities. Archbishop T. A. Ganguly was sent to West Pakistan to talk with Justice Cornelius, a Catholic, the Chief Justice of the supreme court of Pakistan, about the possibility of issuing a protest. He told Archbishop T. A. Ganguly: "Don't you dare make a protest! This is a civil War, an uprising against the legitimate authority that is being put down with necessary force. Soldiers

45. en.banglapedia.org/index.php?title=Rahman,_Bangabandhu_Sheikh_Mujibur bangabandhu sheikh mujibur rahman

will be soldiers at times and overdo things, but that is not a sufficient basis to protest."⁴⁶ He realized that 'soldiers often exceed their bounds in trying to put down a rebellion quickly, but to protest against it was going much too far in his estimation.'⁴⁷

During the liberation war of Bangladesh, the Catholic Church had adopted a policy that we came to know from the memoirs of Fr. R. W. Timm, CSC.⁴⁸ According to his account, the policy was as follows:

> Thousands of Hindus came to Catholic missions begging to become Christians. The Catholic policy was to enroll them "in the community", give them a cross to wear and tell them that when things settled down they could make up their minds about accepting baptism and becoming Christians. (I don't know of any who did.) . . .⁴⁹

One of the eyewitnesses, Hubert Arun Rozario, described the role of Archbishop T. A. Ganguly in the liberation war in such a way:

> I remember Archbishop Ganguly in the days of our Liberation War when he was trying frantically to pass letters and money from Bangali workers in West Pakistan, specially from Karachi to their families in our remote villages of Dohar and Nawabganj Thanas, to sustain their livelihood and help their children to continue studies. At the risk of his life he wanted to give our distressed people protection and consolation in our battered country where death was everywhere. He did the miracle and a new channel was opened to communicate between their families and the workers in Pakistan and send money via London. I was with him helping in small way and reminding him each day not to take this risk as the general post office, would ultimately find out and he would be picked-up by Pakistani army. He just remained silent and I knew his silence was speaking to me loud and clear at his second floor office in Archbishop's House. As Mukti Juddha escalated conflicts throughout our country, the Archbishop took courageous and prudent actions to assist the freedom movement. He instructed all Christian hospitals and clinics to render loving care and proper treatment to our freedom fighters and our people.

46. Timm, CSC, *Father Edmund Goedert, C.S.C.*, 88; Quinlivan, CSC, Ibid., 24.

47. Timm, CSC, Ibid., 88.

48. For details about the role of Fr. R. W. Timm, CSC in the struggle for liberation war of Bangladesh, see my article, "Father Timm and His Role in the Liberation War of Bangladesh," 119–28.

49. Timm, C.S.C., *Forty years in Bangladesh*, 181–82.

Many Christian hospitals and clinics treated wounded freedom fighters throughout the border areas of Mymensingh, Jessore, Khulna, Sylhet, Rangpur, Dinajpur and Chittagong. In this noble service three Christian fathers and one sister was brutally killed by the occupying Pakistani army. He allowed and requested Parish Priest of Bhoberpara Catholic Church, Fr. Francis Gomes, now retired Bishop of Mymensingh, to set up all logistics to the formation of Shadhin Bangla Sarkar in Baidyanathpur, Kushitia, which was renamed Mujibnagar. The first cabinet of Bangladesh was set up at the church compound and the Independence Document of our motherland was signed on the dining table of the priest-in charge, Rev. Fr. Francis Gomes. His timely actions and the vision of Bangladesh shone as the beacon of light and hope to all Bangalees.

I left for Melaghar Mukti Bahani camp in Agortalla in the month of May and before my departure I saw Archbishop Ganguly, he just asked me, "Do you realize that you are taking a most dangerous path?" I did keep silent, and then he softly said, "It is the most effective and glorious path to liberate our occupied country." He then put his hand on my head and just said, "God be with you, wherever you are posted." I felt strength in my soul and with that overwhelming love of Christ he bade me farewell. Guess what? In the course of the Liberation war, I met the present Editor of The Daily Star, my school friend Mahfuz Anam, in Kalyani camp, near Benapole border, where we were being brushed-up again and again for a special assignment, every day, by a great freedom fighter and officer, Major Manzur, later Lt. Gen. Manzur.

I had the privilege to work for the formation of "Trebeni Chatra Kalyan Sangha," "Suhrid Sangha," during my student days in Dhaka University. Many a time when I was overburdened with problems to organize our youth, I came to the Archbishop, told him about our shortcomings and difficult problems, and he put himself under our burdens. The fact is he always wanted to be with the youth in the field, in the difficult situations when nobody came forward to help them in our motherland.

Archbishop Ganguly worked hard during the Liberation war in extreme conditions. He traveled from village to village and spoke to our people. He spoke of hope and his homilies were simple and direct. He never cared for his comfort in order to share in the sufferings of our people in the hands of Pakistani soldiers. Till his death, he was always willing to take on the burden of the common people and tried to share their sufferings and anxieties.[50]

50. Rozario, "Lest We Forget Archbishop Theotonius A. Ganguly."

The Role of Archbishop T. A. Ganguly

During the liberation war, four Catholic priests were martyred by the Pakistani occupation force. The four Christian martyrs were Father Mario Veronesi, SX, (4th April, 1971),[51] Father Lucas Morandi of Dinajpur Diocese (21st April, 1971)[52], Father William Evans, CSC (14 November, 1971)[53] and Sister Emmanuel, SSMI (8th June, 1971).[54]

---

51. Father Mario Veronesi, SX, was a Xaverian missionary and came here (East Pakistan) from Italy. He was killed by the Pakistani Army On April 4, 1971, Palm Sunday; he was in the mission of Jessore, serving as much as he could the poor suffering people during that time. Soldiers appeared and he stood in front of them, his arms spread wide in a gesture of defense of his people. He was shot in the chest and killed. He died at the beginning of Holy Week (according to the catholic Christianity). He was 58 years old, and had been a spiritual for twenty eight years, nineteen of which he had spent in East Pakistan (Bangladesh). He was buried at first in Jessore then, later, his body was moved to Shimulia. Garello, S.X., *Bangladesher Tin Bandhu,* (Three Friends of Bangladesh), 12–79. For details see also, www.xaviermissionaries.org/M_Stories/Martyrs/VernIntro.htm

52. Father Lucas Marandi was all alone in the Ruhea church, which was under the Dinajpur Diocese in a compound separated from a few Catholics living close by. On April 21, 1971, a West Pakistani army jeep heaved up at the priest's house. Father welcomed them and offered them tea and biscuits. They then left for the north. He relieved from of his bout of nervousness, but that was only for a while. After three hours, the jeep came back again. Father Marandi appeared once more, but the soldiers manhandled him, surrounded his residence and tortured him for the next five minutes or so. They bayoneted his face beyond recognition. Blood splashed all over the walls. When they left the compound, fatally injured Father was dying.

A few Catholics who lived nearby hurried in to see what had occurred. Finding him critically injured, they determined to take him to India by a bullock farm cart that Father had used earlier. Before they could move him, Father Lucas Marandi died. His dead body was taken to the Catholic Church at Islampur on the Indian side of the border where he has been buried. Pinos, P.I.M.E., *Catholic in North Bengal,* 26–27. See also, Hemrom, *Fr. Lucas Marandi,* 7–9.

53. For detail, see also, Alonzo, C.S.C., Ph. D, *The Story of Fr. William Evans, C.S.C.*; see also, Costa, *Bangladeshe Catholic Mondoli* (The Catholic Church in Bangladesh), 302–3.

54. On June 8, Sister Emmanuel was killed in Baromari when her jeep ran over a land mine. Homrich, CSC, "*History of the Liberation War*"; *Chronicles of Jalchatra Mission,* 1.

CHRISTIAN MISSIONS IN EAST BENGAL

Photo Courtesy: Father Evans (Holy Cross Church, Luxmibazar, Dhaka), Father Veronesi (Bishop's House Archives, Khulna), Father Marandi (Catholic Beginnings in North Bengal by by Luigi Pinos, P.I.M.E.) Layout and Design: Joachim Romeo D'Costa. Source: of http://www.genocidebangladesh.org/bangladesh-war-of-independence-west-pakistani-soldiers-kill-catholic-priests/

After the brutal killing of Fr. William P. Evans, CSC, Archbishop T. A. Ganguly, CSC presented a report at the Golla Mission on 14th November 1971. The report is given below:

> We, the under signed, certify that the young men of the local Christian Community brought to Golla the dead body of Rev. Fr. William P. Evans, C.S.C., Pastor of St. Francis Xavier Church, Golla, P.S. Nawabganj, Dt. Dacca, from Barra where it was recovered from the river Ichhamati by a certain Md. Ali and his associates, We received the body of Father Evans at Golla Church at 12:45 p.m. Sunday, 14th November, 1971.
>
> We inspected the body of Father Evans and noticed that he had received deep cuts on the side of the mouth and lower lip. There were two bullet wounds on his body (one bullet entered the body below the ribs on left side, passing through the body

emerging above hp sideways) and cuts on the inner side of both arms; in addition there were scratches on his palm and feet.

Sister M. Charles, R.N.D.M. and M. Cornelius, R.N.D.M., Mrs. Margaret Gomes, Nurse's aide, and Messrs Hubert Gomes, Gregory Gomes and Peter Gomes of Golla who helped was the body and clothe it for the funeral service, recognized and identified the body of Fr. Evans, as also thousands of people, men and women and children—Christian, Hindu and Muslim—approximately five thousand in number, who had come to pay their last respects to their beloved pastor, recognized the body of Rev. Father William P. Evans, C.S.C.

The funeral service for Fr. Evans was held in St. Francis Xavier Church, Golla at 4:10 p.m. with a Concelebrated Mass with Archbishop Theotonius Ganguly, CSC as president and the following concelebrants: Rev. Fathers William Hickens, James Solomon, Urban Corraya, Walter Michalik and Theodore Majumder.

Immediately following the Concelebrated Mass which was attended by thousand faithful of the locality, the remains of Rev. Fr. Evans was laid to rest at 4:50 p.m. on Sunday, November 14, 1971, next to the grave of a former Pastor of Golla Church Rev. Father Adolf Francais in the cemetery at Golla.

May he rest in peace.[55]

As the war neared its end, a concluding attempt to wipe off the country's intellectuals took place, mostly planned between 12 and 14 December to eliminate potential leaders of the new nation.[56] Archbishop T. A. Ganguly was also included in the list of Bengalee intellectuals who would be killed by the Pakistani occupation force and their local collaborators. According to former Archbishop of Dhaka Paulinus Costa, who was residing in an adjacent room with Archbishop at the Ramna Bishop House during the liberation war of Bangladesh:

> In the mid-November, a winter morning, a Pakistani Army officer, who happened to be a Catholic, came to the Bishop's House and informed me (Paulinus Costa) that the Pakistani Army had listed Archbishop's name as a Bengalee intellectual for his activities in favor of the Muktis (freedom fighters). Therefore, the Army officer suggested [to] me (Paulinus Costa) to inform Archbishop that he would [best] leave his residing place, take place in a secured shelter for few days and come back again when the situation would

---

55. *The Report on the Death of Rev. Fr. William p. Evans, C.S.C.*
56. Hensher, Philip, "The War Bangladesh can never forget."

come to normal position. When Archbishop came to know the reality, he opposed the proposal [saying] 'if I abandon my home what will happen with my people, and I would rather wait to die and stay here but could not leave this place.'[57]

At last, independence came in 16 December 1971. It was a triumph of the Bengali nationalism, which inherent here under the Bengali culture.[58] At the end of war, Archbishop Ganguly wrote to one of the priests in January 1972, after the conclusion of a war that had been nine months of terror and brutality:

> We have survived the ordeal but the church did not go unscathed. Three of the finest priests (Fathers Mario Verencai, Bill Evans, and Lucas Maradndi) and Sister Emmanuel and scores of our own Catholics have sacrificed their lives along with hundreds and thousands of our non-Christian brethren, as a price of peace. A number of our institutions (churches, convents, schools, dispensaries, rectories) have been either totally destroyed or badly damaged . . . The government and the people of Bangladesh are now faced with many serious problems, mainly the economic problem. The rehabilitation of the millions of refugees who had taken shelter in India and have already started to come home is indeed a colossal problem.[59]

RECOGNITION OF BANGLADESH BY THE VATICAN AND ROLE OF ARCHBISHOP T. A. GANGULY

To gain diplomatic recognition of newly born Bangladesh was very important during that time, and Archbishop of Bangladesh T. A. Ganguly played a significant role. Detailed information depended on Father Enzo Corba, PIME who had visited with Archbishop T. A. Ganguly during that time at the Vatican. He gave an interview to the researcher where he stated that:

> After the liberation war of Bangladesh, Archbishop Ganguly along with Bishop Michael Rozario of Dinajpur, put pen to paper urging the Vatican to grant Bangladesh diplomatic identification on

---

57. Interview with the former Archbishop of Bangladesh the Most Rev. Paulinus Costa, , DD, at his present residing place at Holy Rosary Church, Tejgaon, Dhaka-1215 on 14 August 2014.

58. For details about the Bengali Culture, see also, Murshid, Ibid.

59. Quinlivan, CSC, Ibid., 25–26.

The Role of Archbishop T. A. Ganguly

February 15, 1972. Later, Archbishop Ganguly, Bishop Michael Rozario and I (Fr. Corba) went to Rome to meet with the Pope Paul VI, asking for funds and the recognition of newly born Bangladesh by the Vatican. Both demands were accepted by the Vatican.[60]

The Vatican was to recognize Bangladesh as an independent country on September 25, 1972.[61]

Father Corba Enzo, PIME, Archbishop of Dhaka Theotonius Amal Ganguly, CSC, and the Bishop of Dinajpur Michael Rozario and father Badlands visit to Pope Paul VI. Photo Courtesy: Piero Gheddo, *Missione Bengala I 155 anni del Pime in India e Bangladesh*, **Editrice Missionaria Italiana, 2005.**

REHABILITATION PROGRAM

In a letter dated March 1972, the Archbishop described the situation after the end of the war:

> As to the general situation in our newborn country, the housing problem is truly critical. The thousands upon thousands of returning refugees have simply no shelter at all. This is all. This is all more worrying as coupled with the fact that food supplies are getting

60. Interview with Father Corba Enzo P.I.M.E. at Singra Forest Ashram (Hermitage), Birgonj Upazilla, Dinajpur District, Bangladesh on 10 July, 2011.

61. www.londoni.co/index.php/history-of-bangladesh?id=155

more scare every day, increases our concern. The major rice storehouses were either destroyed or looted and months of April and May are really going to be critical if massive aid does not start entering our lifelines.[62]

The huge task of relief and reconstruction after the liberation war was greatly aided by CORR[63] (the Christian Organization for Relief and Rehabilitation), founded after the cyclone of 1970. Its initial headquarters were in Chittagong and, then it was shifted to Dhaka. Archbishop Ganguly was elected by the bishops' conference as national chairman.[64]

After the liberation war of Bangladesh, the country faced a very critical situation, as all the refugees returned to their ancestors' land—the newly born Bangladesh. Almost immediately after independence, the 10 million refugees in India began pouring back over then borders. Government had set up over 250 reception centers to welcome them and gave them temporary shelter and care. But in India they had received a one-week supply of food and transport money, so most of them headed directly towards home. This thoughtful arrangement averted huge problems of dependency and logistics. By February 15, 1972, the refugees had returned completely.[65]

It took a week for the government-in-exile to come over from Calcutta. It was 18 days before CORR got verbal approval to carry on relief work and another eight days before Fr. Labbè availed the same in writing on January 11, 1972. Without waiting for help of others, they had started their works and CORR set to work immediately after liberation war to convert their 55-project relief and rehabilitation program into a nationwide war reconstruction program. They drew up a $30 million "Skeleton Program" and Fr. Labbè rushed off to Rome to meet the Disaster Relief Committee of Caritas International at Vatican, which pledged some $12 million in cash and kind on the spot. By the end of the year, their program was already underway, even before the banks opened for the first time on January 1, 1972. With Fr. Labbé and the late Joachim Dessai, the first CORR administrator, they had presented their Skeleton Program to the Secretary of Relief and

---

62. Quinlivan, CSC, Ibid., 26.

63. Caritas was founded in 1967 as the Eastern branch of Caritas Pakistan. Following the cyclone of November 1970 it was re-organized and became known as CORR (Christian Organization for Relief and Rehabilitation) and took on the character of a national organization on January 13, 1971. The name Caritas was re-introduced in 1976. According to the website: www.caritas.bd.org

64. Quinlivan, CSC, Ibid., 26.

65. Timm, C.S.C., *Forty years in Bangladesh*, 200.

Rehabilitation on December 28, 1972 and received his verbal permission to carry on work and to bring in goods from India.[66]

The CORR Skeleton Program was designed to rehabilitate 200,000 war-devastated families, including housing (average cost Tk.300), professional rehabilitation (average cost Tk.500), test relief work and, if necessary, food, clothing and cooking utensils. Their main objective was to get people back to work as soon as possible so that they could earn their own food in the face to face the grim situation. The beneficiaries were to be only those whose house and means of livelihood (cattle, plough, sewing machine, carpenter tools, etc.) had been plundered or destroyed.[67]

In February 1972, Archbishop Ganguly, along with Bishop Michel Rosario of Dinajpur, went to the Vatican to meet the Papal Secretary of State, the Congregation for the Evangelization of People, Pope VI, and the Papal Relief Coordinating Commission, Cor Unum. They also met representatives of Caritas International, U. S. Catholic Relief Service, and Miserere. Archbishop Ganguly told them that conditions in Bangladesh were tragic because of the return of ten million refugees and damage done to the homes of millions of others. Fr. Benjamin Labbé had gone to meet with Caritas International earlier, which was mentioned before.[68]

Archbishop Ganguly also came forward to help the newly formed Bangladesh Government in its rehabilitation efforts. He met the Prime Minister of Bangladesh and the father of the nation Bangabandhu Sheikh Mujibur Rahman on February 2, 1972. During that time, he donated Tk. 20 lac and his episcopal golden chain and cross for post-independence war relief and rehabilitation in Bangladesh to the Prime Minister. He also presented a short report on the activities of CORR. Among others, Bishop Michael Atul D' Rozario, CSC of Khulna and Bishop Joachim Rozario of Chittagong and Bishop Blair of Anglican Church of Bangladesh also were present at the program.[69]

---

66. Ibid., 201–2.
67. Ibid., 201–2.
68. Quinlivan, CSC, Ibid., 27.
69. Interview with Bishop Michael Atul D' Rozario, CSC and Fr. Joseph S. Peixotto, CSC, at the Provincial House of Holy Cross Fathers at Rampura, Dhaka on 17 July 2015; Photograph of the ceremony of hanging over of the event of the donation to Bangabandhu Sheikh Mujibur Rahman. Here to be mentioned that Pereira, CSC, Ibid.,113, mentioned that the ceremony was held in 1973, but according to the interview and photography the program was held on 2 February 1972.

(L-R: Second from left) Archbishop T. A. Ganguly, C.S.C. of Dhaka, Bishop Michael Atul D'Rozaio, C.S.C. of Khulna and Bishop Joachim Rozario of Chittagong met with Prime Minister Bangabandhu Sheikh Mujibur Rahman of the newly independent Bangladesh (first from left) on February 2, 1972 and donated a cheque for 200,000 takas and his episcopal gold chain and cross for post-independence-war relief and rehabilitation work in Bangladesh. Photo Courtesy: Moreau House, Rampura, Dhaka.

The new Bangladesh church needed quickly to organize seminary formation. Archbishop Ganguly wrote in April of 1972:

> Twenty-one of our seminarians are still at the seminary in Karachi, Pakistan. Three of them were to come here and be ordained last December, but were unable to leave due to the war. Now all the twenty-one might be considered as "political prisoners" awaiting exchange with Pakistani prisoners here in Bangladesh and India.[70]

He also asked for prayers for their quick and safe return to home. He mentioned how hard they are trying to get them back as soon as possible.[71]

By the June of 1973, an intermediate seminary had been organized at the Archbishop's House. The total number was 45 seminarians from the (then) four dioceses of Bangladesh. Five major seminarians, repatriated from Pakistan, had begun studies at Papal Seminary in Poona, India. The National Major Seminary for Bangladesh would open in August with Father Paulinus Costa as rector.[72]

70. Quinlivan, CSC, Ibid., 28.
71. Ibid., 28.
72. Ibid., 27–28.

Plans were in place to build an intermediate seminary building on the grounds of the Archbishop's House by the middle of 1974 and to construct a major seminary building at the same time.[73]

The Archbishop was clearly a man beset with many worries, pressures, and needs. Again, in June of 1973, he wrote:

> over and above all of our other problems and projects, we are duty bound to contend with the daily stream of those who, due to the present state of the economy (i.e. spiraling prices, gross inflation, and all the rest of it), do not have enough, nay, who do not even have one full meal a day.[74]

He also wrote, "our headaches and heartaches" and aspirations in a "newborn nation still in the tottering stage" as "we started from absolute zero in everything." In another letter, he speaks of these "critical days of stress and want."[75]

During his time as an Archbishop, the new National Major Seminary was one of the finest works, with the Holy Spirit Seminary in Dhaka, Bangladesh enjoying one of the highest ordination rates in the world. Before the birth of Bangladesh, the seminarians had been trained at "Christ the King Seminary" in Karachi. After a difficult struggle to find an adequate number of teaching staff, financial aid and a building, on August 23, 1973 the then apostolic nuncio, Archbishop Edward Cassidy (later a Cardinal and President of the Pontifical Council for Promoting Christian Unity), and four Bangladeshi Bishops established the Holy Spirit Seminary in Dhaka Cathedral. Two years later, the foundation stone of the present Seminary in Banani, Dhaka, was laid by the first native Bishop of Bangladesh, Archbishop Theotonius Ganguly, CSC.[76]

By the August of 1972, however, there was growing concern about the Archbishop's health. He was worn down physically and emotionally. The Superior General of the Congregation of Holy Cross wrote to the Archbishop inviting him to come to Rome where he could take rest. In a letter to the Provincial of the Indiana Province, the superior General wrote that there was concern that the Archbishop might have TB because he was so rundown indicating that the psychological and emotional stress was probably the greatest cause. The Archbishop responded on September 4, 1972,

73. Ibid., 28–29.
74. Ibid., 28.
75. Ibid., 28.
76. *DAILY CATHOLIC*, WEDNESDAY; June 16, 1999. vol. 10, no. 116.

"I feel that it [going to Rome to recuperate] would be a rather uncommon measure not available to the generality of our people. If God should want me to continue to spend myself for his people, I am ready, be it even in sickbed."[77]

---

77. Quinlivan, CSC, Ibid., 29.

9

The Early Phase of Reformation in Christianity in East Bengal and Archbishop T. A. Ganguly, CSC: 1959–1977

RELIGIOUS REFORMATION OF CATHOLIC Christianity was one of the most important events in the history of the Catholic Church in East Bengal. It is well known that the religious reformation in East Bengal began soon after the Second Vatican Council in which Archbishop Theotonius Amal Ganguly, CSC participated along with other three Bishops of East Pakistan, naming Most Rev. Raymond Larose, CSC, Bishop of Chittagong Diocese; Most Rev. Joseph Obert, PIME, Bishop of Dinajpur Diocese; Most Rev. Dante C. Battaglierin, SX, DD Bishop of Khulna Diocese.[1] The official language of the council was Latin. Later on, the documents of the council were translated into different languages.[2] The modern Church is working with the documents of Vatican-II. This chapter deals with some questions regarding the role of T. A. Ganguly, CSC behind the implementation of Vatican-II in East Bengal together with all Bishops of the country at that time. This chapter tries to clarify these relevant questions. To find out the answers of these questions, we have to look at the efforts of inculturating the Catholic Church in East Pakistan at that time. The questions are:

I. What is the Second Vatican Ecumenical Council?

II. Why did Pope John XXIII convoke the Vatican Council?

1. The name of the Bishops found at the *Catholic Directory*, 2011, 69, 159, 188.
2. Abbott (General Editor), *The Documents of Vatican-II*, ix.

III. How had the documents of Vatican-II been implemented in the Catholic Church in East Pakistan?

IV. What was the impact of Vatican-II in East Bengal?

WHAT IS VATICAN-II?

Vatican-II is the Second Vatican Ecumenical Council (original title in Latin: Councilum Oecumenicum Vaticanum Secondum). There have been 20 Ecumenical Councils, in the Catholic Church, before the Second Vatican Council, which was the 21st Ecumenical Council.[3] The word 'Ecumenical' means a Council that deals with important issues of the universal Church. The Council before Vatican-II was Vatican-I was held in 1869–1870.[4] It was a brief council, as it was interrupted by Franco-Russian war[5] and invasion of Papal States by the Piedmontese armies. Vatican-I rejected all the erroneous teachings of that time, and gave a definition of the infallibility of the Pope, a more important Council was the Ecumenical Council of Trent held in 1542–1563, almost four hundred years before Vatican-II. That was a time when the Catholic Church had to face many problems in regard to her authentic teachings, which had been changed or distorted by some Protestant Churches at that time. All these false teachings were rejected by the Council of Trent. The Catholic Church at that time tried her best to safeguard its teachings regarding the Sacraments, explanation of the texts of the Bible, original sin of Adam and Eve, devotion to the saints and regulation for Pastoral ministry of the Catholic Church.[6]

Vatican-II exclusive of 992 footnotes of various lengths, the sixteen promulgated document contain around 103,014 words. There are five basic sources of these Latin texts:

---

3. Ibid., 110.
4. Shehan, Lawrence Cardinal, 'Introduction' in Abbott, Ibid., 9.
5. For details on Franco-Russian war, see also, Howard, *Franco Prussian War*.
6. According to the written documents of Fr. Francis Shima, Fr. Gaberial provided this to the researcher at the Bishop House, Kakrial Dhaka, 14 July 2015. It is also to be noted that Fr. Francis worked for the committee of Liturgical development in East Bengal as the Secretary and Archbishop T. A. Ganguly, CSC, nominated him for this post. He also was sent abroad for his study on Liturgy. So, he was very much connected with the development of Liturgical works.

I. the final versions distributed at the Council just before the last vote on a text and the actual promulgation of it by the Holy Father;

II. the Vatican newspaper *L'Osservatore Romano*, which printed the full Latin texts, one at a time, shortly after each one was promulgated;

III. the official Vatican periodical, *Acta Apostolicae Sedis*, from February 1964 through December 1966;

IV. individual booklets printed by the Vatican polyglot Press (1964–1966);

V. The collected texts edited by the Secretary General of the Council and printed by the Vatican Polyglot Press (1966).[7]

THE CHRONICLES OF VATICAN-II

Catholic Church throughout the whole world underwent tremendous changes on account of the Second Vatican Council, which was held in Vatican City in the years of 1959, 1962 and 1965. This council dealt with vital issues of the life and works of the Catholic Church. The aim of Vatican-II was "aggiornamento" (in the words of Pope John XXIII, who convoked the council). This Italian words means updating, renovation, reformation etc. i.e. which means adaption of the Catholic Church to modern time and to various culture of different peoples and race in the world.[8] The chronicles of Vatican-II as follows:

1. Announcement:

On 25 January 1959, Pope John XXIII had first sudden declaration of his intention to convoke an Ecumenical Council of the Catholic Church. That was only after about three months after his election as the Roman Pontiff.[9]

2. Preparation:

On June 5, 1960, Pope John established the necessary commissions and secretariats to make all the preparation for the Ecumenical Council. Then on December 25, 1961, Pope John convoked the Twenty first Ecumenical Council, which is the Second Vatican Council. (The first Vatican Council was held in 1869–1870).

7. Abbott, Ibid., ix.
8. Fox, *Vatican Council II*.
9. Sima and Palma, *Dewitiya Bhatican Mohasabar Dalil Samuha*, 668; Abbott, Ibid., 15.

On July 20, 1962, invitations were sent to those Christian Churches and Communities, which are operated from Catholic Church, asking them to send those Christian Churches and communities, which are separated from the Catholic Church, asking them to the Council. On September 5, 1962, the norms of the Council were established.[10]

3. First Session:

The Second Vatican Council was solemnly opened by Pope John XXIII on October 20, 1962 "a message to Humanity" was issued by the Council. This first session was closed on December 8, 1962. Then after about six months Pope John XXIII died on June 3, 1963. After that Pope Paul VI was elected as the Roman Pontiff on June 21, 1963. He immediately announced his decision to continue the Council inaugurated by Pope John XXIII.[11]

4. Second Session:

The second session of the Council was opened by Pope Paul VI, on September 29, 1963. Then on October 30, 1963, an orientation vote was taken, which favored sacra mentality and collegiality of Bishops, the divine right of the Episcopal college, restoration of the diaconate as a distinct and permanent order.

During this session the first two documents of the Council were promulgated:

a. Constitution on the Sacred Liturgy,

b. Decree on the means of social communication.

This second session closed on December 4, 1963. After that, on January 4–6, 1964, Pope Paul made an ecumenical journey to the Holy Land (homeland of Jesus and of St. Peter) and met Patriarch Athenagoras (Chief Orthodox Patriarch of the East). Then on May 17, 1964, the Secretariat for no-Christian Religions was created.[12]

5. Third Session:

The third session of the council opened on September 14, 1964. During this session, three documents were promulgated:

---

10. Sima and Palma, Ibid., 668.
11. Ibid., 668.
12. Ibid., 668–69.

a. Dogmatic Constitution on the Church;

b. Decree on Ecumenism;

c. Decree on Eastern Catholic Church.

This third session ended on November 21, 1964.[13]

6. Fourth Session:

The fourth session of the Council (which was the final session) was opened on September 14, 1965. The following day (September 15, 1965), Pope Paul set forth the norms governing the new Episcopal Synod established to help him in governing the Church.

On October 4–5, 1965, Pope Paul went to New York and addressed the several assembly of the United Nations. After his return, he gave reports of it to the council Fathers.[14]

During this final session, the following documents were promulgated on October 28, 1965:

1. Decree on the Pastoral Office of Bishops in the Church;

2. Decree on the appropriate Renewal of the Religious Life;

3. Decree on Priestly Formation;

4. Declaration on Christian Education;

5. Declaration on the Relationship of the Church to non-Christian Religions.

Two more documents were promulgated during this session on November 18, 1965. These are:

1. Dogmatic Constitution on Divine Revelation;

2. Decree on the Apostolate of the Laity.

In this session, announcement was made by the Pope Paul VI about the beginning of the reform of the Roman Curia.[15] The introduction of the process for the ratification of Pope Pius XII and Pope John XXIII, Jubilee Period, and convocation of the synod of Bishops not later than 1967.

---

13. Ibid., 669.

14. Cardinals and Bishops who participated in the Council, are Known as Council Fathers, Ibid., 669.

15. The holy of Cardinals who help the Pope in his administration works.

A liturgical celebration titled "a prayer service for promoting Christian unity" took place, on December 4, 1965, at which the Holy Father, Paul VI, assisted along with the Fathers of the Ecumenical Council as well as the Observers and guests delegated to attend the Council".

On December 7, 1965, four more documents of the Council were promulgated. These are:

1. Declaration on Religious Freedom;
2. Decree on the Ministry and Life of Priests;
3. Decree on the Church's Missionary activity;
4. Pastoral Constitution on the Church in the modern world.[16]

After long four sessions, the Second Vatican Ecumenical Council was officially adjourned on December 8, 1965. At this concluding session "Message of the council" were given: to Rulers, to men of thought and science, to artists, to women, to the poor, the sick, and the suffering, to workers and to the youth.[17]

Image of Vatican II (Source: Internet)

16. Sima and Palma, Ibid., 669.
17. Ibid., 669.

The Early Phase of Reformation in Christianity

WHY DID POPE JOHN XXIII CONVOKE THE SECOND VATICAN COUNCIL?

Up until the Second Vatican Council, the notion of the church was like pyramid[18] wherein the Pope was at the top-most level, below that level come the Cardinals, then followed by, step by step, the Archbishops, then Bishops, then Monsignors, after which came the Priests, the Deacons, after them come the Brothers and Sisters, and family at the base of the pyramid come the vast majority of the numbers of the Church known as Laity or Lay-people. This notion of the Church gave much importance to the clergy who took care of all the important activities of the Church. The lay people were to come to the Church for liturgical and functional celebrations and remain inactive instead of taking active part in the celebration. The drawing below may help us to understand the place and rank of the members of the Church.

The pyramid system can be portrayed in such way:

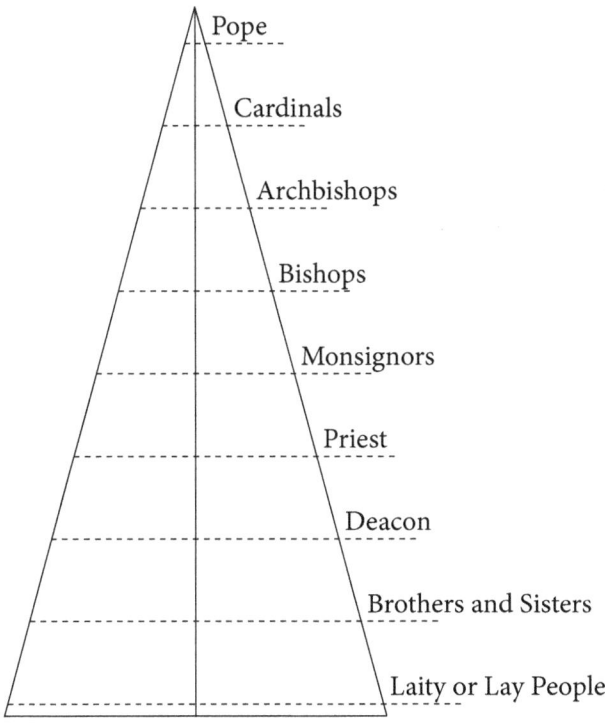

18. D' Rozario, CSC, "Dogmatic Constitution on the Church," 15–29.

Pope John XXIII saw this situation and wanted to do something about it. He kept pondering on this notion of the Church and compared it with the original Church established by Jesus Christ as described in the Bible. It is written in the Bible that Jesus Christ called twelve men to become His disciples (known as Apostles, meaning persons pent). These twelve were the men who always accompanied Jesus and witnessed what He was doing and heard what He was saying.[19]

From among these twelve Apostles[20], Jesus selected Peter as the representative of Himself in order to give leadership to the Church after His death on the cross.[21]

Thus, Peter was the first Pope (Roman Pontiff) and the other Apostles were Bishops.[22]

The notion of the Church before Vatican-II was known to the Cardinals and Bishops who participated in the Vatican-II are known as the Fathers of the Council. Hence with the inspiration given by Pope John XXIII, they described the Church as the 'people of God.'[23] According to this notion the entire Christian Church is the 'people of God' from which some members are called by the Holy Spirit to give the necessary services to the Church which is People of God.[24]

According to this view or notion of the Church (as people of God), Vatican-II reviewed the notion of the local or indigenous church. It reminds us that it is the local churches which together constitute the universal church, whereas the previous notion, before Vatican-II, gave us the idea that the universal church is divided into local Churches, which therefore are parts of the universal church.[25] The following drawing will clarify what has been said above.

---

19. *Holy Bible*, Mark 3:13–19.
20. In Greek Episcopes means an elder of a society.
21. *Holy Bible*, Mathew, 16:15–19.
22. Abbott, Ibid., 397.
23. Ibid., 12, 56–57, 488, 491.
24. Ibid., 12, 56–57, 488, 491.
25. Ibid., 36, 50.

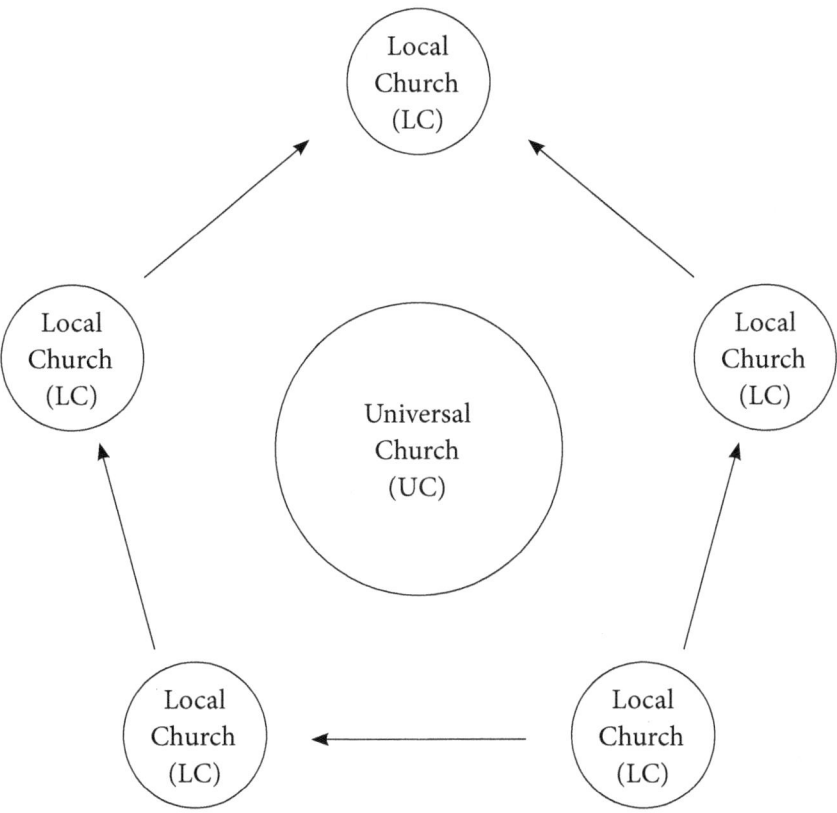

Pope John XXIII convoked the council of Vatican-II in view of bringing about some reformation to the Catholic Church. This is because the Catholic Church did not undergo any change since the Ecumenical Council of Trent held in the middle of the sixteenth century (1542–1563). The main intention of Trent was to protect the Roman Catholic Church from any erroneous teachings of various persons and groups of People whose opinions were not acceptable to the doctrine of the Roman Catholic Church. Moreover, there was a need to give directive about the true teaching of the Church in regard to the Sacraments,[26] genuine explanation of the Bible texts, Original sin of Adam and Eve, and devotion of Saints. Trent had to take decisions which were appropriate and necessary in the context of that time. Trent had to face problems of emanating from various opinions and teachings which were against the teachings of the Catholic Church. These teachings were rejected by Trent. In order to safeguard the Catholic

---

26. Religious rites regarded as channels and signs of receiving grace.

Church, the Council of Trent had to emphasize some sort of uniformity for the sake of unity in the Catholic Church, although uniformity and unity are not synonymous. Actually what is visible in the Church and in the world is that, unity exists in diversity or pluriformity. All the people in a society or in a country are not uniform; nonetheless there can be unity among them. On the other hand, there is some kind of uniformity in address, size, style of searching etc. but there may not be unity among them. For a long time unity and uniformity have been seen as necessary for each other's relationship, i.e., there has to be uniformity for the sake of unity, and vice versa. This view of that age (16th century) kept the Catholic Church almost unchanged for four hundred years. As a result many practice of the Church were not understandable for the people of the 20th century. Before the Second Vatican Council, it was noticeable that during the four hundred years between Trent and Vatican-II, many things had changed in the world, whereas the church did not undergo any serious change. Pope John XXIII were aware of this situation, which inspired him to summon an Ecumenical Council in order to update, renovate, inculturate and revitalize the Church in her life and activities so that the church may become a "Church in the modern world"[27] and a church of the people where in the lay people could have active participation in all the activities of the Church. Hence, later on, when Vatican-II was going on, it was said that Pope John opened the doors and windows of the Church in order to get fresh air.[28]

With this awareness in his mind, Pope John XXIII on January 25, 1959, announced his intention to convene an Ecumenical Council. After that, on June 5, 1960, Pope John established the preparatory Commissions and Secretariats in view of the Council. Then on October 11, 1962, the Ecumenical Council of Vatican-II was solemnly opened by Pope John XXIII.[29]

HOW WERE THE DOCUMENTS OF VATICAN-II IMPLEMENTED IN EAST BENGAL?

The Second Vatican Council promulgated sixteen documents. All these documents have given directions for renovation, restoration and up-dating

27. Ibid., 199.

28. According to the hand written description of Father Francis Gomes Sima, the hand written document was provided by Father himself to the researcher at the Archbishop House Kakrail, Dhaka on 26 September 2014.

29. Ibid.

of the life and activities of the Catholic Church. These directives have inspired all the countries of the world where the church is present. Thus the directives also inspired the Church in East Bengal.

The most important document of Vatican-II is the constitution on the church. However, it was the liturgy of the church, which was the first publically discussed in the Council of Vatican-II. This is because the celebration of liturgy keeps the Church living by worshipping God and by nourishing God's people. It is said in the constitution on Liturgy, "The Liturgy in the summit towards which the activity of the church is directed; at the same time it is the foundation from which all her power flows."[30]

After the Second Vatican Council was closed on December 8, 1965, Archbishop T. A. Ganguly became aware of the fact that something has to be done in order to renovate and activate the church in East Bengal and thus adopt the church to the local situation so that the church in this country became truly a local and indigenized church. Up to Vatican-II, the people (the laity) were not aware of their active role in the activities of the Church.[31] Vatican-II made it clear that the lay people also have an active part to play in the life and activities of the church.[32] Before Vatican-II, the lay people were inactive in the liturgical celebrations because of the liturgical language (Latin) which they did not understand, and also because of the liturgical regulations of that time of uniformity.

The Second Vatican Council was put much emphasis on the liturgical life of the Catholic Church in every country of the world. Archbishop T. A. Ganguly realized that it is very important to inculturate the liturgy of the local Church in East Bengal in order to bring it close to the people so that they may understand what is going on in the liturgical celebrations. Up to Vatican II the liturgy of the Catholic Church was in Latin language, which the people did not understand at all. Hence, in order to inculturate liturgy, local language should be used. There are four signs used in liturgy. These are:

a. Person (like Priest, servers, singers, servers, people etc.);

b. Things (like liturgical dress, flowers, candles, incense, bell, liturgical utensils, etc.);

c. Speech and Language (like reading, prayer, songs, homily etc.)

30. Abbott, Ibid., 26.
31. Ibid., 394, 397, 399.
32. Ibid., Decree on the apostolate of the Laity, no. 3.

d. Posture and Gesture (like sitting, standing, kneeling, raising of hands, etc).[33]

In order to implement the instructions of the Second Vatican Council, Archbishop Ganguly, together with all the Bishops of East Bengal, took some steps. Some of these steps are:

a. Collegiality of Bishops emphasized Vatican-II; was made more effective in the church in East Bengal in the form of Bishops' Conference.

b. The Oriental Institute in Barisal, under Chittagong Diocese, was established to renew and to indigenize the church in East Bengal to the local situation. This Institute emphasized the creation and use of songs in accordance with local culture. The Institute organized music courses with special emphasis on oriental (Hindustani) classical music so that the participants of this course may be able to read and write the notation of songs, and also be able to compose music and songs.

c. All the sixteen documents of Vatican-II were supposed to have been translated in Bengali language. Six of them were translated and printed in booklet form in 1969. The rest could not be done on account of the Liberation War, which began in March 1971.

d. Lay people were invited to take active part in the activities of the church. Priests in charge of the Parish churches were told to form a Parish Council[34] in each parish. These Councils are to have meetings to diocese about the well-being and the needs of the Parish. It also tries to solve problems of the Parish and takes decisions about the future program of the Parish. This way the lay people can take part in the decisions, plans and programs of the local church.

e. Usually, an altar (table) is used for some Liturgical celebrations, especially mass.[35] Before Vatican-II, this later would be placed against the back wall, and thus the presiding priest had to face the back wall instead of facing the people in the church during the liturgy. Vatican-II

---

33. According to the hand written description of Father Francis Gomes Sima.

34. A Parish Council is a committee whose numbers are: The Parish Priest (President), representatives taken from people of various walks of life, e.g. teachers, village leaders, women groups, students, Religious Brothers and Sisters, etc. If necessary, some persons can be selected from the active groups of the people. A parish is an area of the Diocese with a Priest in charge of it.

35. Eucharistic Celebration.

has turned the alter away from the wall so that the priest may face the people while presiding over liturgical functions. This was also done in the Church in East Bengal.[36]

THE IMPACT OF VATICAN-II IN THE CATHOLIC CHURCH IN EAST BENGAL

As we have seen above, the documents of Vatican-II brought many changes in the Church. Up until Vatican-II, the Catholic Church was thought to be "Semper idem" (always the same). That means, no changes are ever to be made to the life and activities of the church. The Council Fathers, with the help of famous theologians of the day managed to analyze the actual situation of the church at that time in the light of the Scriptures (Bible). They saw that the church had gone away from the original notion of an institution established by Jesus Christ and also from the notion of the Church in the first several centuries. That is why Vatican-II wanted to restore all the valuable realities of the early church of Jesus Christ. It is seen in all the documents of Vatican-II. Although there were some objections to the forthcoming documents from the conservations, nevertheless, the Council Fathers went ahead and made the necessary changes. Similarly, in an effort to indigenize the Church in East Bengal, there were oppositions from some conservative Priests and Lay People which made it a difficult task to accomplish at that time. Yet the Church in East Bengal went ahead making the necessary changes as indicated by Vatican-II. Archbishop Ganguly, together with the other Bishops of East Bengal took steps for the reformation and indigenization of the Church in East Bengal according to the directing of Vatican-II.

First of all, in regard to the restoration and reformation of liturgical celebrations, the altar for Mass (i.e. Eucharistic Celebration) was turned from facing the back wall of the Church to several feet away from the back wall so that the Priest may be able to face the people while celebrating Mass. This is how Mass was celebrated in the Church for the first several centuries. The altar had been turned towards the wall during the middle ages. This restoration encouraged better participation of the people in the liturgical services.

---

36. According to the unpublished written documents of Fr. Francis Sima, Ibid.

Archbishop Ganguly also encouraged the use of local languages in the liturgical celebrations that the people may be able to understand what is being said in the celebration. He encouraged the creation of an indigenous clergy in order to make the church more local. He formed several commissions for the local church. Among them: Biblical Commission, Liturgical Commission, and Catechetical Commission.[37]

However, the impact of Vatican-II, under the leadership of Archbishop T. A. Ganguly, pursued it as the reformation of Catholic Church in East Bengal, where it turned from pyramid based Church to local and indigenous Church, which I mentioned earlier. He along with his associates showed maturity to start reforms in and out sides of Catholic Church from his tenure, which is still being continued. There was no doubt that it was a religious and social reform for Catholic Church but when he was started to implement it, showed his political consciousness through his activities, which focused on my preceding chapter. So it could be argued that it was not only a very tough situation for the Catholic Church but also for this region, because of the circumstances from his appointment as an auxiliary bishop to last day of his life as an Archbishop. The most important event in the history of Bengal, the liberation war, occurred during his tenure in 1971, where he took his position in favor of people of the region with the help of a constitution, implemented under the guidance of Vatican-II. He reformed local Catholic Church, which indicated closer to local people.

---

37. According to the unpublished written documents of Fr. Francis Sima.

The Early Phase of Reformation in Christianity

Archbishop Ganguly along with common people. Photo Courtesy: Christian Communication Centre, Luxmibazar, Dhaka.)

The religious reformation of the Catholic Church under the light of Vatican II, in the latter part of the twentieth century, led to large-scale transactions and transformations of Christian society as well as the thinking process of Catholic Church in East Bengal. The people began to think of the Church as their Church-'Indigenous Church'.

10

Death and Aftermath

DEATH

THE MOST REV. THEOTONIOUS Amal Ganguly, CSC the Catholic Archbishop of Dhaka, died on 2 September 1977 at 4:15 pm, of heart failure in front of Dr. Nural Islam's clinic on Dilu Road. In spite of attempts for artificial respiration, conducted by Fr. Charles Gillespie, CSC and Sr. M. Progga, SMRA who were accompanied with the Archbishop to the clinic, he breathed his last. He was 57.

The news of the death of Archbishop T. A. Ganguly, CSC spread like wildfire among the Catholic Community of Dhaka and a grieving crowd of about thousand people rushed to the Archbishop's House at Ramna to pay homage to their religious leader. His body was brought to the Church at 7:00 PM and a mass was offered in the Ramna Cathedral.[1]

---

1. *Weekly Pratibeshi*, September 2, 1977, 2.

Archbishop Theotonius Amal Ganguly's grave in Ramna Cathedral Premises, Photo Courtesy: Christian Communication Centre, Luxmibazar, Dhaka.

THE AFTERMATH

There was a popular demand among the Catholics of Bangladesh that the canonization process be started as soon as possible after the death of Archbishop Ganguly. The similar scenario is also found in the history of Catholic Church when Pope John Paul II died on April 2, 2005. During the time, thousands of people gathered in St. Peter's Square for mourning the death of Pope. The people rose up banners demanding "Santo subito!"- Saint immediately.[2] Archbishop Ganguly's canonization process started in 2006. Archbishop Paulinus Costa, DD of Dhaka, on September 2 of that year, 29 years later after his death, in an official ceremony at St. Mary's Cathedral in Dhaka, introduced the causes and opened the diocesan inquiry on Archbishop Theotonius Amal Ganguly. The process of his canonization is, at the first stage, known as "Servant of God". The head of the Catholic Church, Pope Benedict Sixteenth had earlier approved this declaration. He is the first Bangalee who received such a rare honor in the process of canonization.[3]

According to the system of Roman Catholic Christianity, after the death of a person, a minimum of five years has to pass before taking up the

2. D' Costa, *Archbishop Theotonius Amal Ganguly, C.S.C.*
3. www.asianews.it/news-en/Bangladesh

causes of his or her canonization. The common faith in the Christianity requires that there are three steps to become a Saint, but in the Catholic Church taught that it has four steps:

1. Servant of God,
2. Venerable,
3. Blessed, and
4. Saint.[4]

Firstly, when the subject matter would arise for the canonization process the local bishop of the diocese, placed an official letter, contained life of the person, and looked for the Pope's authorization to initiate the canonization process. Subsequent to obtaining the permission or no-objection from the Vatican, the local bishop formally initiated the foreword of the foundations and the aperture of the diocesan investigation. The question of canonization is then called the "Servant of God." The bishop also, shaped a diocesan committee where spectators would provide evidences to the Christian virtues of the person measured epic. These are *theological virtues* (faith, hope and charity), *cardinal virtues* (prudence, justice, temperance and fortitude), and *other virtues* precise to the person's state of life. The committee also composed all accessible papers (the person's own handwritten, typewritten, and printed writings as well as other writers' books and writings on him or her).[5]

Secondly, on the achievement of the diocesan process, the bishop sends all documentations to the Congregation for the Causes of Saints in the Vatican. The Congregation then studies the same and, if satisfied with the heroic virtues of the person, issues a decree announcing him or her as the "Venerable."[6]

Thirdly, if the Venerable *dies a martyr's death*, the Pope himself officially announces the person a martyr through a decree and consent to the beatification formal procedure. Later in the procedure, the person is called the "Blessed." If the Venerable *dies a normal death*, the Congregation necessitates a substantiation of a phenomenon that had taken place through his or her arbitration. The Pope himself provides recognition to the sensation

---

4. www.catholicdoors.com/faq/qu221.htm, for details see also, C., Beccari. "Beatification and Canonization."

5. Ibid.

6. Ibid.

and permits the Congregation to issue a decree for the beatification. Following the beatification ceremony, the person is called the "Blessed." A feast day is also allowed to be observed in the Blessed's own diocese and certain other places.[7]

Fourthly, in the last stage, another miracle is required to be established after the beatification. The Pope then solicits the Congregation to get ready for the canonization of the person. The canonization ceremony authenticates that the person is sacred and is in heaven. Then he or she is identified as the "Saint" and is allowed to be venerated throughout the Catholic Church.[8]

Archbishop T. A. Ganguly belonged now to the first step of the canonization process as the 'Servant of God'.[9]

---

7. Ibid.

8. Ibid.

9. Interview with former Archbishop of Bangladesh the Most Rev. Paulinus Costa, DD, at his present residing place at Holy Rosary Church, Tejgaon, Dhaka-1215 on 8 August 2014.

11

Conclusion

ARCHBISHOP THEOTONIUS AMAL GANGULY, CSC became the central figure in the history of Catholic Church in East Bengal, during the second half of the 20th century. From a common origin, he moved to one after another, and ultimately to be nominated by the highest authority of Catholic Church (Pope) to the high position as the first Bengali Archbishop in the history of Bengal and south Asia. This was largely due to his being in the right place at the right time, yet ably assisted by his dynamic character.

But his appointment was not to take place in a calm background, but rather in the midst of terrible turmoil for the Catholic Church, which I have described in the preceding chapter. He served the Catholic Church as bishop and the Archbishop of Dhaka in a most challenging time for the Church[1] and for the country as well. In the year of 1960, he was appointed as the Auxiliary Bishop of the Archdiocese of Dhaka and became the Archbishop in 1967. As the Archbishop of Dhaka Archdiocese, he faced a crucial period in the history of Catholic Church, as the people of Bengal had been struggling to get their democratic rights against the military ruler Ayub Khan throughout the decades of the seventies. The country went through indescribable turmoil and tribulations during the period of late seventies. His appointment as the Archbishop of Dhaka looked like an accident from the context of Catholic Church. The background was created under the circumstance of a conflicting situation regarding the state policy of Pakistan towards the indigenous people. The government had adopted a policy against the local indigenous people in the northern districts of

1. Costa, C.S.C., "Reflections on the Life of Archbishop Ganguly."

East Pakistan, during the war of India-Pakistan in 1965, treating the indigenous as the enemy of the state of Pakistan. As a result, many of them had to abandon the country and took shelter in the border region of India. Archbishop L. L. Graner, CSC took a public position in favor of the victims of those districts against the government's actions and protesting in the form of a letter, which was published in a newspaper. That created such an impact that the Indian representative held a debate on the issue at the United Nations. Under such circumstances, Archbishop Graner had to leave this country, and T. A. Ganguly was appointed as the Archbishop. After undertaking the responsibilities, he would have the Second Vatican Council to guide the local Church into a phase of regeneration, as in fact, an indigenous Church.

In the year of 1970, the Bengali people had faced a devastating cyclone and tidal surge, during which time he played a very important role to rehabilitate the affected people. The following year, in 1971, the struggle for the liberation war of Bangladesh started, where he took his position in favor of the people. This led to his being enlisted as another Bengalee intellectual who must be annihilated by the Pakistani occupation force. Despite receiving a message from a Pakistani Army officer, who happened to be a Catholic, he refused to abandon his residence, choosing to remain in the Archbishop's House at Kakrail, Ramna throughout the entire period of the liberation war. He probably realized that the central command of Pakistan state by the West Pakistani military ruler would not continue for long in the face of the people's war in 1971. Therefore, all his steps and policy, implemented in favor of the people, enabled many lives to be saved during the liberation war. The most important part from the context of this newly born country was to obtain recognition from the Vatican, in which he played a significant role, which I mentioned in my preceding chapter.

The most important part after the War of Liberation was to rehabilitate the people. In this aspect, he requested Pope Paul VI to provide funds and recognition for his country, and both demands were fulfilled. The critical time in his tenure was sadly to hand over the ownership of Holy Family Hospital. The reason why he handed over the hospital is also clearly explained in a preceding chapter.

To examine his life and times Brother Jarlath D'Souza, CSC gave following description of Archbishop T. A. Ganguly, CSC:

> He played a prophetic role to change the life of the Church here; it was not his charisma but he played his rightful role with the help of God.[2]

The present Catholic Church in Bangladesh reaps the fruits of his prudent and farsighted philosophy and hard labor. He acted in every step of his life and times according to the *vocation of life*. So while his role for the Catholic Church and for different sectors of this country may never be made manifest in a glorious way, his name will remain in the history of the country as a remarkable religious and social reformer who shaped the Catholic Church for its people so that they could look up to it as their- "Indigenous Church."

It could be said that the philosophy and activities of T. A. Ganguly reflected Christian humanism. To define 'humanism' within his philosophical thoughts, it could be argued that while the concept was Christian, its content was local. Moreover, he had written on Indian philosophy as his PhD dissertation, which he sought to reconcile and reconstruct with Christianity. So his philosophy is necessarily a blend of his universal Catholic faith with his understanding of the local philosophy, bringing a new dimension for the local people of East Bengal. Thus, his conscious mind was prepared to play a significant role for the localization of the Catholic Christianity when he became the first Bengali Archbishop for East Pakistan under the inspiration of Vatican-II. At last, it could also be said that his philosophy was one of reconciliation and reconstruction of Catholicism with the local philosophical thoughts, where human being is the central character in his writings and the vocation of life is the source of the development of human life. In this respect, he could be compared with the Hindu religious reformer in Bengal in the nineteenth century Ramakrishna Paramahamsa, whose philosophy insisted:

> Jato mat tatapath (there are as many ways as there are views).[3]

But the goal is the same. This simply connoted that the various religions provided so many avenues leading to a spiritual goal. T. A. Ganguly drew attention to the inner harmony of religion rather than its external variety of religions, much as what Ramakrishna did for Hindu society, and

---

2. Interview with Brother Jarlath D'Souza C.S.C. at his office Muhammadpur Zakir Hossain Road, Dhaka-1207 on 13 August 2014.

3. Mitra, "Hindu Reform Movements," 234.

CONCLUSION

Sufis did for Islamization in Bengal,[4] T. A. Ganguly did for the Catholics in East Bengal. His works helped to shape the Church into a new phase, as the people of the land looked at the Church as their own Church—an 'Indigenous Church'. He not only accommodated Bengali songs of non-Christian writers for prayer, but also used Bengali songs and local instruments for the programs of the Church. Even the prayer system and an all the public activities were carried out in Bengali Language instead of the previous language—Latin. He also sent abroad a number of Catholic priests for higher study on the liturgical development of religion, so that they could play important roles for the development of the Church. Archbishop Theotonius Amal Ganguly, CSC would be considered as a social and religious reformer for Christian society in 20th century Bengal through his missionary activities and philosophical thinking. Therefore, he would be considered as a man of wisdom, vision and vigor who reshaped the very core values and universality of the Christian Church in Bangladesh and brought Church close to the common people, within the sense and sensitivity of the local culture and heritage.

---

4. For detailed on Islamization in Bengal see also, Eaton, *The Rise of Islam and the Bengal Frontier*.

Appendix I

Holy Cross Priests in East Bengal, 1853–2003

THE HOLY CROSS MISSIONARIES activities in East Bengal could be divided into three phases. Firstly, from 1853 to 1947 they worked in British India's Bengal Province, Secondly, from 1947 to 1971 they worked in East Pakistan and thirdly, they have been working in Bangladesh from 1971 till now. The names of the region were changed due to political causes or influences thereof but the geographical locations remain same.

B=Bangladesh, Bur=Burma, C=Canada, F= France, G=Germany, P=Philippines, US=United States, += those who died in the subcontinent or shortly after leaving. * indicates those who left the community (some becoming diocesan). Local Holy Cross priests are dated from the year of their ordination and Brothers, Sisters and seminarians from the date of their First Profession.

Name	Birth & Death	In E. Bengal
Adelsperger, John (US)*	4.3.1857–	1891–95
Altenhofen, Peter + (US)	?1882–23.11.1915	1907–15
Anjus, Eugene T. (B)	18.4.59–	1986
Askins, Robert (US)	23.2.21–14.3.88	1948–58, 1964–69
Aubě, Henri-Paul (C)	10.7.1922–17.6.99	1946–58
Aussant, Jean (C)* 1963	20.12.1925–	1953–54 (Haflong)
Badier, Leon J. + (F)	22.3.1877–31.3.1909	1903–09
Banas, James T. (US)	1.4.30–	1959

Appendix I

Name	Birth & Death	In E. Bengal
Baroi, Nicholas S. (B)	23.10.61	1993–
Barrosse, Thomas +(US)	3.6.26–14.6.94	1986–94
Barroux, Louis E. (US)*	15.3.1817–14.9.97	1853–58
Bauer, Lawerence T. (US)	5.9.06	1935–75
Benoit, Pierre (C)	30.7.38–	1965–
Bergmann, Frederick + (US)	6.2.13–24.3.99	1940–99
Birkmeyer, John (US)	25.6.24–	1957–71, 1976–85
Bleau, J. Albert (C)	11.6.01–29.4.1988	1930–39
Blin, Albert E+ (C)	26.1.1885–21.3.23	1911–23
Boarman, James Leon Albert (US)	25.1.07–	1937–48
Boeres, Ftrancis J. (US)	17.2.1862–13.9.1938	1888–1910
Boivin, Raymond (C)	11.11.1914–13.1.92	1942–52
Botlero, Francis Hamlet (B)	22.12.63–	1999
Boucher, Gilbert (C)	–2.1.69	
Boudreau, Henri (C)	12.8.19–13.6.75	1933–73
Bougeard, Luis M. (F)*?	3.10.1874–	1900–13
Boulay, Philĕas (C)	2.4.1885–17.4.1968	1912–51
Bourque, Andrĕ T. (C)	26.7.1855–28.6.1914	1891–96
Breault, Guy (C) * 1974	6.7.1931	1960–72
Breen, Harold (C)	11.0408–2.2.1964	1935–60, 1964–68
Breen, Msgr. George D. (C)	26.1.1898–10.11.97^	1935–51
Bride, Harold L. (US)	3.9.19–	1953–60, 1964–68
Brooks, Christopher (US)	25.12.1948–21..1967	1920–46
Brouillard, Claude (C) * 1972	5.4.1933	1960–71
Brunelle, Benoit (C)^	–10.6.97	1948–52
Burke, Eugene A. (US)	23.12.22–	1955–70
Burrell, David (US)	1.23.33–	1975, 1977, 1986, 1994, 2014–2016
Burton, Francis J. (US)	11.5.02–13.9.82	1941–70
Campers, Edmund V. (US)	21.11.11–	1940–40
Canon, Joseph F. (US)*	28.6.24–	1951–57
Chassĕ, Sinaï A. + (C)	12.6.1890–10.3.1930	1921–30
Cle´ment, Raymond J. (C)	5.8.1883–30.3.1960	1918–46
Costa, Benedict + (B)	16.6.57–19.12.93	1986–93

Holy Cross Priests in East Bengal, 1853–2003

Name	Birth & Death	In E. Bengal
Costa, Benjamin (B)	7.9.42–	1971–
Costa, Bp. Moses M. (B)	11.17.50–	1981–
Costa, Subash Joseph (B)	1.5.77–	1.2.02
Couë, Louis + (F)	8.2.1809–24.12.58	1857–58
Croce, Albert A. (US)	15.7.18–	1952–58
Crowley, Bp. Timothy J. + (US)	16.1.1880–2.101945	1907–45
Cruze, Edmund (B)	17.11.59	1989
Cruze, James C. (B)	30.5.66–	1998–
Cruze, Luis Samar (B)	6.11.48–	1978–
Cruze, Prashanta N. (B)	11.11.74–	22.1.99
Cruze, Donel Stephen (B)	24.4.80–	1.2.02
Das David Bipul (B)	25.12.74	28.1.00
Das, LawrenceNoresh (B)	31.1.66–	1996–
Das, Sudhir (B)	14.5.70–	22.1.99
DeGrace, Noman J. (US)	6.1.01–	1927–33
Delaunay, John Baptist (US)	8.7.1886–16.2.1953	1922–28
Delavy, Vincent B. (US)		1946–60
Demers, Paulin (C)	11.9.28–	1955–74
DeMontigny, Alexandre+ (F)	16.10.1826–15.8.55	1855
DeMontigny, Alphonse (C)	1.7.17–15.3.53	1923–35
DeMontigny, Jean A. (C)	5.4.1900–22.11.1949	1926–28
Desrochers, Frank (C)		1963–68
Desrochers, Francois-Xavier	18.5.1847–1.6.1912	
Desmoudt, René-Winoe+ (F)	16.12.1873–27.6.1911	1903–11
Desrochers, Omer (C)	17.12.1882–14.1.59	1910–47
Devers, John(US)		
Dorwart, Wliiam D. (US)	.10.49–	1975–76
D'Costa, Anol Terence (B)	9.63.69–	2002–
D'Cruze, Maurice (B)	6.4.29–	1959–
D'Rozaraio, Dominie J. +(B)	29.9.7899–28.11.77	1928–77
D'Rozaraio, Rt. Rev. Michael (B)	23.11.25–	1953–
D'Rozaraio, Rt. Rev. Patrick (B)	1.10.43–	1972
D'Rozaraio, Peter + (B)	28.8.1890–7.101935	1927–35
Duane, James (US)		1986–87

Appendix I

Name	Birth & Death	In E. Bengal
Duclos, Aimé (C)+	20.11.87–26.8.02	1931–49
Dubois, B		
Dufal, Bp. Pierre (F)	12.8.1822–14.3.98	1858–76
Dusaulx, Émile A.[1]	11.12.1820	1860–62
Evans, William P. + (US)	15.1.19–13.11.71	1945–71
Faineau, Louis H. (F)	31.10.1885–12.4.1952	1858–76,1888–07
Fallize, Michael (US)	24.2.1855–28.4.1920	1888–1910
Fichet, Pierre-Marie+ (F)	8.2.1873–20.8.1951	
Fourmond, Aime-Marie+ (C)	6.3.1834–12.4.1907	1858–76, '88–1907
Fournelle, Yvan (C)		1953–61
Français, Adolphe M. +(F)	9.7.1860–28.11.1920	1894–1920
Ganguly, Rt.Rev. Theotonius A. +(B)	18.2.20–2.9.77	1947–77
Garand, Benoit (C)	17.4.1857–	1891–1900
Gaudon, Adolphe +(F)	26.2.1876–14.7.1902	1899–1902
Gaudon, Paul-Alphonse +(F)	20.9.1880–25.5.1911	1907–11
Genevrier, Albert J. (F)[2]	5.7.71855–?	1903–?
Gillespie, Charles P. + (US)	28.93.22–5.1.96	1949–96
Goedert, Edmund N. (US)	8.9.18–	1946–79
Goggin, Léo (C)	1.3.1897–11.11.1957	1925–47
Gomes, Anthony (B)	6.9.1900–	1920–25
Gomes, Anthony Susanta (B)	4.3.67–	1997–
Gomes, Edward Subrata (B)		1986–93
Gomes, Hubert Robi (B)	1986–1.3.64	1995–
Gomes, Lazarus (B)		1972–
Gomes, Liton Hubert (B)	17.12.70–	2001–
Gomes, Richard Chandon (B)	27.9.74–	2.2.01
Gomes, Robert D. (B)	14.9.75–	7.2.97
Gomes, Stephen G. (B)	19.1.36–	1967–
Gomes, Sudhir Jacob (B)	14.11.70–	
Gomes, Rt. Rev. Theotonius M.(B)	9.4.39–	1965–
Gonsalves, Theotonius A.(B)	25.8.73–	28.1.00
Goodall, Francis P. (US)	9.2.1897–	1926–32
Graham, William L. (US)	27.10.22–	1955–69
Graner, Rt. Rev. Lawrence L.(US)	3.4.1901–21.4.82	1928–66

Holy Cross Priests in East Bengal, 1853–2003

Name	Birth & Death	In E. Bengal
Grandmaison De, Germain (C)	15.3.28–	1954–87
Gregoire, Marcel (C) 1968	27.12.1930	
Guimond, Jean (C) 1971		1963–1972
Hamon, Jean (F)	13.7.1874–14.5.1938	1903–05
Harel, Joseph R. –A. (C)	23.2.1886–23.8.1942	1911–30
Harrington, John J. (US)	7.1.06–1.1.67	1933–40,1946–58
Hemborn, Elias, M. (B)	30.10.74–	7.2.97
Hennessy, John J. (US)	1.4.1879–4.3.65	1907–1961
Herckés, Philippe (F)³	8.2.1877–6.11.1915	1899–1915
Hickens, William F. (US)	21.5.19–	1946–79
Himbeault, Albert (C)	19.2.06–19.12.94	1945–73
Hoffman, Robert M. (US)	31.5.21–	1947–56, '60–65
Homrich, Eugene E. (US)	8.12.28–	1956–
Houser, Charles + (US)	10.9.19–22.12.97	1946–9
Howlader, LawrenceSubrata (B)	11.9.65–	1994–
Hurth, Bp. Peter (US)	30.3.1857–1.8.1935	1894–1910
Jean, Silvio (C)⁴		
Jolly, Yvon 1972		19612–66
Jourdain, Gerard (C)⁵	22.12.14–	1945–51
Just, Alphonse (F)?	17.5.1879–17.6.1934	1903–
Kane, John W. (US)	28.9,.1993–25.7.1974	1928–68
Kearns, Mathew S. (C)	16.8.1888–21.11.1946	1911–46
Kehoe, Francis+ (US)	16.12.1891–3.9.1923	1920–23
Kennerk, Terence D. + (US)	13.10.14–1.2.2001	1953–2001
Kieffer, Peter (US)	17.1.1876–	1899–1912
Kleem, Ferris A. (US)	1.1.26–	1959–60
Krill; Philp D. (US)	12.11.49–	1979–80
Kubi, Paul Ponen (B)	29.6.56–	1986–
Kuzur, Subal (B)	24.10.73–	28.1.00
Labbé, Benjamin + (C)	18.5.23–15.6.98	1950–98
Lafond, F. –X.-Emile + (C)	10.93.1854–26.2.1925	1890–1925
Lagüe, Gilbert (C)	29.11.39–	1966–
Langelier, Fabian-Edouard (C)	14.7.1863–23.8.1900	1891–96
Lapierre, Gervais (C)	11.7.74–	1936–56

Appendix I

Name	Birth & Death	In E. Bengal
Laprade, George P. (US)	23.10.31–	1957–2003
Larbiou, Bernard + (F)	9.5.1832–22.10.67	1855–67
Larose Bp. Raymond + (C)	10.1.1896–17.5.84	1926–1984
Lavoie, Robert (C)	18.3.07–7.3.76	1939–51
Lazarus, Luis (I)	20.8.1882–5.4.1959	1903–14, 1919–59
Lecavallier, Laurent (C)	19.8.24–	1952–80
Lefebvre, Jean (C) 1957?	17.9.24–	1949–51
Legault, Maurice (C) +	5.5.17–21.12.48	1947–48 (Aizawl)
Legrand, Isaie P. (F)	5.6.1835	1861–65
Legrand, Bp. Joseph A. (F)	19.4.1853–10.4.1937	1903–29
Lehane, Joseph S. (US)	30.5.23–	1957–
LePailleur, Rt. Rev. Alfred + (C)	9.8.1886–12.4.1952	1914–1951
Le Roux, ? Henri (F)		1865–?
Linneborn, Bp. Frederick+ (US)	27.5.1864–21.7.1915	190–1915
Lorusso, Joseph A. (US)	20.8.22–	1960–65, 1967–70
Louage, Bp. Augustine J. + (US)	18.9.1829–8.6.94	1890–94
Lucia, Louis M. + (F)	19.9.1841–25.1.72	1865–72
MacGregor, Donald (US)	29.6.1888–6.4.1967	1924–40
Madden, James P. (US)	15.7.29–	1958–62
Mangan, Michael A. + (US)	28.4.1897–24.11.1943	1925–43
Maniel, Jean-Baptiste (F)	30.11.1829–6.1.77	1856–76
Marcotte, Jean-Doris (C)	–6.3.93	1947–52
Marks, Walter R. (US)	4.9.1899–19.5.1975	1934–68
Marmoiton, Mr. André (F) +		1865–68
Marois, Roger (C) 1967		1954–59
Martin, James + (US)	19.9.07–21.3.60	1943–60
Martin, Jean (C) 1930	29.6.1905	
Martin, John (C)		1957–58
Mascarenhas, Augustin +(Bur)	3.1.1890–10.2.1960	1919–60
Massart, Edward F. (US)	21.9.02–1.2.92	1930–56
Massart, Raymond A. (US)	10.12.03–	1931–47, 1952–60
McCauley, Rt. Rev. Vincent J. (US)[6]	8.3.06–1.11.82	1936–45
McClure, Alfred (C) 1967	31.3.1922	
McClure, Joseph A. (C)	31.3.22–	1949–61

Holy Cross Priests in East Bengal, 1853–2003

Name	Birth & Death	In E. Bengal
McFarland, Francis L. (US)	19.10.24–	1951–59
McGarvey, James P. + (US)	30.10.05–3.5.66	1932–66
Mckee, Robert F. (US)	27.12.12–9.2.8	1946–75
McMahon, Gerald F. (US)	28.2.13–18.8.97	1946–93
Mercier, Benoit A. (F)	28.1.1832–	1853–76
Metivier, Alhonse (C)	17.6.1893–12.11.1963	1924–34
Meyer, Louis L. (US)	14.5.17–	1945–54
Michalik, Walter G. (US)	21.2.18–	1956–75
Michaud, Camille (C)	30.3.97–30.7.1979	1927–45
Milot, Jean R. (C) 1971	171.11.1937–	1962–66
Monaghan, William A. (US)	21.10.00–26.5.76	1938–72
Monette, Jean-Guy (C) 1972		1966–70
Moreau, Leonidas J. (C)	9.12.09–4.2.75	1928–38
Murphy, William (C)	20.2.59	1927–39
Murphy, Joseph F. (US)	3.6.16–	1946–52
Nadeau, Charles (C) 1987	15.4.1928–	1967–75
Nanni, Philippe + (I)	24.2.1845–29.12.1926	1892–1926
Neff, Alfred J. (US)	7.10.11–20.3.97	1941–52,1958–91
Nelson, Bertram (B)	16.5.34–	1962–
Nirad, Célestin F.-A. (F)	19.12.1878–15.5.31938	1903–23
Noakes, Bro. George (E)	–17.7.81	1961–80
Norckauer, Maurice + (US)	4.11.1891–13.2.1957	1921–57
Novak, Richard T. + (US)	2.8.35–16.1.64	1962–64
O'Hara, Thomas J. (US)	16.3.49–	1974–75
Oswald, Matthias J. (US)	15.4.1880–10.8.53	1906–06
Ouimet, Pierre (C)* 1971		1961–66
Pagé, Michael (C)*		1960–72
Palma, Elias (B)	15.10.56–	1986–
Hubert Joseph Palma (B)	1983–	
Patrick, Richard D. (US)	28.2.08–7.3.71	1935–53
Patenaude, Joseph + (C)	3.7.1924–18.3.94	1954–94
Payant, Philippe (C)	23.8.27–19.7.2000	1945–62
Peeters, Hubert + (C)	15.9.1855–4.3.1915	1889–1915
Peixotto, Joseph S. (US)	28.5.33–	1962–

Appendix I

Name	Birth & Death	In E. Bengal
Pellegrin, George J. (US)	28.11.05–12.4.79	1932.42
Pereira, Adam S. (B)	14.9.54–	1986–
Pereira, Francis. Parimal (B)	10.10.51–	1981–
Pereira, Richard Shekor (B)	9.11.67–	2002–
Picard, André (C)	22.2.1917–30.1.98	1946–69
Pinson, Jean-Baptiste (F)	26.6.1873–23.9.1955	1897–1903
Poirer, Eugene + (C)	6.9.02–29.2.76	1932–43
Poirer, Gérlard H. (C)	21.1.28–18.2.98	1982–89
Poirer, Joseph (F)		1953–68
Pope, George F. (US)	17.7.29–	1958–77, 1981–
Quinn, Francis X. (US)	20.5.1899–26.1.1991	1932–35
Quinlivan, Frank J. (US)	4.8.43–	1979–85, 1994–
Rabinal, Alejandro R. (P)	11.1.34–	1988–
Raulet, Pierre M (F)	3.3.1865–22.8.1934	1894–1919
Rebeiro, James Bikash (B)	11.7.76–	2.2.01
Rebeiro, Lawrence (B)	15.10.68–	7.2.97
Reith, Herman R. (US)	14.8.15–	1977–79
Rick, Joseph M. (US)	1.6.00–29.10.79	1929–56
Rinckes, Bernard (C)*	25.11.1830–	1857–58
Roche, Bonnet + (F)	6.1.1832–12.8.97	1860–76, 188–97
Rondet, Jacques (F)	17.7.1830–24.12.58	1857–68
Roux, L. (came with Fr. Lucia)[7]		1865–?
Rouzoul, Alexis (F) *	9.6.1831–	1861–63
Roy, Joseph J. (US)	30.3.1874–?.3.05	1900–05
Rozario, Amol Augustine (B)	24.2.69–	7.2.97
Rozario, George Komol (B)	26.3.64–	2000–
Rozario, Bp. Joachim + (B)	2.9.30.9.6.96	1962–96
Rozario, James Kiran (B)*	1950–	1989–97
Rozario, Leonard Apollo (B)	23.12.68–	2000–
Rozario, Leonard Shankar (B)	11.2.67–	1998–
Rozario, Placid P. (B)	23.2.74–	7.2.97
Rozario, Pius Hemanto (B)	5.5.61–	1989–
Rozario, Stanislaus Bakul (B)	18.7.59–	1986–
Rozario, Vincent B. (B)	1.5.69–	2003–

Holy Cross Priests in East Bengal, 1853–2003

Name	Birth & Death	In E. Bengal
Rozario, Ujjal L. (B)	28.7.72–	7.2.97
Saint-Martin, Joseph (C)	15.5.1890–1.7.1970	1921–24
Saint-Onge, Paul (C)	17.8.1929–2.8.99	1963–69
St-Pierrre, Martial + (C)	14.2.29–5.1.85	1947–85
Salgada, Bro. Aloysius E. + (B)	–18.12.89	1920–1989
Sarkar, Dominie S. (B)	15.3.71–	7.2.97
Sarker, Michael C. (B)	27.7.72–	28.1.00
Saulnier, Auguste E. (F)	6.9.1843–8.1.1916	1865–76, 1890–99
Schlaver, David E. (US)	5.12.42–	1972–74, 1979–81
Schneider, Chester J. (US)	26.3.19–13.8.80	1947–64
Secor, Orel B. (US)*	22.12.45–	1955–69
Shea, Paul + (US)	30.6.03–14.2.55	1931–55
Sherer, James M. (US)*	29.5.33–	1961–66
Steigmeyer, Gregory (US)	27.9.17–5.12.85	1945–63, 1967–69
Steigmeyer, Robert C. (US)	15.4.20–	1949–70
Ste. Marie, Adrian J. (US)	17.7.18–	1952–62
Sullivan, Leo J. (US)	17.12.16–7.10.94	1946–79
Switalski, Raymond (US)	3.6.1900–18.11.76	1926–53
Thorp, John P. (US)*	28.3.41–	1968–70
Tiemey, Joseph O. (US)	2.10.23–19.12.71	1950–66
Tighe, James (F)*	11.11.1838	1861–63
Timm, Richard W. (US)	2.3.23–	1952–
Tobin, James E. (US)	26.9.20–	1947–76
Tolentino, Boniface S. (B)	16.2.55–	1984–
Toppo, Gabriel Michael (B)	16.9.65–	2001–
Tourangeau, Guy-Marie (C)	26.2.22–	1947–2003
Tripi, Ronald R. (US)	14.5.35–	1962–86
Valée, (came with Mr. Mormoiton)		1865–?
VandenBossche, John V. (US)	18.5.24–	1953–70
Vérité, Louis A. +(F)	11.10.1815–26.4.59	1853–59
Voisin, Michel +(F)	11.12.04–11.2.94	1933–94
Waichuls, Robert J .+ (US)	7.3.08–10.2.77	1937–58
Wetzel, Edward M. (US)	7.4.02–21.11.87	1929–49, 1951–59
Wheeler, Ambrose (US)	6.9.18–	1968–76

Appendix I

Name	Birth & Death	In E. Bengal
Wilkirson, Richard S. (US)	3.6.51–	1976–77
Wyss, Francis S. (US)	1.3.1894–19.12.1982	1924–80
Young, Charles J. (US)	3.5.04–15.11.88	1933–88
Zimmerman, Thomas + (US)	2.3.26–17.5.93	1953–1993

1. Left the Congregation.
2. Joined military service.
3. Left in September and died on December 17 in Rome of chronic dysentery.
4. Ctg.
5. Chittagong.
6. Later bishop of Fort Portal, Uganda.
7. Worked in Chittagong in 1868, according to *Souvenir: Great Jubilee: Chittagong Diocese-200, Chittagong,* 2000 (Jubilee Central Committee, Chittagong, 2000).

Source: The list is verbatim from, R. W. Timm (ed.), *150 Years of Holy Cross in East Bengal Mission,* Dhaka, Congregation of Holy Cross, 2003, 76–86.

Appendix II

Holy Cross Priest Religious Superiors, 1920–1982

USUALLY, THE VICAR APOSTOLIC or Bishop would be in addition to a local superior of the Fathers and Brothers, up to the General Chapter of 1920. There are, however, exemptions to be found for a short time, e.g. Father Sorin was desired by the Chapter of 1852 as Superior of the Dacca Mission, but refused it. Father Voisin was named as the Superior of the first group but did not depart until the second group transpired. Father Vérité, the substitute Superior, did not assume the position of the first Holy Cross Pro-Vicar Apostolic until May 21, 1856, after Father Moreau established the Vicariate of Chittagong.

The Canadian and American religious superiors were divided from 1923. Besides, subsequent to the Fathers and Brothers established separate authorities in 1946, every society had its own religious superior, until 1984 when the Dhaka and Chittagong Districts turned into one.

Joint Superiors	Year
Albert Blin	1920–23
Dhaka Superiors	
Timothy Crowley	1923–27
Maurice Norckauer	1927–32
Benjamin Labbé	1972–82
Michael Mangan	1932–38

Appendix II

John Kane	1938–50
Joseph Rick	1950–56
Robert McKee	1956–68
Thomas Zimmerman	1968–82
Joint Superiors	
Richard Timm	1982–88
Thomas Zimmerman	1988–91
Benjamin Costa	1991–97 Vice Provincial
Stephen Gomes	1997 Provincial
Canadian Superiors	
Alfred LePailleur	1927–32
Leonidas Moreau	1932–38
GervaisLapierre	1950–58
Laurent Lecavalier	1958–64
Joseph Patenaude	1964–70
Benjamin Labbe	1970–76
Patrick D' Rozario	1976–82

Source: The list is the verbatim from, R. W. Timm (ed.), *150 Years of Holy Cross in East Bengal Mission*, Dhaka, Congregation of Holy Cross, 2003, 87.

Appendix III

Former Archbishops of Dhaka, 1947–2005 (Archdiocese est. 15 July, 1950)

1947–1967	Most Rev. Lawrence Leo Graner, CSC
1967–1977	Most Rev. Theotonius Amal Ganguly, CSC
1978–2005	Most Rev. Michael Rozario CSC

Source: *Catholic Directory*, 2011, 70.

Appendix IV

Holy Cross Bishops of East Bengal, 1891–2011

Year	Name	Working place
1891–1894	Most Rt. Rev. Augustine Joseph Lou age, CSC	Dhaka Diocese
1894–1909	Most Rt. Rev. Peter Joseph Hurth, CSC	Dhaka Diocese
1909–1915	Most Rt. Rev. Francis Frederick Linneborn, CSC	Dhaka Diocese
1916–1929	Most Rt. Rev. Joseph Armand Legrand, CSC	Dhaka Diocese
1927–1951	Most Rev. Alfred Le Pailleur, CSC	Chittagong Diocese
1929–1945	Most Rt. Rev. Timothy John Crowly, CSC	Dhaka Diocese
1947–1950	Most Rt. Rev. Lawrence Leo Graner, CSC	Dhaka Diocese
1952–1967	Most Rt. Rev. Raymond Larose CSC	Chittagong Diocese
1960–1967	Most Rt. Rev. TheotoniusAmalGanguly, CSC	Dhaka Diocese
1968–1994	Most Rt. Rev. Joachim Rozario CSC	Chittagong Diocese
1970–2005	Most Rt. Rev. Michael A. D' Rozario CSC	Khulna Diocese
1978–1996	Most Rev. Theotonius Gomes CSC	Dinajpur Diocese
1995–2010	Most Rev. Patrick Rozario CSC	Chittagong Diocese
1996–2011	Most Rev. Moses Costa CSC	Dinajpur Diocese

Source: *Catholic Directory*, 2011, 69; 129;159; 189.

Appendix V

PIME Missionaries in West Bengal and East Bengal Bangladesh, 1855–2012

THE LIST IS DEVELOPED based on their arrival year in East and West Bengal.

Arrival Year	Name
1855	Albino Parietti
1855	Giovanni Sesana
1855	Luigi Limana
1855	Antonio Marietti
1855	Francesco Pozzi
1859	Paolo Mauri
1859	Luigi Brioschi
1859	Luigi De Conti
1859	Angelo Curti
1860	Enrico Longa
1863	Remigio Pezzotti
1866	Jacopo Broy
1866	Giuseppe Bersani Dossena
1866	Angelo Galimberti
1868	Ambrogio Giuliani
1868	Alessandro Molteni

Appendix V

Arrival Year	Name
1868	Mose Pozzi
1868	Giovanni Battista Scatti
1870	Alberto Cazzaniga
1874	Giuseppe Galesi
1874	Gianpietro Marzi
1877	Paolo Rigamonti
1878	Vincenzo Corga
1879	Santino Taveggia
1880	Candido Uberti
1885	Carlo Cedri
1885	Carlo Laboranti
1885	Giovanni Battista Nava
1888	Ambrogio Grassi
1892	Francesco Rocca
1892	Giuseppe Macchi
1893	Gaetano Ponzoni
1893	Giuseppe Armanasco
1896	Giovanni Garrovi
1897	Francesco Morassi
1902	Rustico Picchi
1903	Serafino Donzelli
1905	Alessandro Beretta
1906	Carlo Rho
1906	Ottorino Pedrotti
1906	Teodore Castelli
1907	Giuseppe Reschini
1907	Fermo Crotti
1910	Edoardo Ferrario
1910	Giuseppe Lazzaroni
1910	Ste fano Monfrini
1911	Pietro Costa
1912	Giovanni Battista Anselmo

PIME Missionaries

Arrival Year	Name
1912	Gaetano Curioni
1913	Luigi Mellera
1914	Valentine Belgeri
1919	Giuseppe Obert
1919	Guido Margutti
1919	Ambrogio Galbiati
1920	Tommaso Cattaneo
1922	Michele Bianchi
1923	Paolo Carnevale Miino
1923	Adamo Grossi
1924	Angelo Negrini
1924	Giacomo Ceroni
1924	Luigi Brambilla
1925	Luigi Martinelli
1926	Terenzio Bucari
1926	Emilio Pigoni
1927	Arsenio Favrin
1928	Lorenzo Moscato
1928	Angelo Re
1928	Angelo Del Corno
1929	Ferdinando Sozzi
1929	Guerrino Campagnolo
1929	Giuseppe Milozzi
1929	Massimo Teruzzi
1930	Ruggero Bibini
1930	Alessandro Bottinelli
1931	Vittorio De Giusti
1931	Francesco Ghezzi
1932	Luigi Bigoni
1933	Fortunato De Psoli
1933	Giuseppe Naroni
1933	Giuseppe Cavagna

Appendix V

Arrival Year	Name
1934	Vittorio Pellegrini
1934	Antonio Bonolo
1935	Francesco Villa
1935	Ambrogio Dell'Orto
1936	Giacomo Forte
1936	Ettore Bellinato
1937	Pietro Crivelli
1937	Amatore Artico
1938	Alessandro Perico
1938	Luigi Bello
1938	Angelo Maggioni
1938	Luigi Oggioni
1938	Luigi Pinos
1938	Cesare Pesce
1938	Luigi Scuccato
1950	Teofilo Lucatello
1950	Eugenio Petrin
1950	Luigi Marcato
1951	Ovidio Gerlero
1951	Enrico Vigano
1951	Salvatore Di Serio
1952	Luigi Acerbi
1953	Angelo Canton
1954	Luigi Verpelli
1954	Luigi Carrea
1954	Luigi Pussetto
1955	Giovan Battista Vanzetti
1956	Angello Villa Giovanni Barbe
1956	Mario Alvigini
1956	Carlo Calanchi
1958	Ovidio Nebuloni
1958	Enzo Corba

Arrival Year	Name
1958	Paolo Poggi
1959	Nicola Manca
1960	Faustino Cescato
1960	Luigi Brun
1961	Antonio Mapelli
1962	Fabiano Licciardi
1964	Andrea Mies
1964	Giovanni Pessina
1965	Giulio Schiavi
1965	Gregori Schiavi
1965	Mario Fardin
1966	Sandro Giacomelli
1968	Angelo Rusconi
1969	Franco Cortesi
1969	Adolfo L'Imperio
1970	Enrico Bertazzoli
1972	Onofrio Spinosa
1972	Andrea Branca
1972	Guglielmo Colombo
1972	Giovanni Zonta
1972	Luciano Cordarri
1972	Nocita Rosario
1972	Giulio Berutti
1972	Ettore Caserini
1972	Giuseppe Gariboldi
1972	Luigi Malocchi
1972	Emanuele Meli
1972	Arturo Speziale
1972	Paolo Ciceri
1972	Giovanni Bernardo Pillonetto
1973	Giancarlo Bozzini
1974	Gianantonio Baio

Appendix V

Arrival Year	Name
1974	Carlo Dotti
1974	Quirico Martinelli
1975	Carlo Buzzi
1975	Vito Del Prete
1975	Emilio Spineili
1975	Antonio Vendramin
1975	Gian Battista Zanchi
1975	Achille Formiga
1975	Gino Goduto
1978	Carlo Menapace
1978	Achille Boccia
1978	Franco Cagnasso
1979	John Patoilc
1983	James Fannan
1984	Stefano Castaldi
1984	Pier Parolari
1985	Livio Prete
1987	Mariano Ponzinibbi
1988	Lucio Beninati
1991	Pier Luigi Pizzamiglio
1991	Dino Giacominelli
1991	Mario Zappella
1991	Gianluigi Taller
1992	Silvio Morelli
1993	Gian Paolo Gualzetti
1993	Luca Galimberti
1993	Roberto Valenti
1994	Daniele Zonta
1996	Fabrizio Calegari
1996	Gabriel Amal Costa
1997	Francesco Rapacioli
1999	Natale Brambilla

PIME Missionaries

Arrival Year	Name
2001	Fabio De Jesus Arcilla Giraldo
2001	Luis Ferney Lopez Jemenez
2001	Josue De Jesus Ochoa Castano
2004	Massimo Cattaneo
2005	Paolo Ballan
2005	Henry Ignacio Ginaldo Pineda
2005	Ruben Dario Oquendo Lopez
2006	Hector Ramirez Montes
2006	Jose Albeiro Posada Orozco
2006	Amado Higuita Gomez
2007	Micelle Brambilla
2007	Alberto Malivemo
2008	Bishop Mollick (Africa)
2009	Joseph Aind (Africa)
2011	Giovanni Gnaldi
2012	Adoiphe Ndouwe
2012	Almir Magno Trindade Azevedo

Source: Fr. Biplob Mollik (Translated), (Father Silvano Garello, SX, edited), *Bangladeshe PIME Missionarygon Abong Fr. Pinos and Fr. Enzo Corba r mission Ovigata*, (PIME Missionaries in Bangladesh and the mission experience of Fr. Pinos and Fr. Enzo Corba), PIME Bangladesh, 2014, 90-92.

Appendix VI

Former Bishops of Dinajpur Diocese, 1927–2011

1927–1928	Most Rev. SantinoTaveggia PIME (Formerly of Krishnagar 1906–1927)
1928–1947	Most Rev. John Baptist Anselmo PIME
1948–1968	Most Rev. Joseph Obert PIME
1968–1978	Most Rev. Michael Rozario
1978–1996	Most Rev. Theotonius Gomes CSC
1996–2011	Most Rev. Moses Costa CSC

Source: *Catholic Directory,* **2011, 159; Fr. Biplob Mollik (Translated), (Father Silvano Garello, SX, edited),** *Bangladeshe PIME Missionarygon Abong Fr. Pinos and Fr. Enzo Corba r mission Ovigata,* **(PIME Missionaries in Bangladesh and the mission experience of Fr. Pinos and Fr. Enzo Corba), PIME Bangladesh, 2014, 88.**

Appendix VII

Xaverian Missionaries in East Bengal, 1952–2010

THE LIST OF THE Xaverian missionaries are given below, who worked in East Bengal according to their arrival date. *indicates for Bangladeshi Xaverians.

Name	Arrival Date	Departure Date
Mons. Battaglierin Dante	03/07/1952	15/05/1969
Fr. Tessaro Albino	03/07/1952	20/10/1965
Fr. Chiofi Mario	03/07/1952	10/07/1970
Fr. Alberton Antonio	03/07/1952	10/11/1987
Fr. Dagnino Amatore	03/07/1952	29/06/1956
Fr. Dalla Valle Vittorio	03/07/1952	09/07/1967
Bro. Scalet Leonarodo	17/12/1952	15/04/1964
Fr. Veronesi Mario	17/12/1952	04/04/1971
Fr. Rigon Marino	05/01/1953 06/12/1979	22/25/1976
Fr. Spagnolo Francesco	13/03/1953	30/06/1974
Fr. Guarniero Bruno Aldo	13/03/1953 01/07/1977	26/03/1974 09/08/2005
Fr. Gittti Giuseppe	13/03/1953	25/08/1970

Appendix VII

Name	Arrival Date	Departure Date
Bro. Masolo Giuseppe	03/09/1953 28/10/1987	30/061986 16/06/2000
Fr. Miklavcic Albino	08/11/1954	02/01/1960
Fr. Bello Domenico	27/04/1955	01/10/1966
Fr. Crestani Silvio	27/04/1955	01/10/1966
Fr. Dri Bruno Luigi	30/04/1955 02/04/1985 29/10/1999	02/09/1980 30/09/1996 13/01/2003
Fr. Tomaselli Francesco	30/04/1955	09/04/1991
Fr. Pelizzo Amedeo	27/09/1955	05/12/1958
Fr. Rota Benito	27/09/1955	11/08/1960
Br. Stocco Lio	16/01/1956	11/01/1965
Fr. Dalla Vecchia Serafino	29/11/1956 08/11/1967	19/11/1965 17/02/1979
Fr. Villa Francesco	30/011958	30/06/1963
Fr. Ceci Lucidio	30/01/1958	21/03/1979
Fr. Bertoli Dante	30/06/1958	30/10/1960
Fr. Bizzeschi Bruno	10/11/1958	18/04/1967
Fr. Rossi Arduino	28/12/1958 06/09/1989 23/01/2007	23/03/1975 12/06/1996
Bro. Zen Giuliano Isacco	30/12/1958	12/09/1961
Fr. Gugliotta Francesco	07/02/1959	05/04/1966
Fr. Gasparotto Ampelio	29/07/1959	14/07/2005
Fr. Lamanna Edmondo	30/10/1959	30/06/1968
Fr. Maloney Robert Sarsfield	07/11/1959	20/06/1968
Fr. Sella Guerrino	21/12/1959	08/01/1962
Fr. Pais Giacomo	30/01/1960	04/03/1976
Fr. Tirloni Antonio Mario	16/01/1961	19/10/1969
Fr. Fantini Lorenzo	30/01/1961	10/07/1964
Bro. Bucari Remo	30/09/1961	
Fr. Bernacchi Rinaldo	30/11/1961 03/06/1977	07/11/1968 15/05/1987
Fr. Polidori Vittori	22/02/1962	30/10/1966

Xaverian Missionaries in East Bengal, 1952–2010

Name	Arrival Date	Departure Date
Fr. Zennari Silvano	22/02/1962	28/01/1965
Fr. Rinaldi Giuseppe Luigi	28/02/1962	15/01/1963
Fr. Salvetti Livio Rinaldo	30/08/1962 12/07/1972	01/02/1969
Fr. Parmiggiani Alessandro	01/09/1962	30/08/1965
Fr. Cobbe Valeriano	03/10/1962	14/10/1974
Fr. Ghirardi Orlando	25/11/1965	06/12/1981
Fr. Mattevi Pio	01/01/1966 13/02/1992	10/10/1985
Fr. Cruder Mario	08/08/1967	30/06/1972
Fr. Zucchinelli Luigi	19/08/1967	05/08/1970
Fr. Tedesco Sebastiano	13/11/1968 03/05/1991	30/06/1985 27/11/1999
Fr. Colombara Pietro Antonio	19/04/1969	01/08/01983
Fr. Garello Silvano Oreste	20/10/1970	10/03/1973 01/07/1980
Fr. Fogliani Antonio	15/10/1971 01/12/1990	08/08/1978 10/01/1994 27/05/2004
Bro. Gamba Giovanni	16/10/1971 01/07/1979	30/06/1977 26/02/2006
Fr. Spiga Gabriele	26/09/1972	
Fr. Storgata Marcello	26/09/1972	14/07/1993
Fr. Signorini Domenico	26/09/1972	23/12/1976
Fr. Luvie Ernesto	26/09/1972 30/01/1983	01/06/1977 31/05/1991
Fr. Burbello Bruno	29/09/1972	29/01/1983
Bro. Tasca Alessandro	05/10/1973	01/08/1994
Fr. Boscato Attilio	17/10/1973	
Fr. Coni Alfio	17/10/1973 04/01/1983	01/06/1978
Fr. Caldognetto Domenico	25/11/1974 16/05/1987	08/08/1979 07/10/1992
Fr. Abbiati Giovanni	13/01/1975 04/09/1985	19/03/1983

Appendix VII

Name	Arrival Date	Departure Date
Fr. Rubini Carlo	14/01/1975	26/01/1992
Fr. Paggi Luigi	14/01/1975	
Fr. Falcone Vincenzo	23/02/1975	06/12/1986
Fr. Mantovani Claudio	11/11/1975 01/06/1988	10/10/1984 04/06/2006
Fr. Alberton Antonio	03/07/1952 14/12/1975	14/12/1975 10/11/1987
Fr. Fagan John	16/12/1975 14/03/2001	10/05/1994
Fr. Casey Archibald	01/10/1976	08/02/1990
Fr. Rigali Giacomo	10/10/1976 15/03/1996	18/07/1989 20/03/1999
Fr. Germano Antonio	24/04/1977	
Fr. Bernacchi Rinaldo	30/11/1961 03/06/1977	07/11/1968 15/05/1987
Fr. Guarniero Bruno Aldo	13/03/1953 10/07/1977	26/03/1974 09/08/2005
Fr. Lupi Pietro Luigi	24/01/1978	04/07/1986 18/09/1990
Fr. Zannini Francesco	12/03/1979	26/11/1994
Bro. Gamba Giovanni	16/10/1971 01/07/1979	30/06/1977 26/02/2006
Fr. Decembrino Antonio	05/05/1980	28/12/1997
Fr. Gobbi Giacomo	05/05/1980	
Fr. Garello Silvano Oreste	20/101970 10/07/1980	10/03/1973
Fr. Gaudenzi Italo	07/07/1980 21/12/1995	31/05/1988 04/07/1997
Fr. Felotti Pierluigi	30/10/1980	11/06/1987
Fr. Martoccia Giovanni	01/11/1980	04/12/1995
Fr. Oprandi Giasnalfonso	08/11/1980	12/12/2002
Fr. Valoti Lorenzo	29/01/1981 19/02/1992	01/02/1985
Fr. Tobanelli Riccardo	11/01/1982 15/10/1994	16/12/1989

Xaverian Missionaries in East Bengal, 1952–2010

Name	Arrival Date	Departure Date
Fr. Torresani Osvaldo	11/01/1982 05/01/1998	01/07/1990 25/07/2002
Fr. Zene Cosimo	20/09/1982	30/11/1992
Fr. Bradanini Pierfrancesco	28/10/1982	30/07/1991
Fr. Flores Osuna Juan Antonio	17/11/1982	13/09/1991
Fr. Gracia Mandillo Eduardo	17/11/1982	06/03/1993
Fr. Nava Rinaldo	07/02/1984	04/07/2001
Bro. Cperchio Gildo	05/02/1985	
Fr. Abbiati Giovanni	13/01/1975 04/09/1985	13/03/1985
Fr. Alvardo Pacheco Diego	15/11/1985	14/10/1999
Fr. Pietanza Domenico	15/11/1985	
Bro. Modonutti Claudio	07/02/1986	
Fr. Nitti Gianvito	15/03/1987	
Fr. Caldognetto Domenico	25/11/1974 16/05/1987	08/08/1979 07/10/1992
Bro. Masolo Giuseppe	03/09/1953 28/10/1987	30/06/1986 16/02/2000
Fr. Mantovani Claudio	11/11/1975 01/06/1988	10/10/1984 04/06/2006
Fr. Gomez Salas Benjamin	19/10/1989 05/03/2003	18/08/1994
Fr. Lupi Pietro Luigi	24/01/1978 18/09/1990	04/07/1986
Fr. Matteazzi Giovanni	01/05/1991	19/01/2006
Fr. Dela Torre Ruiz De Chavez	03/05/1991	01/07/1998
Fr. Targa Sergio	15/01/1992 15/02/2000	02/02/1998
Fr. Mattevi Pio	01/01/1966 13/02/1992	10/10/1985
Fr. Tebar Ramirez Maximino	30/05/1992	11/06/1996
Fr. Murguia Cardenas Hector	01/11/1992	01/08/1998
Fr. Reguero Perez Javier	25/06/1995	28/05/1999
Fr. Mattiazzi Marco	29/11/1995	05/09/1998

Appendix VII

Name	Arrival Date	Departure Date
Fr. Rigali Giacomo	30/10/1976 15/03/1996	18/07/1989 20/03/1999
Fr. Moroni Paulo	15/11/1996	21/09/2000
Fr. Lopez Lopez Jose De Jesus	03/01/1997	08/03/1999
Fr. Wasyudiyanto Antonius	01/07/1997	
Fr. Rantetana Gerpasius	01/07/1997	19/10/2004
Fr. Gomes Polash Henry*	12/02/1999 10/09/2004	14/08/1999 24/02/2006
Mondol Philip	12/02/1999	14/08/1999
Fr. Escobar Rodriguez	21/07/1999	
Fr. Gonzalez Delgadillo	12/01/2000	
Fr. Targa Daniele	16/02/2001	
Fr. Succa Ezio	16/02/2001	13/01/2003
Bro. Mantellini Paolo	16/12/2001	
Fr. Rondi Filippo	07/12/2001	
Fr. Albor Ortiz Agustin	26/09/1987 15/01/2002	15/05/1995
Sarker Soroj Martin*	26/07/2002	01/09/2002
Fr. Gomes Rocky David*	26/07/2002	13/09/2002
Gomes Khokon Lawrence*	26/07/2002	01/09/2002
Tripura Satyarang*	11/07/2003	31/10/2003
Fr. Suhud Budi Pranoto	21/05/2004	
Biswas Patrick Sagar*	09/07/2004	16/08/2004
Halder Khokon Milton*	09/07/2004	01/10/2004
Das Saul Gaurango*	01/07/2005	28/08/2005
Marandi Lucas*	01/10/2005	28/08/2005
Fr. Gargano Giovanni	16/02/2007	
Fr. Garduno Arias Marcos	09/04/2008	
Fr. Cuevas Contreras Melecio	09/04/2008	
Fr. Ramos Vieira Luis Augusto	09/04/2008	
Fr. Tangke Bandaso Yulius	29/09/2009	

Source: Daniel Dante Talukdar, *Amar Chokhe Xaverian missionarygon (1952–2010)*, Publication place and time did not mention, 22–28.

Appendix VIII

Former Bishops of Khulna Diocese, 1952–2005

1952–1969	Most Rev. Dante C. Battaglierin, SX, DD
1970–2005	Most Rev. Michael A. D'Rozario, CSC, DD

Source: *Catholic Directory,* **2011**, **188.**

Appendix IX

Population by Religious Communities in Percentage, 1901–2001

Census Year	Total	Muslim	Hindu	Buddhist	Christian	Others
1901	100.0	66.1	33.0	..	..	0.9
1911	100.0	67.2	31.5	..	..	1.3
1921	100.0	68.1	30.6	..	..	1.3
1931	100.0	69.5	29.4	..	0.2	1.0
1941	100.0	70.3	28.0	..	0.1	1.6
1951	100.0	76.9	22.0	0.7	0.3	0.1
1961	100.0	80.4	18.5	0.7	0.3	0.1
1974	100.0	85.4	13.5	0.6	0.3	0.2
1981	100.0	86.7	12.1	0.6	0.3	0.3
1991	100.0	88.3	10.5	0.6	0.3	0.3
2001	100.0	89.7	9.2	0.7	0.3	0.2

Source: Bangladesh Bureau of Statistics, 2003.

Appendix X

Archbishop's Easter Message (March 29, 1964)

DEARLY BELOVED,

ONCE AGAIN I have the opportunity to send you Easter Greetings. It is always a real pleasure for the shepherd to speak to his flock, particularly on the occasion of great feasts. You have been most devoted during the Holy Season of Penance, these forty days of Lent. And now that the dawn of Resurrection Sunday is soon to show itself, we shall be able to rejoice with our Risen Saviour. He brings us joy in victory, and a peace that He wishes to share with us always.

Our Lord's Passion was a terrible thing to have to undergo. You have been reading and thinking about those sorrowful days, and His almost limitless sufferings. Lent is the time to arouse yourselves to the real meaning of sin, that horrible treason which is so offensive to the good God. It is the time for sorrow of heart and for real penance.

Perhaps never has there been so much real physical and mental suffering in this Archdiocese as during the past month or two. As you know, the Catholic and other Christian communities in the District of Mymensingh have suffered very much. They have been the victims of harassment, of mental affliction, of physical mistreatment. Their homes have been violated, their security of body and peace of mind lost. Conditions were so bad that the Christians, almost 30,000 of them, fled from their homes into India, leaving behind all their earthly possessions. Some lost their lives; others were wounded; some are still under treatment in hospitals and camps. Almost all your Catholic brethren of the parishes of Maiamnagar, Baramari,

Appendix X

Biroidakuni and Bhalukapara fled. The parishes of Ranikhong, Balachora and Jalchatra have lost a smaller number.

It has been a sad experience for these refugees, a time of real sorrow. Likewise has it been difficult for those who have remained behind. The sorrow of the Priests, Brothers, Sisters, and of myself, is hard to put into words. Not all of you are aware of these happenings. But I was aware of the danger long ago, and I warned the Government of what was likely to happen if strict measures were not taken to stop these injustices. Unfortunately, my warnings were not heeded, I have spent a great deal of time during these months in the border area, trying to keep our people from going away. You would not believe that such things could happen in such a short time. You will pray for these afflicted ones, asking the good God to give them the grace to know and to do His Holy Will.

Of course, the whole Christian community is now troubled in mind. But do not lose confidence or become pessimistic. Efforts are now being made to correct the evils; too late for those who have gone away, but heartening to those still here. A minority group in any country has a difficult time. For the most part their peace and security will depend on the efforts they themselves make to bring home to the civil authorities that they are an intelligent group, aware of their rights and duties, ready to demand the one and fulfill the other. Remember, finally, there is no substitute for unity,-that unity of mind and purpose which draws together all Christians, no matter what their origin, for timely action.

And now after the sorrow, the joy of Easter. We must go forward, as did the Apostles and early Christians, as have so many other thousands who have found deep sorrow on their lives' path. Christ is the giver of peace. *"Peace is my bequest to you, and the peace which I will give you is mine to give; I do not give peace as the world gives it"* (John 14/27). Thus, may He bless you and your families, instilling in your hearts great peace, courage, unselfishness, and all those virtues needed to make of you worthy citizens, unafraid to meet the problems with which you must be confronted, always aware that you are aiding in building not your own kingdom, but the Kingdom of God.

Sincerely yours in Christ,

+ LAWRENCE
Archbishop of Dacca.

Source: *The Pratibeshi*, Vol. XXIV, No. 11, March 29, 1964.

Appendix XI

Archbishop's Pastoral Letter (July 26, 1964)

DEARLY BELOVED,

TWO YEARS AGO, under the leadership of Pope John XXIII, the Bishops of the world gathered in Rome. For the opening session of the Second Vatican Council. Last year Pope Paul VI called the second session of the council; and now preparations are nearly complete for the third session which begins on September 14th.

You realize the importance of a General Council. For the Council is more than just a series of meetings of the 2,500 Bishops from all countries of the world. The decisions of the Council represent the teaching of the Universal Church and are therefore the infallible voice through which we can know God's holy will for us.

Consequently I ask each of you to pray daily for the success of the Council, that through it the Holy Spirit may clearly manifest how we in this twentieth century can best understand and follow that eternal truth which our divine Saviour revealed during His life on earth. Along with your prayers, add little acts of self-denial; for as the Archangel told holy Tobias, "Prayer is good with fasting and alms." Surely we expect great graces from God if 500 million Catholics daily lift their hands in prayer, and purify their hearts ever more by mortification.

In their annual meeting held in Dacca after Easter this year, the Bishops of Pakistan discussed some of recommendations of the Council. Before long, we shall publish general directives that will help to make the Holy Sacrifice of the Mass and Sacraments more meaningful to you.

Each one of you must look for ways to pattern his own life ever more faithfully according to Christ's teaching. Circumstances may change; eternal truth remains the same. This is the only safe guide for us to follow.

Appendix XI

Recently I spent a month in several of parishes in Mymensingh District. I had occasion to encourage our Garo Catholics who have been returned to their homes, and I myself was pleased to see them settle down again. A great deal has been done by the authorities, and more will be done, to make this possible. There is much that we also can do, as I mentioned in my Easter Message.

My Easter Letter was written to comfort those who had suffered and reassure all of you, by recalling the suffering of Christ and the joy that followed on Easter Sunday. Unfortunately, my words of encouragement were overlooked by some who quoted out of context only that part of my message which referred to suffering, in order to prove their claim, not mine, that Pakistan persecutes Christians. In the bitter controversy that followed, the Government of Pakistan and I myself were both blamed.

Now the controversy has subsided, let me remove from your minds any douts you may have had. Contrary to reports, I did not go abroad, foreign press. My only message was directed to you, as this one is. I did not speak of persecution. And you yourselves know, dearly beloved, that Christians in Pakistan enjoy religious freedom. No one can deny that.

This very freedom means that you, as loyal citizens, must play your part in the tremendous progress that is taking place. Along with the rights and privileges, you must also share in the responsibilities that are common to all citizens. Opportunities are plentiful, provided you are prepared, by study and hard work, to make use them.

Let this thought be the subject of the usual essay contests held in our schools for Independence Day, and I ask headmasters and teachers to emphasize the need for education and the opportunities that await those who are well trained for their life's work.

In conclusion, let me encourage you once again to draw both inspiration and strength from Christ, making Him the model of your lives. Read daily and study Sacred Scripture, especially the Gospels. Often receive our Blessed Lord in Holy Communion so that you may find in this most Blessed Sacrament not only one-ness with Christ, but also that strength which comes from unity with one another. Asking this blessing for you, I remain,

Devotedly yours in Christ

+ Lawrence
Archbishop of Dacca

Source: *The Pratibeshi*, Vol. XXIV, No. 27, July 26, 1964.

Appendix XII

Archbishop Ganguly's Address at Reception on Jan. 21, 1968

IT IS NOT DIFFICULT for me to find words to express my sentiment today, for the simple words THANK YOU sum up all my thoughts.

THANK YOU, first of all, to Almighty God. In the words of our Blessed Mother, "He who is mighty has done great things for me."(Luke 1:49)

THANK YOU to my parents and family who so often sacrificed themselves in countless ways for my welfare and well-being.

THANK YOU to my teachers, to the congregation of Holy Cross, to those Bishops who have gone before me, and particularly to my predecessor, and in so many ways my friend and helper: Archbishop Graner . To him and to the others before us, you and I owe a debt of gratitude for the heritage which we have received.

My thanks to you, priests, religious, laymen, who assist me by your prayers and devoted service to god and to the works of the church.

My THANKS to you, friends from other churches who have come here today to join with us in our happiness. I pray that today's meeting here may be only one of many more meetings to come that will bring us ever closer to one another in the days ahead.

To you who have worked so hard in preparing this function: THANKS from all of us for the pleasure your hard work brings us.

Before my consecration in 1960, I went to Rome and was privileged to have a private audience with Pope John XXIII. In his kindly warmth, the Holy Father welcomed me with a question: "How old are you? .Are you only 13?" After seven years as Bishop, I am sure no one, even with the

Appendix XII

kindness of Pope John could ask that question. The hair is thinner now, for one thing, and I know that in the years ahead there will be more signs of age and care.

Indeed, the thought of the cares ahead would make me fearful if I had to face them alone. But your generous assurances today give me courage; and I know that we—you and I together, with the help of God, can go forward in the years and the work ahead.

Others in the past have had worries and difficulties perhaps in many ways greater than the ones we face. But see the work they have done; see the wonderful heritage we have received, see the treasure those others have entrusted to us.

Dearly beloved in Christ, we must not bury that treasure nor let it slip from our fingers. We take it with gratitude from those who went before us; we will enrich it and hand it on to those who follow. This is our task.

As your Archbishop, I welcome this opportunity to greet you, to thank you for your cooperation, and to assure you that I, for my part, will dedicate myself entirely to the work God has entrusted to me. In the months ahead we will have occasion and opportunity to plan our work more carefully. The synod of priests will be organised; the Laity will have their parish organisations; we shall hope for a diocesan group of priests, religious and Laity working together in planning and undertaking various programmes.

For all this, we need time and effort. And therefore I ask you to have patience with me and with one another. We can neither neglect the present while planning for the future, nor be so absorbed in the present that we forget the future. Our efforts must include them both. We must not waste our engines in vain quarrels and useless discussions about details. There are too many and too important works to be done. I know—and we all know—that there are many things that need improvement; let us go about this task in an atmosphere of peace and charity, working together and not pulling our separate ways. Unless we have unity, there is little hope for improvement.

To every priest, brother and sisters, to every Catholic man, woman and child, to each of our Christian brethren and to everyone of good will, extend my greeting and my invitation: let us join together to seek solutions for the serious problems that face us. May god bless our country, our leadless, our people. With them, we shall seek without rest to bring God's blessings to the poor and the hungry and the sick and the needy. May the love of God not be a cloak that hides our laziness or indifference; may the love of neighbour not be an excuse for rashness and impatience. Rather, may love of God and of neighbour be the inspiration that urges us on to greater efforts in the service first of God and then of our fellowmen.

Friends, it is this love that fills my heart today; it is this love that I want to have and to share with you and with all. With this love I end these few words as I started them: with a THANK YOU for your love and your loyalty today.

Source: *The Dacca Letter*, VOL. XIX, No. 1, January 1968, 4.

Appendix XIII

Muhammad Ali Jinnah's First Presidential Address to the Constituent Assembly of Pakistan (August 11, 1947)

'Mr. President, Ladies and Gentlemen!

I cordially thank you, with the utmost sincerity, for the honour you have conferred upon me—the greatest honour that is possible to confer—by electing me as your first President. I also thank those leaders who have spoken in appreciation of my services and their personal references to me. I sincerely hope that with your support and your co-operation we shall make this Constituent Assembly an example to the world. The Constituent Assembly has got two main functions to perform. The first is the very onerous and responsible task of framing the future constitution of Pakistan and the second of functioning as a full and complete sovereign body as the Federal Legislature of Pakistan. We have to do the best we can in adopting a provisional constitution for the Federal Legislature of Pakistan. You know really that not only we ourselves are wondering but, I think, the whole world is wondering at this unprecedented cyclonic revolution which has brought about the clan of creating and establishing two independent sovereign Dominions in this sub-continent. As it is, it has been unprecedented; there is no parallel in the history of the world. This mighty sub-continent with all kinds of inhabitants has been brought under a plan which is titanic, unknown, unparalleled. And what is very important with regards to it is that we have achieved it peacefully and by means of an evolution of the greatest possible character.

Muhammad Ali Jinnah's First Presidential Address

Dealing with our first function in this Assembly, I cannot make any well-considered pronouncement at this moment, but I shall say a few things as they occur to me. The first and the foremost thing that I would like to emphasize is this: remember that you are now a sovereign legislative body and you have got all the powers. It, therefore, places on you the gravest responsibility as to how you should take your decisions. The first observation that I would like to make is this: You will no doubt agree with me that the first duty of a government is to maintain law and order, so that the life, property and religious beliefs of its subjects are fully protected by the State.

The second thing that occurs to me is this: One of the biggest curses from which India is suffering-I do not say that other countries are free from it, but, I think our condition is much worse-is bribery and corruption. That really is a poison. We must put that down with an iron hand and I hope that you will take adequate measures as soon as it is possible for this Assembly to do so.

Black-marketing is another curse. Well, I know that black-marketeers are frequently caught and punished. Judicial sentences are passed or sometimes fines only are imposed. Now you have to tackle this monster, which today is a colossal crime against society, in our distressed conditions, when we constantly face shortage of food and other essential commodities of life. A citizen who does black-marketing commits, I think, a greater crime than the biggest and most grievous of crimes. These black-marketeers are really knowing, intelligent and ordinarily responsible people, and when they indulge in black-marketing, I think they ought to be very severely punished, because the entire system of control and regulation of foodstuffs and essential commodities, and cause wholesale starvation and want and even death.

The next thing that strikes me is this: Here again it is a legacy which has been passed on to us. Along with many other things, good and bad, has arrived this great evil, the evil of nepotism and jobbery. I want to make it quite clear that I shall never tolerate any kind of jobbery; nepotism or any influence directly of indirectly brought to bear upon me. Whenever I will find that such a practice is in vogue or is continuing anywhere, low or high, I shall certainly not countenance it.

I know there are people who do not quite agree with the division of India and the partition of the Punjab and Bengal. Much has been said against it, but now that it has been accepted, it is the duty of everyone of us to loyally abide by it and honourably act according to the agreement which is now final and binding on all. But you must remember, as I have said, that this mighty

Appendix XIII

revolution that has taken place is unprecedented. One can quite understand the feeling that exists between the two communities wherever one community is in majority and the other is in minority. But the question is, whether it was possible or practicable to act otherwise than what has been done, A division had to take place. On both sides, in Hindustan and Pakistan, there are sections of people who may not agree with it, who may not like it, but in my judgement there was no other solution and I am sure future history will record is verdict in favour of it. And what is more, it will be proved by actual experience as we go on that was the only solution of India's constitutional problem. Any idea of a united India could never have worked and in my judgement it would have led us to terrific disaster. Maybe that view is correct; maybe it is not; that remains to be seen. All the same, in this division it was impossible to avoid the question of minorities being in one Dominion or the other. Now that was unavoidable. There is no other solution. Now what shall we do? Now, if we want to make this great State of Pakistan happy and prosperous, we should wholly and solely concentrate on the well-being of the people, and especially of the masses and the poor. If you will work in co-operation, forgetting the past, burying the hatchet, you are bound to succeed. If you change your past and work together in a spirit that everyone of you, no matter to what community he belongs, no matter what relations he had with you in the past, no matter what is his colour, caste or creed, is first, second and last a citizen of this State with equal rights, privileges, and obligations, there will be no end to the progress you will make.

I cannot emphasize it too much. We should begin to work in that spirit and in course of time all these angularities of the majority and minority communities, the Hindu community and the Muslim community, because even as regards Muslims you have Pathans, Punjabis, Shias, Sunnis and so on, and among the Hindus you have Brahmins, Vashnavas, Khatris, also Bengalis, Madrasis and so on, will vanish. Indeed if you ask me, this has been the biggest hindrance in the way of India to attain the freedom and independence and but for this we would have been free people long long ago. No power can hold another nation, and specially a nation of 400 million souls in subjection; nobody could have conquered you, and even if it had happened, nobody could have continued its hold on you for any length of time, but for this. Therefore, we must learn a lesson from this. You are free; you are free to go to your temples, you are free to go to your mosques or to any other place or worship in this State of Pakistan. You may belong to any religion or caste or creed that has nothing to do with the business of the State. As you know, history shows that in England, conditions, some time ago, were much worse than those prevailing in India today. The Roman Catholics and the Protestants persecuted each other. Even now there are some States in existence where there are discriminations made and bars imposed against a particular class. Thank God, we are not starting in those days. We are starting in the days where there is no discrimination, no distinction between one community and another, no discrimination between one caste or creed and another. We are starting with this fundamental principle that we are all citizens and equal citizens of one State. The people of England in course of time had to face the realities of the situation and had to discharge the responsibilities and burdens placed upon them by the government of their country and they went through that fire step by step. Today, you might say with justice that Roman Catholics and Protestants do not exist; what exists now is that every man is a citizen, an equal citizen of Great Britain and they are all members of the Nation.

Now I think we should keep that in front of us as our ideal and you will find that in course of time Hindus would cease to be Hindus and Muslims would cease to be Muslims, not in the religious sense, because that is the personal faith of each individual, but in the political sense as citizens of the State.

Well, gentlemen, I do not wish to take up any more of your time and thank you again for the honour you have done to me. I shall always be guided by the principles of justice and fairplay without any, as is put in the political language, prejudice or ill-will, in other words, partiality or favouritism. My guiding principle will be justice and complete impartiality, and I am sure that with your support and co-operation, I can look forward to Pakistan becoming one of the greatest nations of the world.

I have received a message from the United States of America addressed to me. It reads:

I have the honour to communicate to you, in Your Excellency's capacity as President of the Constituent Assembly of Pakistan, the following message which I have just received from the Secretary of State of the United States:

On the occasion of the first meeting of the Constituent Assembly for Pakistan, I extend to you and to the members of the Assembly, the best wishes of the Government and the people of the United States for the successful conclusion of the great work you are about to undertake.

Source: *Dawn*, Independence Day Supplement, August 14, 1999. www.pakistani.org/pakistan/.../constituent_address_11aug1947.html

Appendix XIV

Demographic Difference between East and West Pakistan, 1951 and 1961

THE DEMOGRAPHIC DIFFERENCE BETWEEN two wings is given below:

	Total Population (Millions)		Population Density (Persons/ SQ.MI.)		Urbanization (Percentage)		Literacy (Percentage)	
	1951	1961	1951	1961	1951	1961	1951	1961
East Pakistan	41.9	50.8	701	922	4.3	5.2	21.1	21.5
West Pakistan	33.7	42.9	109	138	17.8	22.5	16.4	16.3

Source: Adapted from Pakistan, Ministry of Home and Kasmir Affairs, Home Affairs Division, *Population Census of Pakistan*, 1961, Vol. I, pt. ii, statements 2.3, 2.11, 2.14, pt. iv, statements 4.1, 4.4. Rounaq Jahan, *Pakistan: failure in national integration*, Columbia University Press, New York and London, 1972.

Appendix XV

Frequency of Languages Commonly Spoken as Mother Tongue in Pakistan (Percentage of population)

THE FREQUENCY OF LANGUAGES is common spoken given below according the census of Pakistan in 1951 and 1961:

Language	East Pakistan		West Pakistan		Pakistan	
	1951	1961	1951	1961	1951	1961
Bengali	98.16	98.42	0.02		56.40	55.48
Punjabi	0.02	0.02	67.08		28.55	29.02
Pushtu	-	0.01	8.16	8.47	3.48	3.70
Sindhi	0.01	0.01	12.85	12.59	5.47	5.51
Urdu	0.64	0.61	7.05	7.57	3.37	3.65
English	0.01	0.01	0.03	0.04	0.02	0.02
Baluchi	-	-	3.04	2.49	1.29	1.09

Source: Adapted from Pakistan, Ministry of Home and Kasmir Affairs, Home Affairs Division, *Population Census of Pakistan*, 1961, Vol. I, pt. IV, statement5.3. Cited in, Rounaq Jahan, *Ibid*, 12.

Appendix XVI

Twenty-One Point Programme, 1954

THE 21 POINT PROGRAMME for the election manifesto in 1954 was adopted by the United Front. The Programme is as follows:

1. To recognise Bangla as one of the State Languages of Pakistan;

2. To abolish without compensation zamindari and all rent receiving interest in land, and to distribute the surplus lands amongst the cultivators; to reduce rent to a fair level and abolish the certificate system of realising rent;

3. To nationalise the jute trade and bring it under the direct control of the government of East Bengal, secure fair price of jute to the growers and to investigate into the jute-bungling during the Muslim League regime to punish those found responsible for it;

4. To introduce co-operative farming in agriculture and to develop cottage industries with full government subsidies;

5. To start salt industry (both small and large scale) in order to make East Bengal self-sufficient in the supply of salt, and to investigate into the salt-bungling during the Muslim League regime to punish the offenders;

6. To rehabilitate immediately all the poor refugees belonging to the artisan and technician class;

7. To protect the country from flood and famine by means of digging canals and improving irrigation system;

Twenty-One Point Programme, 1954

8. To make the country self-sufficient by modernizing the method of cultivation and industrialisation, and to ensure the rights of the labourer as per ILO Convention;

9. To introduce free and compulsory primary education throughout the country and to arrange for just pay and allowances to the teachers;

10. To restructure the entire education system, introduce mother tongue as the medium of instruction, remove discrimination between government and private schools and to turn all the schools into government aided institutions;

11. To repeal all reactionary laws including those of the Dhaka and Rajshahi Universities and to make them autonomous institutions; to make education cheaper and easily available to the people;

12. To curtail the cost of administration and to rationalise the pay scale of high and low paid government servants. The ministers shall not receive more than 1000 taka as monthly salary;

13. To take steps to eradicate corruption, nepotism and bribery, and with this end in view, to take stocks of the properties of all government officers and businessmen from 1940 onward and forfeit all properties the acquisition of which is not satisfactorily accounted for;

14. To repeal all Safety and Preventive Detention Acts and release all prisoners detained without trial, and try in open court persons involved in anti-state activities; to safeguard the rights of the press and of holding meetings;

15. To separate the judiciary from the executive;

16. To locate the residence of the chief minister of the United Front at a less costly house, and to convert Burdwan House into a students hostel now, and later, into an institute for research on Bangla language and literature;

17. To erect a monument in memory of the martyrs of the Language Movement on the spot where they were shot dead, and to pay compensation to the families of the martyrs;

18. To declare 21st of February as 'Shaheed Day' and a public holiday;

19. The Lahore Resolution proposed full autonomy of East Bengal leaving defence, foreign affairs and currency under the central government. In the matter of defence, arrangements shall be made to set the

Appendix XVI

headquarters of the army in West Pakistan and the naval headquarters in East Bengal and to establish ordnance factories in East Bengal, and to transform Ansar force into a full-fledged militia equipped with arms;

20. The United Front Ministry shall on no account extend the tenure of the Legislature and shall resign six months before the general elections to facilitate free and fair elections under an Election Commission;

21. All casual vacancies in the Legislature shall be filled up through by-elections within three months of the vacancies, and if the nominees of the Front are defeated in three successive by-elections, the ministry shall resign from office.

Source: en.banglapedia.org/index.php?title=Twenty_One_Point_Programme

Appendix XVII

Six-Point Programme, 1966

SIX-POINT PROGRAMME IS AS follows:

1. The Constitution should provide for a Federation of Pakistan in its true sense on the Lahore Resolution, and the parliamentary form of government with supremacy of a Legislature directly elected on the basis of universal adult franchise.

2. The federal government should deal with only two subjects: Defence and Foreign Affairs, and all other residuary subjects shall be vested in the federating states.

3. Two separate, but freely convertible currencies for two wings should be introduced; or if this is not feasible, there should be one currency for the whole country, but effective constitutional provisions should be introduced to stop the flight of capital from East to West Pakistan. Furthermore, a separate Banking Reserve should be established, and separate fiscal and monetary policy be adopted for East Pakistan.

4. The power of taxation and revenue collection shall be vested in the federating units and the federal centre will have no such power on the issue. The federation will be entitled to a share in the state taxes to meet its expenditures.

5. There should be two separate accounts for the foreign exchange earnings of the two wings; the foreign exchange requirements of the federal government should be met by the two wings equally or in a ratio to be fixed; indigenous products should move free of duty between the two

Appendix XVII

wings, and the Constitution should empower the units to establish trade links with foreign countries.

6. East Pakistan should have a separate militia or paramilitary force.

Source: en.banglapedia.org/index.php?title=Six-point_Programme

Appendix XVIII

Some Economic Indicators between East Pakistan and West Pakistan

	East Pakistan	West Pakistan
Area (in square miles)	54,501	310,236
Population (1970 estimate)	70 million	60 million
Five-Year Plan Allocation		
1st	32%	68%
2nd	32%	68%
3rd	36%	64%
4th (unlikely to be implemented)	52.5%	47.5%
Foreign aid allocation	20–30%	70–80%
Export earning	50–70%	30–50%
Import expenditure	25–30%	70–75%
Industrial assets owned by Bengalis	11%	
Civil service jobs	16–20%	80–84%
Military Jobs	10%	90%
Resources transferred from East to West between 1948-9 and 168-9	Rs.31, 120 million	

Appendix XVIII

	East Pakistan	West Pakistan
Per Capita Income, Official		
1964–5	Rs.285.5	Rs. 419.0
1968–9	Rs.291.5	Rs. 473.4
Regional Difference In P.C.I., Official		
1959–60	32%	
1964–5	47%	
1968–9	62%	
Real difference in p.c.i., 1968–9	95%	
Real difference in average standard of living 1968–9	126%	
Proportion of imcome spent on food by industrial workers (1955–6 survey)	69–75%	60–63%

Source: Tariq Ali, *Can Pakistan Survive? The Death of A State*, Penguin Books Limited, London, 1983, 86.

Appendix XIX

Representation of the Civil Service of Pakistan in East Pakistan and West Pakistan, 1948–1967

Year	Total No. of Officers	East Pakistan		West Pakistan	
		No.	% of Total	No.	% of Total
1948	18	2	11.1	16	88.9
1949	20	9	45.0	11	55.0
1950	20	6	30.0	14	70.0
1951	11	4	36.4	7	63.6
1952	17	5	29.4	12	70.6
1953	13	3	23.1	10	77.9
1954	25	7	28.0	18	72.0
1955	17	5	29.4	12	70.6
1956	21	11	52.4	10	47.6
1957	20	7	35.0	12	65.0
1958	24	10	41.7	14	58.3
1959	24	12	50.0	12	50.0
1960	31	10	32.3	19	67.7
1961	27	10	37.0	17	63.0

Appendix XIX

Year	Total No. of Officers	East Pakistan		West Pakistan	
		No.	% of Total	No.	% of Total
1962	27	12	44.5	15	55.5
1963	31	13	41.9	18	58.1
1964	33	14	42.2	19	57.8
1965	30	15	50.0	15	50.0
1966	30	14	46.6	16	53.4
1967	30	13	43.3	17	36.7

Source: Mustafa Chowdhury, *Pakistan-Its Politics and Bureaucracy*, Associated Publishing House, New Delhi, 1988, 51.

Glossary

Apostle to the Gentiles: All the people of the world who are not Jews are Gentiles.

Apostolate of the Laity: active participation in church affairs by those who are not priests.

Archepiscopal: Connected with the Archbishop.

Augustinian: Member of the Augustinian order (a religious group in Catholic Christianity).

Bartal: Local musical instrument of Bangladesh.

Bhajan: is any type of Hindu devotional song. It has no fixed form: it may be as simple as a mantra or kirtan, or as sophisticated as the dhrupad or kriti with music based on classical ragas and talas. It is normally lyrical, expressing love for the Divine. The name, a cognate of bhakti, meaning religious devotion, suggests its importance to the bhakti movement that spread from the south of India throughout the entire subcontinent in the Moghul era.

Concelebrate: two or more priests celebrating eucharist together.

Ecumenical Council: Church council affecting entire Catholic world.

Episcopal blessing: blessing of people or things effected by a bishop.

Episcopal vestments: dress of the bishop.

First Friday confessions: the practice of confessing sins to a priest on first Friday of each month.

Glossary

Jesuits: The name of religious order: Society of Jesus, prominent in Catholic culture.

Khol: A clay double-headed drum of eastern India, or the wooden double-headed drum of southern India.

La Salette: Name of a town in Belgium, where people believed that Mary, the mother of Jesus, came and spoke to the people.

Legion of Mary: a Catholic lay association active in church affairas.

Liturgy: official order of worship established by church.

Mondira: Musical instrument.

Monsignori: plural for 'monsignor,' an ecclesiastical dignitary.

Mukti-Juddha: Freedom fighter.

Namjop: A form of prayer by singing, contemplating God's name.

O.P.: Dominican pertaining to the 'Order of Preachers'.

Orthodox Patriarch: presiding Bishop of the eastern Church.

Our Lady of Guadeloupe: The place of South America where faithful believe that Mary, the mother of Jesus, came and talked to the people.

Our Lady of Success: Or Our Lady of Good Success (Spanish: Nuestra Señora del Buen Suceso; Filipino: Ina ng Mabubuting Pangyayari), also called Our Lady of Good Events, is one of the titles of Blessed Virgin Mary. This title is shared among numerous images around the world—a number of images in Spain, one in Quito, Ecuador, and one in Parañaque City, Philippines. It is claimed that Quito's image had produced an apparition-to Mother Mariana de Jésus Torres. [Source: Wikipedia]

Our Lady of the Rosary: title for Mary, mother of Jesus.

Prefect of Studies: Director of studies in a religious congregation or diocese.

Sacred Congregation for Propaganda: Roman office in charge of spread of Christianity.

Salesian Missionaries: Missionaries of the religious order of Don Bosco (S.D.B.)—Salesians.

S.J.: Society of Jesus.

Glossary

SMRA: Title of a group of Catholics women with religious vows, in east Bengal.

Spiritual Legion of Mary: A lay Catholic group serving the church.

Suffragan: Request for prayer.

Tanpura: Musical instrument. The tanpura (or tambura, tanpuri) is a long-necked plucked string instrument found in various forms in Indian music; it does not play the melody yet supports and sustains the melody of another instrument or singer by providing a continuous harmonic bourdon or drone. A tanpura is not played in rhythm with the soloist or percussionist: as the precise timing of plucking a cycle of four strings in a continuous loop is a determinant factor in the resultant sound, it is played unchangingly during the complete performance. The repeated cycle of plucking all strings creates the sonic canvas on which the melody of the raga is drawn. The combined sound of all strings, each string a fundamental tone with its own spectrum of overtones, is a rich and vibrant, dynamic-yet-static tone-conglomerate, due to interactive harmonic resonances that will support and blend with the external tones sung or played by the soloist.

The name tanapura is derived from tana, referring to a musical phrase, and pura, which means "full" or "complete". Hindustani musicians favour the term 'tanpura' whereas Carnatic musicians say 'tambura'; 'tanpuri' is a smaller variant used for accompanying instrumental soloists. [Source: Wikipedia]

Titular Bishop of Oliva: Bishop serving in a subservient capacity and named from an ancient and now vacant diocese.

Xaverian Fathers: a religious order based in Italy, serving in east Bengal and around the world.

Zaminder: landowner, under traditional Portuguese jurisdiction.

Bibliography

Abbott, Walter M. (General Editor). *The Documents of Vatican-II*. America Press Association Press, February 1966.
Ahmed, Abul Mansur. *Amar Dekha Rajnitir Panchas Bachar*. Dhaka: 1975.
Ahmad, Kamruddin. *A Socio-Political History of Bengal and the birth of Bangladesh*. Bangladesh: Zahiruddin Mahmud Inside Library, 1975.
Ahmed, A. F. Salahuddin. *Social Ideas and Social Change in Bengal 1818–1835*. Calcutta, India: Rudhi, 1976.
Ahmed, Moudud. *Bangladesh: Constitutional Quest For Autonomy 1950–1971*. Bangladesh: The University Press Limited, 1979.
Ahmed, Nazimuddin. *Discover the Monuments of Bangladesh-A Guide to Their History, Location and Development*. Dhaka: University Press, 1984.
Ahmed, S. M. Tanveer. "Bangladesher Muktijuddhe Christian Mission o Missionarider Bhumika." (The Role of Christian missions and missionaries in the Liberation War of Bangladesh). In Ajoy Roy, Shamsuzzaman Khan, (Edited), *Bangla O Bangaleer Itihas*, Bangla Academy, Dhaka, (To be Published).
———. 'Father Eugene E. Homrich and His Role in the Liberation War of Bangladesh', *Bangladesh Historical Association*, Vol. XXIII, 2012-2014.
———. *Itihas Gabesona Paddhati* (History Research Methodology), Dhaka: Samhati Publications, 2014.
———. "Father Timm and His Role in the Liberation War of Bangladesh." In *Journal for the Arts faculty of Jagannath University*, Vol. 02, Number-01, July to December, 2012.
Alavi, Hamza. 'India and the Colonial Mode of Production' in Miliband, Ralph and Saville, John (eds.) *The Socialist Registrar 1975*; in Economic and Political Weekly. www.socialistregister.com/index.php/srv/article/view/5384/2283.
Ali, Muhammad Mohar. *The Bengali Reaction to Christian Missionary Activities, 1833–1857*. Chittagong: The Mehrub Publications, 1965.
Allen, B. C. *Eastern Bengal District Gazetteers: Dacca*. Allahabad: The pioneer Press, 1912.
Alonzo, C.S.C., Ph. D, Alfred F. D'. *The Story of Fr. William Evans, C.S.C. Missioner and Martyr*. Indiana: Moreau Seminary, University of Notre Dame. Notre Dame, 2006.
Amin, Tahir. *The Tashkent declaration: a case study: a third party's role in resolution of the conflict*. Islamabad: Institute of Strategic Studies, Pakistan, 1980.

Bibliography

Aziz, K. K. *Party Politics in Pakistan.* Islamabad: 1975.

Bandyopadhyay, Asit Kumar. *Bangla Sahitter Itihas* (History of Bangla Literature). Vol. V, Calcutta: Modern Book Agency Pvt. Limited, 1985.

Bandyopadhyay, Sekhar. *From Palassey to Partition: A History of Modern India.* India: Orient Longman, 2006.

Bangladesh Bureau of Statistics, July 2003.

Bertoci, Peter, J. "Elusive Villages: Social Structure and Community Organization in Rural East Pakistan." Department of Anthropology, PhD Dissertation, Michigan State University, 1970.

Bhadra, Bula. "Marx's views on India: A Sociological Appraisal of the Asiatic Mode of Production," PhD thesis, Sociology, McMaster University, Hamilton, Ontario, 1986. https://macsphere.mcmaster.ca/bitstream/11375/13114/1/fulltext.pdf.

Bible: John 11:25-26 New King James Version (NKJV).

Bloch, Marc. *The Historian's Craft.* A Caravelle Edition, New York: Vintage Books, A Division of Random House, 1953.

Burgh, De W. G. *The Legacy of the Ancient World.* Penguin Books Ltd., 1967.

Burrell, David B. CSC. *Exercises in Religious Understanding.* Eugene, Oregon, USA: Wipf & Stock, 2016.

C., Beccari. "Beatification and Canonization." In *The Catholic Encyclopedia,* New York: Robert Appleton Company. Retrieved, 1907. January 31, 2015 from New Advent: http://www.newadvent.org/cathen/02364b.htm

Campos, J. J. A. *History of the Portuguese in Bengal.* Calcutta: Medical Publishers, 1919.

Camps, Arnulf. *Studies in Asian Mission History, 1956–1998.* Studies in Christian Mission; Vol. 25, Leiden: Brill, 2000.

Chand, Tara. *History of the Freedom Movement in India.* Vol. II. Publication Divn, Ministry of Information and Broadcasting, Government of India, 1967.

Chatterji, Joya. *Bengal Divided: Hindu Communalism and Partition, 1932–1947.* United Kingdom: Cambridge University Press, 2002.

Chattopadhyay, Debiprosad. *Bharatiya Darsan,* (Indian Philosophy). Eight Edition, Calcutta: 2012.

Choudhury, Serajul Islam. "The Language Movement: Its Political and Cultural Significance." www.21stfebruary.org/eassy21_4.htm

Chowdhury, Mustafa. *Pakistan-Its Politics and Bureaucracy.* New Delhi: Associated Publishing House, 1988.

Chronicles of Jalchatra Mission, Pirgacha, Madhupur, Tangail, 1965.

Chronicles of Notre Dame College, Dhaka, 15 December 1954.

Chronicles of Notre Dame College, Dhaka, East Pakistan, 1 May 1959.

Chronicles of Notre Dame College, Dhaka, East Pakistan, 17 September 1956.

Chronicles of Notre Dame College, Dhaka, East Pakistan, 29 March 1959.

Chronicles of Notre Dame College, Dhaka, East Pakistan, 4 December 1956.

Chronicles of Notre Dame College, Dhaka, East Pakistan, 8 January 1958.

Chronicles of Notre Dame College, Dhaka, East Pakistan, 9 January 1960.

Chronicles of Notre Dame College, Dhaka, East Pakistan, February-August 1960.

Chronicles of Notre Dame College, Dhaka, East Pakistan, vol. 1, 14 November 1958.

Chronicles of Notre Dame College, Vol. 1, January 8, 1957.

Chronicles of Notre Dame College, Vol. I, January 12, 1956.

Chronicles of Notre Dame College, Vol. I, September 21, 1953.

Bibliography

Clancy, C.S.C., Raymond J. *The Congregation of Holy Cross in Eastern Bengal, (1852–1876)*. Part-I, Spes. Unica Publication time, place did not mention.

———. *The Congregation of Holy Cross in East Bengal*, 1853–1953. 2 Volumes, Washington: Holy Cross Foreign Mission Seminary, 1953.

Connelly, James T., Ebey, Carl F. James, Ferguson, J., Marceau, Paul D., Schlaver, David E., Warner Richard V., (Editorial Committee), *Holy Cross in Bengal*, 1853–1988. Holy Cross Mission Center, Notre Dame, Indiana, 46556, U.S.A., 1988.

Costa, C.S.C., Fr. Benjamin. "Reflections on the Life of Archbishop Ganguly." In *Weekly Pratibesshi*, 1 September 1996.

Costa, Jerome D'. *Bangladeshe Catholic Mondoli* (The Catholic Church in Bangladesh). Dhaka: Pratibeshi Prakashani, 1986.

———. *Archbishop Theotonius Amal Ganguly, C.S.C.. The Servant of God*. Ahoban-Christmas Issue, Toronto, Canada: Bangladesh Catholic Association of Ontario, 2006. http://issuu.com/jeromedcosta/docs/archbishop_theotonius_amal_ganguly_csc_declared_th

D' Rozario, CSC, Archbishop Patrick. "Dogmatic Constitution on the Church." In *Prodipon*, Vol. XXXVII, no. 3 & 4, 2013, Banani, Dhaka.

DAILY CATHOLIC, Vol. 10, no. 116. June 16, 1999.

Dawn, Independence Day Supplement, August 14, 1999. Transcribed from printed copy by Shehzaad Nakhoda. www.pakistani.org/pakistan/ . . . /constituent_address _11aug1947.html

Declared before the Magistrate of Calcutta on 19th February 1938, Sd/-S. Wajid Ali, Presidency Magistrate. No. 1493 of 1938. True copy to the Secretary, State Medical Faculty of Bengal, 11.08.1938.

Eaton, Richard. *The Rise of Islam and the Bengal Frontier*, 1204–1760. USA: University of California Press, 1993.

Farquhar, J. N., *Modern Religious Movements in India*, New York: The Macmillan Company, 1915. www.vivekananda.net/PDFBooks/Modern_Religious_Movements_in_India.pdf

Fox, Robert. *Vatican Council II and the Church in the Modern World*. www.catholiceducation.com

Ganashakti, 22 and 29 November 1970.

Ganguly, CSC, Father Theotonius Amal. *Jibon Ahban*. Dhaka: Pratibeshi, March 2011.

———. "Purusa and Prakrti (Self and nature): A Philosophical Appraisal of Pātanjala-Samkhya-yoga." PhD Dissertation, Department of Philosophy, Notre Dame Indiana, January 1951.

———. "ST. Thomas and the Human Body." M.A. Dissertation, Department of Philosophy, Notre Dame Indiana, January 1949.

Garello, S.X., Father Silvano (edited). *Christo Dharmio Sabdaratho*. (A Basic Catholic Dictionary by Daniel L. Lowery, C.S.S.R.), Jessore, Bangladesh: Jatiya Dharmya Samajik Prosikhon Kendra, 1996.

———. *Bangladesher Tin Bandhu* (Three Friends of Bangladesh). Dhaka, Bangladesh: Xaverian publisher, 2nd Edition, 1993.

———(edited). *Bangladeshe PIME Missionarygon Abong Fr. Pinos and Fr. Enzo Corbar mission Ovigata* (PIME Missionaries in Bangladesh and the mission experience of Fr. Pinos and Fr. Enzo Corba). Translated by Mollik, PIME, Fr. Biplob. PIME, Bangladesh, 2014.

Bibliography

———. "Introduction," in Talukdar, Daniel Dante. *Amar Chokhe Xaverian missionarygon (1952–2010)*. Publication place and time did not mention.

Gheddo, Piero. *Missione Bengala I 155 anni del Pime in India e Bangladesh*. Italiana: Editrice Missionaria, 2005.

Ghosh, Binoy. *Banglar Samajik Itihaser Dhara 1800–1900*. Dhaka: Sandesh, Bai Mela, 2000.

Ghosh, Shyamali. *The Awami League: 1949–1971*. Dhaka: Academic Publishers, 1990.

Gillespie, CSC Charles P. and Peixotto, CSC, Joseph S. *The Spirit of Notre Dame: A History of Notre Dame College Dhaka, Bangladesh, 1949–2000*. Dhaka, Bangladesh: Provincial House, 28, Zindabahar Lane, 2001.

Goedert, CSC, Rev. Edmund. "Catholic Missions Among the Garos of Bengal, (1909–1959)". (Unpublished work of inside the Catholic Church), collected from Moreau House, Provincial headquarter, Holy Cross priests, Banashree, Rampura, Dhaka, province Archives, Dhaka, Time not mentioned.

———. "History of the Church in East Bengal 1497–1977." (Unpublished work of inside the Catholic Church), collected from Moreau House, Provincial headquarter, Holy Cross priests, Banashree, Rampura, Dhaka, province Archives, Dhaka, Time not mentioned.

Gomej, Rani Cathrine. "Holy Cross Girls' High School," in Islam, Sirajul; Jamal, Ahmed A., Banglapedia: National Encyclopedia of Bangladesh (Second ed.). Asiatic Society of Bangladesh, Dhaka, (2012). http://en.banglapedia.org/index.php?title=Category:Education

Gomes, Father A. Jyoti. "Soaso Bacherer Siri Beya Dhaka Dharma Prodesh" (125 years of Dhaka Diocese). In Gomes, Father Jayanta S. (Edited). *Souvenir: 125th Jubilee anniversary of the naming of the Diocese of Dhaka*. Dhaka: Jubilee Central Committee, 2012.

Gomes, Bernard Sapon. *Bangladesh Mondolir Gourab-Archbishop Theotonius Amal Ganguly, (Life of Archbishop Theotonius Amal Ganguly)*. Dhaka: Archbishop T. A. Ganguly Memorial Trust, 1998.

Gomes, D.D., C.S.C., Rt. Rev. Theotonius. 'Preface,' cited in Timm, CSC, R. W. (ed.). *150 Years of Holy Cross in East Bengal Mission*. Dhaka: Congregation of Holy Cross, 2003.

Guha, Ranajit. *Chirastahi Bandobaster Sutrapat* (The preparatory of Permanent Settlement). Calcutta: Talpata, 2010.

Gupta, Kanti Prasanna Sen. *The Christian Missionaries in Bengal, 1793–1833*. Calcutta: Firma K. L. Mukhopadhyay, 1971.

Hambye, S.J., Rev. Fr. E.R. "Christianity in Bengal of the 17th & 18th Century." In *Indian Ecclesiastical Studies*, Vol. 9, 1970.

Hamid, Abdul (editor). *The Blue and Gold: 1960, Annual Year Book of Notre Dame College*. Motijheel, Dacca: 1960.

Hannan, Md Dr. "Banglaya Christo Dharmer Prochar o Prosar (1501–1947)." (The preaching and spread of Christianity in Bengal: 1501–1947). In M Sahidullah (Executive Editor), *The Journal of the Institute of Bangladesh Studies*, ISSN 1561-798X, No. 21, 1420, 2014.

Hashmi, Taj ul-Islam. *Peasant Utopia, The Communalization of Class Politics in East Bengal, 1920–1947*. Dhaka, Bangladesh: University Press Limited, 1994.

Hemrom, Fr. Haron. *Sahid Sradehao Fr. Lucas Marandi* (Martyred Fr. Lucas Marandi). Naogaon: Beniduar Mission, 1996.

Bibliography

Hensher, Philip, "The War Bangladesh can never forget." *The Independent*, 19 February 2013.

Holy Bible, Mark 3:13–19.

Holy Bible, Mathew, 16:15–19.

Homrich, CSC, Father Rev. Eugene E. "Pirgacha ST. Paul's Church: 1959 to 2010". May 15, 2010.

———, "*History of the Liberation War in East Pakistan or Bangladesh in Madhupur and Local area 1971.*" May 25, 2009, Pastor. St. Paul's Church, Pirgacha, Madhupur, Tangail. (Fr. Homrich, CSC provided the unpublished official documents of Catholic Church to the researcher at St. Paul's Church, Pirgacha, Madhupur, Tangail, on 28 May 2011.)

Hossen, Selina. *Unasattorer Ganoandolon*. Dhaka, Bangladesh: Bangla Academy, December, 1999.

Howard, Michael. *Franco Prussian War: The German Invasion of France*, 1870–71. Dorset Press; 1st edition, 1990.

http://offroadbangladesh.com/places/hasnabad-holy-rosary-church/

http://offroadbangladesh.com/places/hasnabad-holy-rosary-church/

Ingham, K. *Reformers in India, 1793–1833: An account of the work of Christian missionaries on behalf of social reform*. Cambridge University Press, 1956.

Interview with Brother Jarlath D'Souza C.S.C. at his office Muhammadpur Zakir Hossain Road, Dhaka-1207 on 13 August 2014.

Interview with Bishop Michael Atul D' Rozario, CSC and Fr. Joseph S. Peixotto, CSC, at the Provincial House of Holy Cross Fathers at Rampura, Dhaka on 17 July 2015.

Interview with Dr. James Tejosh S. Das at Eskaton Garden Road, Ramna, Dhaka-1000 on 13 August 2014.

Interview with Father Corba Enzo P.I.M.E. at Singra Forest Ashram (Hermitage), BirgonjUpazilla, Dinajpur District, Bangladesh on 10 July, 2011.

Interview with Father Richard William Timm, CSC at the Caritas office of Dhaka on 21 March 2011.

Interview with former Archbishop of Bangladesh the Most Rev. Paulinus Costa, DD, at the Holy Rosary Tejgaon Church of Dhaka on 20 September 2011.

Interview with former Archbishop of Bangladesh the Most Rev. Paulinus Costa, , DD, at his present residing place at Holy Rosary Church, Tejgaon, Dhaka-1215 on 8 August 2014.

Interview with Most Rev. Paulinus Costa (ret.), DD, at his present residential place at Tejgaon Dharmapalli, Dhaka on 28 April 2012.

Interview with Mr. Pius Ganguly at his residence at Indira Road, Dhaka on August 1, 2014.

Interview with the former Archbishop of Bangladesh the Most Rev. Paulinus Costa, DD at his present residing place at Holy Rosary Church, Tejgaon, Dhaka-1215 on 8 August 2014.

Interview with the former Archbishop of Bangladesh the Most Rev. Paulinus Costa, , DD, at his present residing place at Holy Rosary Church, Tejgaon, Dhaka-1215, on 16 August 2014.

Interview with the former Archbishop of Bangladesh the Most Rev. Paulinus Costa, , DD, at his present residing place at Holy Rosary Church, Tejgaon, Dhaka-1215 on 14 August 2014.

BIBLIOGRAPHY

Interviewed with Former Archbishop of Dhaka Archdiocese the Most Rev. Paulinus Costa, DD at his present residing place at Holy Rosary Church, Tejgaon, Dhaka-1215 on 14 December 2014.
Iqbal, Iftekhar. *The Bengal Delta Ecology, State and Social Change* 1840–1943. Cambridge Imperial and Post-Colonial Studies Series, Basingstoke: Palgrave Macmillan, 2010.
Islam, Kazi Nazrul. *Mrittu khuda* (Novel). Dhaka: Mowla Brothers, Eight editions, 2012.
Islam, Mufakharul M. *An Economic History of Bengal 1757–1947*. Dhaka: Adorn Publication, 2012.
Islam, Nazrul. *Bangladesher Gram: Atit O Vobissat (Village of Bangladesh: Past and Future)*. Dhaka: Prothoma Prokashan, 2011.
Islam, Sirajul. *The Permanent Settlement in Bengal-A Study of its Operations 1790–1819*. Dhaka: Bangla Academy, 1979.
Jabeen, Mussarat, Chandio, Amir Ali, and Qasim, Zarina. "Language Controversy: Impacts on National Politics and Secession of East Pakistan." In *South Asian Studies, A Research Journal of South Asian Studies, Vol. 25, No. 1*, January-June 2010.
Jahan, Rounaq. *Pakistan: failure in national integration*. New York: Columbia University Press, 1972.
Jones, Kenneth W. *Socio-Religious Reform Movements in British India*. 1st Indian Ed. New Cambridge History of India 3. New Delhi: Cambridge University Press, 1994. shadowsgovernment.com/ . . . /Socio-religious%20reform%20movements%20in%20 British . . .
Kabir, Nurul. *The Red Moulana, An essay on Bhashani's ever-oppositional democratic spirit*. Dhaka: Samhati Publications, 2012.
Kamal, Ahmed. *State Against The Nation The Decline of the Muslim League in Pre-independence Bangladesh, 1947–54*. Dhaka: The University Press Limited, 2009.
Kamal, Mesba. *Unosouttorer Gono Aovuttthan: Sahid Asad O Sreni Rajniti Prosanga (People's Upsurge of 1969: Martyr Asad and Issues of Class-Politics)*, Dhaka, Bangladesh: Sharabon Prokashani, Second Edition, 2006.
Keegan, John, *The Second World War*, New York: Viking, 1990.
Khan, Hamid. *Constitutional and Political History of Pakistan*. Karachi, Pakistan: Oxford University Press, Second Edition, 2011.
Khan, Muazzam Hussain. *Thousand Years of Sonargaon*. Dhaka: 2009.
Khan, Muin-ud-Din Ahmad. "Muslim Reform Movements," in Islam, Sirjul (Edited), *History of Bangladesh 1704—1971, Social and Cultural History*. Volume, Three, Asiatic Society of Bangladesh, 1997.
Kottuppallil, S.D.P., George. *History of the Catholic Missions in Central Bengal 1855–1886*. Shillong, Vendrame Institute, 1988.
Lapierre, Dominique and Collins, Larry. *Freedom At Midnight*. India: VIKAS Publishing House, 1976.
Sarkar, Louis Probhat. *Christianity and Christian Churches in Bengal* (1573–1960). Vol. 1, Calcutta: Prabhu Jisu Girja (Church), 76, Rafi Ahmed Kidwai Road, 2002.
MacCulloch, Diarmaid. *The Reformation: A History*. US edition: Viking Adult, 2004.
Mamoon, Munatssir. *Nineteenth Century: East Bengal 1857–1905*. Translated by Kingshuk Chatterjee. Dhaka: International Centre for Bengal Studies (ICBS), 2010.
———. *Dhaka Shomogro* (in Bangla). Dhaka: Ananya, 2003.
Marx, Karl. "The British Rule in India," in the *New-York Herald Tribune*, 1853 Source: MECW Volume 12, Written: June 10, 1853; First published: in the New-York Daily Tribune, June 25, 1853; Proofread: by Andy Blunden in February 2005. In writing

this article, Marx made use of some of Engels' ideas as in his letter to Marx of June 6, 1853, https://www.marxists.org/archive/marx/works/1853/06/25.htm.
———. *The Capital.* Vol.1, Moscow: Progress Publishers, 1965.
McBrien, Richard P. *Catholicism.* United States of America: Winston Press, 1981.
Megasthenes. "The Field Marshal from beyond the Grave." In *Forum: A monthly Publication of The Daily Star,* Volume 5 Issue 12| December2011. www.thedailystar.net/forum/2011/December/revolution.htm
Memorandum of the *Bongiya Pradeshik Krishak Sabha* (Bengal Provincial Peasants Association) *to the Floud Commission in* 1939, published by the Bengal Provincial Kisan Sava.
Mitra, Priti Kumar. "Hindu Reform Movements", in Islam, Sirajul (ed.), *History of Bangladesh* 1704–1971: *Social and Cultural History.* Vol. Three, Asiatic Society of Bangladesh, Second Edition, 1997.
Mondal, Father Joseph Rana. *Raro Samotota Christ Dharmo.* Khulna, Bangladesh, 2011.
Mondal, Lipon Kumar. "Social Formation in Bangladesh: An Essay on the Political Economy of State, Class and Capitalism." In *Journal of The Asiatic Society of Bangladesh (Humanities),* Vol. 59, No. 2, Asiatic Society of Bangladesh, 2014.
Morning News, April 6, 1964.
Murshid, Ghulam. *Hajar Bachhorer Bangla Samskriti* (One Thousand Years of the Bengali Culture). Dhaka: ABOSAR, 2010.
Olivelle, Patrick. *The Āśrama System: The History and Hermeneutics of a Religious Institution.* USA: Oxford University Press, 1993. PDF Copy: www.ahandfulofleaves.org/ . . . /The%20Asrama%20System_The%20History%20and% . . .
Pearson, M. N. *The New Cambridge History of India* 1.1, *The Portuguese in India.* New York: Cambridge University Press, Cambridge, Reprint 1990.
Pereira C.S.C., Father Adam S. *Diba Loker Ujjal Nokhtra Theotonius Amal Ganguly, C.S.C.,* Bangladesh: Holy Cross Priests Society, 2011.
Philip, Hensher, "The war Bangladesh can never forget", *The Independent,* 19 February 2013. http://www.independent.co.uk/news/world/asia/the-war-bangladesh-can-never-forget-8501636.html
Pinos, P.I.M.E., Father Luigi. *Catholic Beginnings in North Bengal.* Saidpur: Catholic Church, 1984.
———. *Catholic Beginnings in North Bengal.* Saidpur, Rangpur: Catholic Church, Bangladesh, Second Edition, 1994.
———. *Uttar Bonge Catholic Mondolir Shuvo Suchona O Poroborti Gotona Proboaha* (Catholic Beginnings in North Bengal), Dhaka: PIME Fathers, 1996.
Pirzada, S.S., ed. *Foundations of Pakistan: All India Muslim League Documents,* 1906–1947. Vol. 2. Karachi, National Publishing House, 1970.
Plekhanov, G. V. *Selected Philosophical works.* Vol. 1, Moscow, 1974.
Potts, E. D. *British Baptist Missionaries in India,* 1793–1837: *The History of Serampore and Its Mission.* Cambridge University Press, 1967.
Qanungo, Dr. Sunity Bhushan. *A History of Chittagong, Vol.* 1 *(From Ancient Times down to* 1761). Chittagong: Bilash Printers, 1988.
Quinlivan, CSC, Father Frank. *Strong in His Gentleness Servant of God Theotonius Amal Ganguly, C.S.C. Archbishop of Dhaka, Bangladesh.* Dhaka: Provincial Sacred Heart of Jesus Province Moreau House, 2009.
Rahman, Bangabandhu Sheikh Mujibur. *Oshomapto Atmo jiboni,* (Unfinished Memoirs). Dhaka, Bangladesh: The University Press Limited, 2013.

BIBLIOGRAPHY

———. *6-points Formula, Our Right to Live*. Dacca: Pioneer Press, 1966.
Rahman, Gazi Md. Mizanur. 'Holy Rosary Church', in Islam, Sirajul; Jamal, Ahmed A. (Edited), *Banglapedia: National Encyclopedia of Bangladesh*, (Second ed.), Asiatic Society of Bangladesh, 2012. http://en.banglapedia.org/index.php?title=Holy_Rosary_Church.
Raj. S. J., Fr. John Felix. "Jesuit contribution to Bengal." www.goethals.in/collections/felixrajarticles/JesuitContribution.htm
Rashid, Harun-or. "A Move for United Independent Bengal." In Islam, Sirajul (ed.), *History of Bangladesh 1704–1971*, Vol. 1, Asiatic Society of Bangladesh, Second Edition, 1997.
Richter, D.D., Julius. *A History of Missions in India*. Translated by: Sydney H. Moore. New York: Fleming H. Revell Company, 1908.
Rigon, Father Mariono. *Villaverla Theke Shelabunia* (From Villaverla to Shelabunia). Dhaka: Pritom Prokash, Bangla Bazar, 2011.
Rizvi, MA, S. N. H. *East Pakistan District Gazetteers: Chittagong*. Dacca: East Pakistan Government Press, 1970.
Rozario, Hubert Arun. "Lest We Forget Archbishop Theotonius A. Ganguly." *THE Daily Star*, Vol. 5, 922, Sat. December 30, 2006. www.thedailystar.net/2007/2006/12/30/d612301504115.htm
Runy, Zohra Sultana. "Rajshahi Bivage Christian Samproday: Akti Oitihasik Parjalochana." (The Christian Community in Rajshahi Division: A Historical Observation). PhD Dissertation, Department of History, Rajshahi University, Rajshahi, Bangladesh, 2010.
Samanta, Shakti (Director), *Anand Ashram*, (Bangla Movie), Initial release: 1977.
Sarkar, Sumit. *Modern India, 1885–1947*. New Delhi: Macmillan, 1983.
Seal, Anil. *The Emergence of Indian Nationalism*, Cambridge University Press, 1971.
Sima, Fr. Francis Gomes and Palma, Father Bernard (Editors). *Dewitiya Bhatican Mohasabar Dalil Samuha*. (Bengali Translation of Flannery, O.P., Austin (General Editor) The Documents of Vatican-II, Dominican Publications, Dublin, Ireland, 1975), Dhaka: 1990.
Singh, A.I. *The Origins of the Partition of India, 1936–1947*, Delhi: Oxford University Press, 1987.
Smith, Stefan Halikowski. *Creolization and Diaspora in the Portuguese Indies (European Expansion and Indigenous Response) The social World of Ayutthaya 1640–1720*. Vol. 8, London: Brill, 2011. (PDF copy)
http://libgen.io/get/1BBC6DCC8276339401CB335D78F92656/Arnulf%20Camps-Studies (PDF Copy)
Souvenir, 125th Anniversary of the naming of the Diocese of Dhaka, 2012, (in Bengali), 125th Anniversary Central committee, Dhaka: 2012.
Strong, F. W. *Eastern Bengal District Gazetteers: Dinajpur*. Allahabad: The pioneer Press, 1912.
Tavernier, Jean-Baptiste. *Travels in India*. Vol. II. Translated by V. Ball, LL.D, F.R.S., F.G.S. London: Macmillan and Co., 1889. http://gemology.se/gill-library/gemjewelry/Tavernier_Jean-Baptiste_1605–1689/Travels_in_India_by_Jean-Baptiste_Tavernier_Baron_d_Aubonne_Vol_1–2_Valentine_Ball_1889.pdf
Thapar, Romila. *A History of India:* Volume 1, Penguin Books, 1990.
———. *Early India: From the Origins to AD 1300*. University of California Press, 2004.
The Catholic Directories of Bangladesh 2011, CBCB CENTRE, Dhaka: 2011.

Bibliography

The Chronicles of Notre Dame College 26 October 1956.
The Chronicles of Notre Dame College, 12 January 1956.
The Chronicles of Notre Dame College, 21 September 1953.
The Chronicles of Notre Dame College, 8 January 1957.
The Dacca Letter, November 1, 1952.
The Dacca Letter, October 1, 1952.
The Dacca Letter, Vol. XIX, No. 1, January 1968.
The Dacca Letter, Vol. VII. NO. 11, May, 1957.
The Dacca Letter, Vol. VII. NO. 7, January Issue, 1957.
The Dacca Letter, Vol. VII. NO. 7, January Issue, 1957.
The Dacca Letter, Vol. VIII. NO. 2, July, 1957.
The Dacca Letter, Vol. VIII. NO. 2, July, 1957.
The Dacca Letter, Vol. VIII. NO. 4, September, 1957.
The Dacca Letter, Vol. XI, No. 3, September 1960.
The Dacca Letter, Vol. XI, No. 4, October 1960.
The Dacca Letter, Vol. XIV, No. 5, October 1963.
The Dacca Letter, Vol. XIX, No. 1, January 1968.
The Dacca Letter, VOL. XIX, No 1, January 1968.
The Dacca Letter, Vol. XVI, No. 4, August 1965.
The Dacca Letter, Vol. XVI, No. 4, August, 1965.
The Dacca Letter, VOL. XI, No. 4, October, 1960.
The Dacca Letter, VOL. XVI, No. 4, Aug.1965.
The Dacca Letter, VOL. XVI, No. 4, Aug.1965.
The Herald, September 16, 1977.
The Pratibeshi, Vol. XXIV, No. 27, July 26, 1964.
The Pratibeshi, Vol. XXIV, No. 11, 29 March 1964.
The Pratibeshi, Vol. XXIV, No. 11, 29 March 1964.
The Report on the Death of Rev. Fr. William p. Evans, C.S.C., St. Francis Xavier Church, Golla, P.O. Gobindpur, Dt. Dacca, November 14, 1971. The official report was jointly signed by Archbishop of Dhaka T. A. Ganguly, CSC and Rev. Fr. Hickens, CSC, Golla.
The unpublished Diary of Rigion, S.X., Father Mariono, which was provided by Father himself to the researcher at *Xaverian* House, Asad Ghate, Muhammadpur, Dhaka on 25 August 2012.
Thekkedath, Joseph. *History of Christianity in India, from the middle of the sixteenth century to the end of the seventeenth century.* Vol. II, Bengalore, Church History Association of India.
Theodore, CSC, Brother. *Memories of Bengal, 1939–40.* Notre Dame Indiana, USA, 1945.
Timm, CSC, Rev. R. W. *Master of Disaster: the outstanding Role of Caritas Bangladesh.* Caritas Bangladesh, 2014.
———(ed.). *150 Years of Holy Cross in East Bengal Mission.* Dhaka: Congregation of Holy Cross, 2003.
———. *Father of the Credit Unions in Bangladesh Father Charles J. Young, C.S.C.* Dhaka, Bangladesh: Congregation of Holy Cross Priests Society, Moreau House, 2010.
———. *Forty years in Bangladesh: Memories of Father Timm.* Caritas Bangladesh, November 1995.
———. *A Kind of Legend in Holy Cross Bangladesh Missionary Father Edmund Goedert, C.S.C.* Dhaka, Bangladesh: Sacred Heart of Jesus Province, Moreau House, 2006.

Bibliography

Umar, Badruddin. *Purba Banglar Bhasha Andolon O Tatkalin Rajnity*, (Language Movement and Contemporary Politics in East Bengal) vol. 1, Dhaka: 1970.

———. *Purba Banglar Bhasha Andolon O Tatkalin Rajnity*, (Language Movement and Contemporary Politics in East Bengal) vol. 2, Dhaka: Jatio Grantho Prokash, 2006.

———. *The Emergence of Bangladesh Class Struggle in East Pakistan (1947–1958)*. vol. 1, Karachi, Pakistan: Oxford University Press, 2004.

———. *The Emergence of Bangladesh: Rise of Bengali Nationalism, (1958–1971)*. vol. 2, Karachi, Pakistan: Oxford University Press, 2006.

———. *The Indian National Movement*, Raja Ram Mohan Roy Memorial Lectures. Translated by: Azizul Islam. The University Press, 1993.

Unpublished written document of Mr. Andy Koval.

Unpublished written narratives of Liberatore Jr. R.J. November 12, 2013.

Ware, Father Kallistos. *The Orthodox Way*. St Vladimir's Seminary Press, 2012. (PDF Copy) http://libgen.io/get/A267C7BCEDF2EBD2CBB751766DAA9394/Kallistos%20Ware-The%20Orthodox%20Way-St%20Vladimir%27s%20Seminary%20Press%20%282012%29.pdf

Weekly Pratibeshi, 2 September 1977.

Weeks, Richard V. *Pakistan*. New York, 1964.

Weiner, Myron. "Political Integration and Political Development." In *The Annals of the American Academy of Political and Social Sciences*, CCCLVIII, 1965.

Wheeler, Richard S. *The Politics of Pakistan: A Constitutional Quest*. London: Cornell University Press, 1970.

Written notes of Father Joseph S. Peixotto, CSC through emails on 21 January 2017.

Written unpublished documents of Fr. Francis Shima, which was provided by Fr. Gaberial to the researcher at the Bishop House Kakrial Dhaka, 14 July 2015.

www.asianews.it/news-en/Bangladesh:beatification-process-starts-for-first-native-bishop-7166.html

www.caritas.bd.org

www.catholicdoors.com/faq/qu221.htm

www.ctgdiocese.com/parishes-of-chittagong-region

www.londoni.co/index.php/history-of-bangladesh?id=155

www.newadvent.org › Catholic Encyclopedia ›

www.orthoinfo.aaos.org/topic.cfm?topic=A00521

www.pimeusa.org/

www.stalbertsranchi.org.

www.xaviermissionaries.org/M_Stories/Martyrs/VernIntro.htm

Wylie, LL.D, Rev. J. A., *The History of Protestantism*, London: Cassel and Company Limited, 1878. arcticbeacon.com/books/History_of_Protestantism-Wylie-1878.pdf

Zinkin, Taya. *Caste Today*. Oxford University Press, 1962.

Index

Page numbers in **bold** typeface indicate a photograph.
Page numbers with an 'n' indicate information in the notes.

Agaginian, Gregory Peter, 70, 71, 72–79, 76–77
Agartola Conspiracy trial, 102
Agartola Diocese, 31
Ahmed, Abul Musnsur, 98
Aijwal Diocese, 31
Akbar, Mughal Emperor, 21n26
Alavi, Hamza, 12 N11, 14 N 15
Ali, Chaudhury Mohammad, 99
Ali, Muhammad Mohar, 2
All-Pakistan Philosophy Congress (1960), 70
Aloysius, Brother, 78
altar, orientation of, 128–29
Alvares, Polycarp, 19–20
Anam, Mahfuz, 106
angelism, 57–59
Anglican Church of Bangladesh, 113
Apostles, 17, 124, 172
Arakan, King of, 28
Aristotle, 55
Ashram System, 61–62
"Asiatic Mode of Production" (Marx), 9
Askins, Robert, 51
Athenagoras, Orthodox Patriarch, 120
Augustine Marie, Sister, 71n30
Augustinian missionaries, 20–22, 28–29

Awami League, 98, 99, 102, 103
Badlands, Father, **111**
Bambina, Maria, 33
Bandura Holy Cross High School, 44, 44n1, **45**
Bangladesh
  independence of, 84, 91
  name change, 1n1
  refugees, 112, 113
  Vatican recognition of, 110, 111
Bangladesh Liberation War
  Ayub in power, 99–103, 136
  background of, 95
  doctors affected by, 92
  economic disparity, 100–01
  elections, 101–2
  Ganguly's role, 94–95, 104–11, 111, 137
  language controversy, 97–98
  Pakistan demographic differences, 96–97
  Pakistan movement, 95–96
  post-cyclone relief effort, 88–91
  rehabilitation program, 111–16, **111**, **114**
  six-point formula, for autonomy, 99

207

Index

Bangladesh Liberation War (*continued*)
  student agitation, 102–3
  Vatican recognition, 110–11, **111**
Bangladesh Mondolir Gourab-Archbishop Theotonius Amal Ganguly (Gomes), 5
Battaglierin, Dante C., 35, **36**, 72, 86, 117
Battle of Plassey (1757), 9
Benedict, Sister, 66–67
Benedict XVI, Pope, 133
Benedictine monks of the Anglo-Belgian Province, 24
Bengal Provincial Peasants Association, 12
Bengalee intellectual, 109, 137
The Bengali Reaction to Christian Missionary Activities 1833–1857 (Ali), 2
Bertoci, Peter, J., 15
Bhashani, Abdul Hamid Khan "Maulana Bhashani," 96, 98
Bhutto, Zulfikar Ali, 102
Bishops Conference (1960), 73–74
Bishops Conference (1971), 90, 104
Blair, Anglican Bishop, 113
Borgna, Monsignor, 72
Brahmacharya (student life), 61
Brahmin class, 42
Brambilla, Gerardo, 4
British Baptist Missionaries in India, 1793–1837 (Potts), 3
British colonial rule, 15, 15n17
British House of Commons, 10–11
The British Rule in India (Marx), 11

Calcutta Archdiocese, 25, 35
call, to life vocation, 60
canonization process, 133–35
Carey, William, 3
Caritas Internationalis, 90, 91, 112, 112n63, 113
Carmelite missionaries, 31
Cartesian 'angelism,' 58–59
Cassidy, Edward, 115
Catholic Missionaries, 104–10
Catholic Relief Service (CRS), 90–91, 113
Catholicism, term usage, 17n2
  . See also Roman Catholic Church

Cenni sulla Missione del Bengala Centrale (Roca), 4
Central Bengal, 3
Charles, M., Sister, 109
Chittagong Diocese, Bangladesh, 25, 26, 27–31
Choudhury, Serajul Islam, 97–98
Christ the King Seminary, Karachi, 115
The Christian Community in Rajshahi Division: A Historical Observation (Runy), 4
The Christian Missionaries in Bengal, 1793–1833 (Gupta), 3
Christian Organization for Relief and Rehabilitation (CORR), 112–13, 112n63
Christian virtues, 134
Christian Yoga, 59
Christianity
  branches of, 17
  as monotheistic religion, 16
Church History [Calcutta 1898] (Kottuppallil), 3
Church of Hasnabad, Dhaka, 21, 21n26, 23, 38
Church of Our Lady of Rosary, 21n26
Church of the Holy Name of Jesus, 36
Church of the Immaculate Conception, Jamal khan Parish, 27, **28**
Church of Tuital, Dhaka, 21–22, 22n27
Clarizio, Emmanuel, 72
class system, 20, 20n20, 41
Clement, Father, 51
Cloistered Adoration Nuns, 79
colonial mode of production, 12–15
commerce, expansion of, 11–13
Congregation for the Causes of Saints, 134–35
Congregation of Holy Cross
  Bandura Holy Cross High School, 44, 44n1, **45**
  beginning work in Bengal, Burma, and Assam, 47
  Bishops House, Dhaka, 71, 71N29
  Dhaka, arrival in, 19
  East Bengal, arrival in, 24
  founder of, 19n15, 24, 25, 49

INDEX

Noakhali mission, 29–30, **30**
Notre Dame College, Dhaka, 48, 51n30, 52, 52n34, 64, **65**, 67, 68, 68n15–18, 20, **69**, 70n22–25, 71, 83, **87**, 90
novitiate in Jordan, Minnesota, 47
Vicariate Apostolic of Bengal, 23–24
Congregation of the Catechist Sister of the Immaculate Heart of Mary the Queen of Angels, 33
Connerton, James, **50**
conversions to Christianity
    Portuguese missionaries, 19, 20n19, 39–40n10
    Portuguese surnames, 39–40n10
Corba, Enzo, 110–11
Cordaro, Colonel, 81
Cordeiro, Archbishop, 72, 74
Cornelius, M., Sister, 109
Cornelius, Supreme Court Justice, Pakistan, 104
Corraya, Kamal, 60
Corraya, Urban, 52, 64, 81, 109
Costa, Alex, 81
Costa, Benjamin, 87
Costa, Paulinus, 89, 93, 109, 114, 133
Costa, Ramona (mother), 39
Council of Trent (1542–1563), 118, 125–26
Cousineau, Albert, 46
Croce, Albert A., 49, **50**
Cunningham, Richard, 49, 50
Cyclone Bhola and tidal surge (1970), 88–91, 137

D' Rozario, Michael Atul, 113, **114**
Dacca Mission, 25
Dacca University, 102
DaCosta, Monsignor, 19–20
Das, James Tejosh S., 92–93
Dawson, 55
"day-star," 70–71
de Groote, Dom Gregory, 25
de Rosario, D. Antonio, 20–21
De Souza, Father, 19
Delaunay, John Baptist, 44n2
Dessai, Joachim, 112

Dey, Ramdulal, 13
Dhaka, Romanized spelling of, 99n30
Dhaka Diocese and Archdiocese, 17n7, 18–27, 44
Dhaka University, 70, 106
Dianga
    religious conversions, 29
    slaughter of Christians, 28
Diba Loker Ujjal Nokhtra Theotonius Amal Ganguly (Pereira), 6
Dinajpur Diocese, Bangladesh, 26, 31–34, 106–7
Directorate of Health, 92
diversity of human life, 60
Dominican missionaries, 22
Downey, Dom Cuthbert, 24
D'Souza, Jarlath, 137–38
Dufal, Pierre, 24

East Bengal
    Cardinal's arrival in, 72–73
    Chittagong Diocese, 27–31
    Dhaka Diocese and Archdiocese, 17n7, 18–27
    Dinajpur Diocese, 31–34
    Khulna Diocese, 35–37
    name change, 1n1
    part of Pakistan, 15
    social structures, 6–14
    village structure, 14–15
East India Company, 9, 11–12
East Pakistan
    as colony of West Pakistan, 15
    description of, 97
    name change, 1n1
East Pakistan District Gazetteers, 29
East Pakistan Rifles, 81
'Easter Message' (Graner), 82–83
Eastern Bengal District Gazetteers, 33
Eastern Orthodox Church, 17n3
economic disparity, Pakistan, 100–01
Ecumenical Councils
    described, 118
    Trent (*See* Council of Trent (1542–1563))
    Vatican I (*See* Vatican Council I)
    Vatican II (*See* Vatican Council II)

Index

election (1954), 98
election (1959), 99
election (1964–65), 101
election (1970), 103
Emmanuel, Sister, 107, 107n54
Ershad, Hussein Muhammad, 99n30
Evans, William, 107–9, **108**

Fallize, Michael, 25
Fell, Arnold "Gus," 49
Fernandez, Francesco, 19, 28
Floud Commission (1939), 12
Foreign Missionaries of Milan, 35
Francais, Adolf, 109

Ganguly, Bimal (brother), 39, 42, 42n18
Ganguly, Nicholas Kamal [originally Gomes] (father), 39, 40
Ganguly, Pius (nephew), 39, 42n18
Ganguly, Theotonius Amal
   baptism, 38
   birth of, 38
   as Bishop, 70–80, **76–79**
   books written about, 5–6
   canonization process, 133–35
   Cardinal's arrival in East Bengal, 72–74
   as central figure In East Bengal, 136–39
   as a child, 39
   conversion to Congregation of Holy Cross, 47, 48
   as a "day-star," 70–71
   death of, 27, 132, 133
   departure ceremony (from US. to Bengal), 48–52, 50
   educational career, 44–52, 63
   fall into a ditch, 65–67
   family members, 39
   first Bangalee Bishop, 26
   first vows, 48
   Notre Dame College (*See* Notre Dame College, Dhaka)
   ordained to priesthood, 45
   as pastor, 80
   philosophical thoughts of, 53–63,138
   as 'Prefect of Studies,' 52, 64
   scholarly activities, 69–70
   as "Servant of God," 133–35
   surname debate, 39–43
   Titular Bishop of Oliva, 26
   University of Notre Dame, Indiana, 46n10
   at Vatican Council II, 80
   as a young priest, **47**
Ganguly, Theotonius Amal, as Archbishop
   as Bengalee intellectual, 109–10
   cyclone impact (1970), 88–91, 137
   funding and role of Archbishop, 88–91
   health concerns, 115–16
   Holy Family Hospital, 92–93
   jurisdiction, 85–87
   major events, 84
   photos, **85–87**
   rehabilitation program, 111–16, **114**
   role during liberation war, 94–95, 94–95N2, 104–11, 111, 137
   seminary formation, 114–15
   Vatican Council II implemented (*See* Vatican Council II)
   Vatican II, implementation of, 126–129
Ganguly, Theotonius Amal, writings of
   article on Catholic youth problems, 70
   "St. Thomas (Aquinas) and the Human Body," 46, 53, 54–56
   Self and Nature [Purush and Prakriti], 46, 53, 56–60
   Vocation of Life [Jibon Ahban], 53, 54, 60–63, 138
   "Yoga Philosophy," 46, 56–59
Ganguly, Xavier [originally Gomes] (brother), 39, 40, 41–43
Garos population, 80, 81, 82, 84
Gauhar, Altaf, 102
Geertz, Clifford, 96
Ghose, Sir Man Mohan, 3
Ghosh, Ramgopal, 13
Gillespie, Charles, 132
Goa, Portuguese colony, 19, 19–20n18
Goiran, Augustus, 29
Golla Mission, 108–9
Gomes, Bernard Sapon, 5
Gomes, Francis, 106

Gomes, Gregory, 109
Gomes, Hubert, 109
Gomes, Margaret, 109
Gomes, Paul, 52, 64
Gomes, Peter, 109
Gomes, Robert, 79
Good, Brian Kenneth, **79**
Gosh, Binoy, 13
Graner, Lawrence Leo
    as Archbishop of Dhaka, 25, **26**, 46, 82
    as Coadjutor Archbishop, 83
    'Easter Message,' 82–83
    establishment of Holy Cross College, 83
    establishment of Notre Dame College, 51n30, 83
    at Ganguly's elevation to Bishop, 70, 72–79, **77**
    during India-Pakistan conflict, 81–84
Grhastha (household life), 61
Gupta, Kanti Prasanna Sen, 3

Haq, Fazlul, 98
Harrington, John J., 51
Hasan, Fida, 102
Henrique, Dom, 22n27
Hettinga, Bishop, 72
Hickens, William, 109
Hill, Charles, 49, **50**
Hindu's and Hinduism
    Brahmin class, 42
    imprisonment of, 29
    revivalism and reformation, 43
Hindus and Hinduism
    Ashram System, 61–62
    conflict with Muslims, 81
    on human body, 55–56
    Samkhya-yoga philosophy, 56–60
    view of God, souls and nature, 59
historical materialism, 5
historical methodology, 5N14
A History of Missions in India (Richter), 1–2
The History of the Catholic Church in Jessore (Marietti & Ghose), 3

History of the Catholic Missions in Central Bengal, 1855–1886 (Kottuppallil), 3
Holy Cross College, 71, 71n30, 83
Holy Family Hospital, Dhaka, 66, 68, 71, 92–93
Holy Rosary Church of Hasnabad, Dhaka, 21, 21n26, **23**, 38
Holy Rosary Church, Tejgaon, 21, 21n23, 21n26, **22**
Holy Spirit Seminary, Dhaka, 115
Homrich, Eugene E., 81
Hossain, Kamal, 51–52, 51–52n32
household life (*Grhastha*), 61
Houser, Charles, 71
human body, St. Thomas on, 54–56
humanism, 62, 138

"Il PIME ele sue Missioni-Bengala" (Brambilla), 4
India
    caste system, 20n20, 41
    independence (1947), 15, 25, 42–43
    partition of, 34
    war with Pakistan, 80–84, 100
indigenous church, 88, 124, 130–31, 137–39
indigenous people, 136–37
industries, expansion of, 11–13
Ingham, K., 2
International Red Cross, 92–93
International Society of Apostolic Life, 32n63
Islam, Nural, 132
Islamic Republic of Pakistan, 1n1

Jacob, Father, 51
Jalchatra Mission, 81
Jamal khan Parish, 27, 28
Jessore Diocese, 26, 35, 107n51
"*Jessorer Katholik Mondolir Itihas*" (Marietti & Ghose), 3
Jesuit missionaries, 19, 22, 28, 29, 35, 36, 45n6
Jesus Christ
    Great Commission, 17n3
    teachings of, 60–61

Index

'Jibon Ahban' *[Vocation of Life]* (Ganguly), 53, 54, 60–63, 138
Jinnah, Mohammad Ali, 96, 97
John Paul II, Pope, 133
John XXIII, Pope, 26, 70, 80, 117, 119–26
Juddha, Mukti, 105
Jude, Brother, 51

Khan, Ayub, 99–103, 136
Khan, Fateh, 28
Khan, Yahya, 89
Khulna Diocese, 35–37
King, Nat, 74
knowledge, in Samkhya-yoga, 58, 59
Knox, James, 72
Kottuppallil, George, 3
Koval, Andy, 90–91
Krishnagar Diocese, West Bengal, 32, 33, 35
Krisnagar Diocese, 3
Kristio Sobhar Sadharon Itihas (Marietti), 3
Kshatriya class, 20, 20n20

La Rose, Bishop, 72
Labbé, Benjamin, 90, 112–13
Lady of Rosary Church, 21n26
Lally, Francis, 72
Landi, Andrew, 90
language
    changes in Liturgical celebrations, 128, 130, 139
    controversy in Pakistan, 97–98
Larose, Raymond, 117
Le Missioni Estere di Milano nel Quadro degli Avvenimenti Contemporanei (Tragella), 4
Le Pailleur, Alfred, 30, **31**
Legrand, Joseph, 44n2, 71n29
Leprosarium tabernacle, 81
Liberation War of Bangladesh. *See* Bangladesh Liberation War
Liberatore, R.J. Jr, 89
Little Flower Seminary, Bandhura, 44, 44n2, 45–46, 52, 64
Liturgy of the Catholic Church, 127–29

local indigenous people, 136–37

Majumder, Theodore, 109
Manzur (Major, later Lt. Gen.), 106
Marandi, Lucas, 107, 107n52, **108**
Marietti, Antonio, 3–4, 35
marriage, importance of, 61
Martin, James, 49, 68
Martinian, Brother, 78
martyred priests, 107–9, **108**
Marx, Karl, 9–11
Marshman, Joshua, 3
Massart, Ray, 49, **50**, 51
material foundation, 15
materialistic philosophy, 54
Mathis, Michael, **50**
Mathis, Mike, **50**
McKee, Robert F., 67, 71
McMahan, Father, 51
Medical Mission Sisters, 66, 78
Mercier, Anthony Beniot, 29
Michalik, Walter, 109
Mirza, Iskander, 99
Miserere, 113
monotheistic religion, 16
Moore, Sydney H., 2
Moreau, Basil Anthony Mary, 19n15, 24, 25, 49
Mullahy, Father, 85
music, changes in Liturgical celebrations, 128, 139
Muslim League, 95–97, 98
Muslim Reformation, 43
Muslims
    conflict with Hindus, 81
    imprisonment of, 29
mystical experience, 56, 59

National Major Seminary for Bangladesh, 114–15
Nazareth Convent, Dhaka, 29
Noakhali mission, Bangladesh, 29–30
Notre Dame College, Dhaka
    ceremony for Bishop Ganguly, 71
    cyclone rehabilitation projects, 90
    establishment of, 48, 51n30, 83

Index

Ganguly's attendance, 48–52
Ganguly's work at, 64, 65, 67–68, 69
Novitiate of the Fathers of Holy Cross, 47

Obert, Joseph, 33, 72, 117
O'Dwver, Ephrem, **50**
O'Laughlin, John, 49, **50**
Olivelle, Patrick, 61
Olliffe, Thomas, 24, 29
Oriental Institute in Barisal, 128
O'Toole, Chris, 50, **50**
Our Lady of Guadeloupe, Rangamati, 29
Our Lady of Lourdes, Noakhali, 29, **30**
Our Lady of Piety Church, Dhaka, 22
Our Lady of the Holy Rosary, Chittagong, 27, **27**, 29

Pakistan
  Bengal movement, 95–96
  Bishops Conference, 72–73, 90, 104, 128
  Cyclone Bhola and tidal surge (1970), 88–91, 137
  demographic differences, 96–97
  East Bengal part of, 1N1, 25
  economic disparity, 100–01
  election (1954), 98
  election (1959), 99
  election (1964–65), 101
  election (1970), 103
  language controversy, 97–98
  Martial Law, 99
  Muslim League, 95–96, 98
  St. Gregory School, 51n30
  six-point formula, for autonomy, 99
  student agitation, 102–3
  two-nation theory, 15, 95
  war with India, 80–84, 100, 137
Papal Relief Coordinating Commission, 113
Paramahamsa, Ramakrishna, 62, 138
Parish Councils, formation of, 128, 128n34
Patanjali (Hindu philosopher), 46
Patanjali's Yoga, 56–60
Paul VI, Pope, 83, 90, 111, **111**, 120–22

Pedrotti, Ottorino, 32–33
Peixotto, Joseph S., 19, 19–20n18, 20n19
people of God, 124
Pereira, Adam S., 6, 39, 41, 92
Permanent Settlement proclamation, 11–14
PIME Missionaries (Pontifical Institute for Foreign Missions), 32–33, 32n63, 35–36
Pius XII, Pope, 35, 121
Plassey Battle (1757), 9
Pontifical Council COR UNUM, 91
Pope, George, **77**
Portuguese missionaries
  Augustinian missionaries, 20–22, 28–29
  beginning of, 19–20
  current population in Bangladesh, 37
  Dominican missionaries, 22
  Jesuit missionaries, 19, 22, 29
  in service of King of Arakan, 28
Portuguese surnames, 39–40n10
potail (head inhabitant), 10–11
Potts, E. D., 3
Pozzi, Francesco, 3, 32
priesthood, virtues of, 60
production, mode of, 11–12
Progga, M., 132
Prome Diocese, Myanmar, 25
Protestantism, 17n4
Purush and Prakriti [Self and Nature] (Ganguly), 46, 53, 56–60

Quinlivan, Frank J., 6, 80N45, 84

Rahman, Ataur, 98
Rahman, Sheikh Mujibur, 98, 99, 103–4, 113, **114**
railway system, 11, 32–33
'Rajshahi Bivage Christian Samproday: Akti Oitihasik Parjalochana' (Runy), 4
Red Cross, International, 92–3
Reformers in India (Ingham), 2
refugees, 80, 111–13
renounced life (Sanyasa), 62

Index

resurrection of the body, 56
retired life (*Vanaprastha*), 62
Richter, Julius, 2
Rigon, Marino, 35, 35n78
Rocca, Francesco, 4, 32, 33
Roman Catholic Church
    angelism, 57–59
    in Bangladesh, map of, 18
    canonization process, 133–35
    Catholic Relief Service, 90–91, 113
    Chittagong Diocese, 27–31, 117, 128
    Dhaka Diocese and Archdiocese, 18–27
    dignity of the human body doctrine, 46, 54–56
    Dinajpur Diocese, 31–34
    Ecumenical Councils (*See* Ecumenical Councils; Vatican Council II)
    Khulna Diocese, 35–37
    martyred priests, 107–9, **108**
    in North Bengal, 32
    recognition of Bangladesh, 110–11
    Trinity doctrine, 16
Rosario, Micheal D, 47, 113, **114**
Rozario, Dominic, **87**
Rozario, Hubert Arun, 105
Rozario, Joachim, **87**, 90, 113, **114**
Rozario, Manoel de, 20
Rozario, Michael, 110, 111, **111**, **114**
Runy, Zohra Sultana, 4–5, 4n12

St. Albert's Seminary, Ranchi, 45, 45n6
St. Francis de Sales, 50–51n28
St. Francis Mission Society, 35
St. Francis Xavier's Church, Golla, 108–9
St. Francis Xavier's Convent, Dhaka, 71, 78
St. Gregory School, Luxmibazar, 51n30, 52, 70–71
St. John Bosco, 50–51n28
St. Lawrence Hostel, Ramna, 51
St. Mary's Cathedral, Dhaka, 70
St. Nicholas Tolentino Church, Nagori, 21, 21n24, **23**
St. Rita's Parish, Mathurapur, 34
"St. Thomas (Aquinas) and the Human Body" (Ganguly), 46, 53, 54–56

Salesian Missionaries of Don Bosco (Salesian Society), 35, 50–51n28
Samkhya-yoga dualism, 57
Samkhya-yoga philosophy, 56–60
Sanyasa (renounced life), 62
School of Oriental African Studies (SOAS), 4n12
Second Vatican Ecumenical Council. *See* Vatican Council II
Self and Nature [Purush and Prakriti] (Ganguly), 46, 53, 56–60
Severin, Oscar, 45, 45n7
Sherer, Bishop, 72
Shima, Francis, 118n6
Silchar Diocese, Assam, 25, 31
Sisters of Charity, 33
Sisters of the Holy Cross, 71n30
six-point formula, Pakistan, 99
Skeleton Program, CORR, 112–13
social structures, East Bengal, 7, 9–14, 42–43
Society of Catholic Medical Missionary, 92, 93
Society of St. Francis de Sales, 50–51n28
socio-psychological background, 42
Solomon, James, 109
Sorin, Edward, 25, 46n10
the soul, 54, 55–59
spirit and matter, dualism of, 57
spiritual and supernatural elements, 54
Spiritual Legion of Mary, 52
Ste Marie, Aldrian, 49, **50**
Strong in His Gentleness Servant of God Theotonius Amal Ganguly, C.S.C., Archbishop of Dhaka, Bangladesh (Quinlivan), 6
student agitation, Pakistan, 102–3
student life (*Brahmacharya*), 61
Suhrawardy, Husen Shaheed, 98
"Suhrid Sangha," 106
supernatural mystical experience, 59
surname changes, 38–43, 39–40n10

Tagore, Dwarakanath, 13
Tashkent Declaration, 99, 102
Taveggia, Santino, 33, **34**
Thapar, Romila, 41

Index

Timm, R. W., 49, **50**, 89, 105
Tragella, Giovanni Battista, 4
"Trebeni Chatra Kalyan Sangha," 106
Trinity doctrine, 16
Trio, Serampore, 3
uniformity versus unity, 126
United Nations, 82, 121
University of Notre Dame, Indiana, 46, 46n10, 48–49

Vanaprastha (retired life), 62
VandenBosche, John, **77**
Vatican Council I (1869–1870), 118
Vatican Council II
   chronological order, 119–22
   description of, 118–19
   documents implemented, 126–29
   Ganguly's attendance, 80
   impact in East Bengal, 129–31, **131**
   implementation of, 88, 126–29
   photo, **122**
   purpose of, 123–25
Vedantic School, 54
Vedic (Chatur Ashram) system, 61–62

Vérié, Louis A., 24, 25, 29
Veronesi, Mario, 107, 107N51, **108**
Vested Property Act, 81
Vicariate Apostolic of Bengal, 23–24
villages, description of, 10–11, 14–15
Vocation of Life [Jibon Ahban] (Ganguly), 53, 54, 60–63, 138
Voisin, Michel, 25
Von Miltenburg, Archbishop, 72
Voorde, Joseph F., 49, **50**

Ward, William, 3
Weiner, Myron, 96–97
West Pakistan, 15, 97, 104–5
Wetzel, Edward M., 51

Xaverian missionaries, 35, 107N51

yoga, 46, 53, 56–60
"Yoga Philosophy" (Ganguly), 46, 56–60
Young, Charles J., 90

Zamindears of Bengal, 12

www.ingramcontent.com/pod-product-compliance
Lightning Source LLC
Chambersburg PA
CBHW070313230426
43663CB00011B/2110